D1570511

*Philosophy
and the Art of Writing*

Philosophy and the Art of Writing

Studies in Philosophical and Literary Style

Berel Lang

Lewisburg
Bucknell University Press
London and Toronto: Associated University Presses

Associated University Presses, Inc.
4 Cornwall Drive
East Brunswick, N.J. 08816

Associated University Presses Ltd
27 Chancery Lane
London WC2A 1NS, England

Associated University Presses
Toronto M5E 1A7, Canada

Library of Congress Cataloging in Publication Data

Lang, Berel.
  Philosophy and the art of writing.

  Bibliography: p.
  Includes index.
  1. Analysis (Philosophy)   2. Discourse
analysis, Literary.   I. Title.
B808.5.L36   101'.4   81-65865
ISBN 0-8387-5030-3   AACR2

PRINTED IN THE UNITED STATES OF AMERICA

For Helen and Ariella and Jessica

Contents

Preface

In the work presented here, I attempt both to demonstrate and to exhibit three related theses. The first asserts that philosophical discourse is a form of making as well as of knowing—more figuratively, that the texts of philosophy have bodies as well as minds. Here too, moreover, dualism fails as an explanation; thus, to understand the writing or reading of philosophy is to take seriously the connection between the literary making of philosophical discourse, on the one hand, and the role of that discourse as philosophical assertion, on the other. The second thesis is that the process of making, of producing artifacts (and thus texts), is itself a version of praxis or doing. Against the still-dominant Kantian tradition in aesthetics and poetics, I suggest that poiesis and praxis are not sharply divided, indeed that in their central features they are not separated at all; that literary structures (including the structures of philosophical discourse) are inevitably distorted in the life of the reader as well as conceptually, on their own terms, to the extent that they are abstracted from their historical contexts where they appear unmistakably as both intentional and caused. The appearance of a text as a physical object tends to obscure its more basic role as a form of action, but this makes even more pressing the need to identify and to analyze the latter form.

My third thesis is that for the artifacts of literary discourse, the role of a persona—a voice, a point of view, a physiognomy—within the individual work is a condition of intelligibility. I do not mean by *persona* the figure of the historical author, certainly not of the historical author alone. Even the most consciously realistic or representational discourse does not yield a "literal" facsimile—and yet, I mean to suggest, no discourse is without *some* representational character. The surest evidence for this claim is the phenomenon of literary style itself. For unless—against all the evidence—we think of style only as a chance occurrence, there is no understanding it or even recognizing its existence except as an embodiment of human agency, including there such features as choice, deliberation, and imagination—as well, of course, as the impulse for repetition and representation that marks the very beginnings of style.

9

Literary discourse is in all of its parts and at all levels (I generalize here from Aristotle's definition of tragedy) the representation of action. It should not be surprising, then, to discover that the role of an agent is significant, first in articulating and then, later, for the understanding of that action. What *is* surprising are the many attempts to construe the modes of discourse—literary, philosophical, scientific—as self-contained and inviolable, as though written texts had a life of their own that was intelligible quite apart from human life or history. That view, I hope to show, is quite unbelievable; the alternative to it is necessary, even inevitable, for the understanding of literary discourse and of the philosophical texts that are only to be grasped as part of that discourse; we see this in the most common and unproblematic objects of literary analysis—in the intentionality of genres, in the representations of figurative language and tropes, in the concepts of narrative point of view and implied reader.

A methodological assumption in this book is that the *form* of a theoretical or systematic argument, as much as anything else embedded in a text, presupposes a substantive decision about the general character of theories or systems. I have taken this claim at its word in proposing what I hope to be a cumulative and consistent line of thought, even if the studies brought together here, a number of them first written for other occasions, do not follow a single line of argument. In Part I of the book, the writing of philosophy is considered, at the level of theory and in practice, as a form of making or art. The emphasis in Part II on the concepts of style and point of view as literary and, more generally, aesthetic categories is meant to provide a basis for what Part I asserts in its more restricted claims for philosophical discourse. The chapters of Part III attempt to show how the act of reading and so the work of the critic (who is certainly *a* reader, if not just another reader) apply the concepts explicated in Parts I and II. The specific readings of texts that I give there (and more occasionally in the first two parts), are not themselves inevitable, of course. But the means they exemplify of "breaking into the text" is in my view native to both texts and readers.

It may seem that in the examples of literary discourse which I choose to consider here I move too quickly not only among genres, but also across the well-earned boundaries of disciplines and of theoretical distinctions—from philosophy to fiction, from a biologist's "note" to the philosophical dialogue to the personal essay. But what is at issue here is a theory of writing and reading whose categories are prior to those of genre or rhetorical figure, and deeper than the distinction between fiction and nonfiction (a distinction that turns out on examination not to be very deep at all). I am not denying that there may be purely literary distinctions, or that extraliterary distinctions may yet be relevant to the understanding of texts. What I hope to show, however, is that in appealing to any such distinctions, we assume a prior choice: we can start from a point outside the text—for example, applying to the analysis of literature independent conceptions of reason or human nature—and then "deduce" a concept of the text from that alien source (thus, for instance, the idea of a text as simply a picture or transcript of thinking, without any intervening medium). Or, we can start *inside* the text—attempting to determine what it implies first about the nature of textuality, and only then about the human and social nature that would have produced such an object in the first place.

The danger in following the latter alternative, as I do, is that, beginning with the text, we may find ourselves fixed or enchanted by it, that we may forget the possibility of life or history outside it, even perhaps conceiving of *ourselves* as texts. This seems in fact the turn that Structuralist and post-Structuralist writers like Lévi-Strauss, Barthes, and Derrida have taken as they reject history first as a category of analysis and then as a feature of the object analyzed. But even this danger, after all, is only a version of a larger one that is ideologically quite nonpartisan: the temptation that has so often captured philosophers, writers, scientists, to mistake the written word (starting of course, with their own) for nature itself. To be sure, no theory is proof against that temptation. But we can at least insist on the admission of evidence and of forms of analysis that would hinder it and force it into the open. I hope that the account in this book, of the connections between philosophy and the art of writing, will contribute to that purpose.

Boulder, Colorado/West Hartford, Connecticut

Acknowledgments

I wish to thank a number of friends and colleagues who have been generous with their help—and sometimes, I should say in fairness to them, with their criticism—in the history of this book. Robert S. Brumbaugh, Ralph Cohen, William Earle, Jim Kincaid, Joel Kraemer, Helen Lang, Irwin C. Lieb, Louis Mink, Howard Needler, Jeffrey Robinson, Paul Shiman, Tuvia Shlonsky, Gary Stahl, Marx Wartofsky, Paul Weiss, the late Morris Weitz, Erik Wensberg, and Forrest Williams all, in different times and ways, provided direction and encouragement. I should be glad to think that the book had at least in part repaid their efforts.

A fellowship from the Council on Research of the University of Colorado enabled me to begin this volume, and as a Research Associate at the Center for the Humanities at Wesleyan University in 1975 and 1978–79, I found the occasion and stimulus to take up many of the questions addressed here. In his own work, Hayden White, past director of the Center, has shown more clearly than almost any recent thinker that to understand the role of writing as significant and 'real' requires that we first understand it as artifact; I am indebted to him for the many ways in which he has followed that theme, as well as for other, more specific help he has provided me. Against the current, both he and Richard Stamelman, the present director of the Center, have sustained there an idea of the humanities at once rigorous and humane.

Earlier or abbreviated versions of a number of chapters in this book have appeared in journals: "Space, Time, and Philosophical Style" and "Style as Instrument, Style as Person," in *Critical Inquiry;* "Nothing Comes of All: Lear-Dying," in *New Literary History;* "The Compleat Solipsist," in *Columbia Forum;* "Presentation and Representation in Plato's Dialogues," in *Philosophical Forum;* "Toward a Poetics of Philosophical Discourse," in *The Monist.* "Philosophy and the Manners of Art" appeared in T. Fuller, ed., *Something of Great Constancy: Essays in Honor of the Memory of J. Glenn Gray* (Colorado Springs, 1979).

13

The group of shapes that can be read as a physiognomy has priority over all other shapes.

E. H. Gombrich

The very form of a literary work . . . is in itself an idea.

Lionel Trilling

Even with a philosopher who gives his work a systematic form, the real inner structure of his system is after all wholly different from the form in which he consciously presented it.

Marx

The method of interpreting Scripture does not widely differ from the method of interpreting nature.

Spinoza

If a man could pass through Paradise in a dream, and have a flower presented to him as a pledge that his soul had really been there, and if he found that flower there when he awoke— Ay! and what then?

Samuel Taylor Coleridge

Philosophy
and the Art of Writing

PART I

Poetics and Philosophical Discourse

1
Toward a Poetics of Philosophical Discourse

> I fear we are not getting rid of God because we still believe in grammar.
> Nietzsche, *Twilight of the Idols*

> God has no particular style in speaking.
> Spinoza, *Tractatus Theologico-Politicus*

The history of Western philosophy is predominantly a history of written texts, but philosophers have lived in that history and looked back at it as if a dependence on such unusual and complex artifacts had nothing to do with the work of philosophy itself. The assumption in this notion of a literary "museum without walls" is that philosophical meaning is self-generating and transparent—that both the medium and form of philosophical texts as they appear to the reader (and before that, of course, to the writer) are accidental causes, with no significant effect on philosophical meaning itself.

It would be dogmatic to rule out a priori this appeal to a recurrent miracle of immaculate conception, but there is no need to: it is perhaps the one case where philosophical writing does speak for itself—bulkily testifying to its own body, artlessly revealing its own historical shape. Insofar as we acknowledge even the slightest distance between philosophy and nature, in fact, we unavoidably confront philosophical writing as a form of making or production; and in arguing here, first for the possibility and then for the necessity of a poetics of philosophical discourse, I propose to discuss one form—the literary form—of this making. If my thesis that the literary appearances of philosophy have an intrinsic relation to the substantive work of philosophy seems all too obvious, I remind the reader that this has as often been taken to be obviously false as it has been held to be true. Certainly the claim has not yet been argued in a sustained view of philosophy as an historical object: philosophers, acutely tuned to the metaphysical categories of space and time, have been notably reticent about their

own locations in space and time. Thus, the argument that philosophical writing is shaped by its historical and formal character as written
discourse as well as by a specifically philosophical impulse (for clarity
or explanation or even for wisdom), and still more, that those two
determinations are related to each other, has in effect to begin at the
beginning. There is little in philosophy or in the historiography of
philosophy for it to build on.[1]

On the other hand, no such lack hinders the general thesis of which
this one is part. The evidence is unmistakable, if it could ever have
been doubted, that writing as such has a history; that that history has
been subject both to internal and to external pressures; and that these
pressures have affected not only the manners or styles of written
discourse, but, before that, the discrimination of what was written
about and even what came to be written about it. As these hold true
for writing in general, they give prima facie status to the same claims
for specific appearances of writing. And *this* means that the question
of what textuality, the embodiment in writing, means for philosophy—like the question "What is philosophy?" to which it then turns
out to be kin—is a philosophical question. Like any other question,
this one too can be begged or ignored; but we can no longer, except as
an article of faith (bad faith at that), act as if there were no risk in
doing so.

Although I have referred to the external pressures that shape
philosophical writing, I shall here only be touching on that issue (I
hope elsewhere to discuss the character of philosophy as ideology).
My primary interest is with the internal question: the status of the
texts of philosophy as "literary," as instances of writing. Even this
focus is narrower than it might be, since I do not propose, except
indirectly, to consider what difference writing *as such* makes to
philosophical discourse, although there is surely a good deal to be
said about that question and although the answer to it circumscribes
anything else asserted of philosophical discourse. Philosophers themselves have on occasion acknowledged the effect on their work caused
by the fact that it is written: Plato, for instance, who in the *Phaedrus*
(274d ff.), after retelling a myth about the origin of writing as a mne-
monic device, claims exactly that "frozen" quality as grounds for his
distrust of philosophical writing; or Merleau-Ponty, who with the
claim that "all great prose is also a re-creation of the signifying instrument" suggests, from the opposite direction, the full implication of
writing as a means of knowing.

And more than this: the classical studies of oral narrative by Millman Parry and writers influenced by him[2] have disclosed significant
differences, not only between the structures of oral and written narra-

tive (as in the formulas of the oral epic), but also in the subjects of those narratives and even in what is said about them. Whether or how such analysis applies to philosophical discourse is not very clear, but the prima facie evidence suggests the pertinence of carrying that analysis forward. The fact that Socrates did not *write* philosophy is surely as native to his conception of philosophy as is his refusal of payment for teaching philosophy (and the two, one supposes, are related: let no fetishes hinder the dialectical swiftness). And there are the other philosophers who *do* write and who explicitly profess a consciousness of the act as well as of their choices among its means: Plato and Merleau-Ponty, who have been mentioned; Wittgenstein, Kierkegaard, Nietzsche, and—looking backwards in time such diverse figures as Rousseau, Leibniz, Spinoza, Bacon, Augustine.

The issues allied to this very general one reach out in many directions. The question of what difference the printing press has made to philosophical discourse, for example, is subordinate to the general question of writing; but it introduces additional causal factors of its own (e.g., canonical texts, the uses of the index, footnoting), and in some cases the two involve identical issues, at the formal as well as at the sociological level.[3] Thus, for one example, we may understand that "posthumousness" is a literary and not only a biological category. We see this in the varieties of literary and philosophical consequence attached to its instances—that Wittgenstein "caused" much the larger part of his writing to be published only after his death; that Spinoza must have taken seriously even in writing it the likelihood that the *Ethics* would be published only after his death (and possibly not at all)—in contrast to his contemporary Hobbes, who published almost all his major works during his lifetime (and then expressed envy of what Spinoza, posthumously, had dared to say); that the 45,000 carefully prepared pages of Husserlian shorthand in the Archives were intended to survive together with the many fewer pages which Husserl himself saw through the press. The a priori likelihood is supported by these writings themselves—that the causes producing such effects did in fact influence the writing (both the published and the posthumous), just as it seems that something more than the accidental prospect of larger circulation makes posthumous writings significant in the history of philosophy only after the advent of printing. To be sure, reasons affect these examples that seem to have little to do with writing (or publishing) as such. But even religious or political wariness may also intrude on the formal issue of writing, founding at one extreme, for example—we cannot know how widespread it is—what Isaac Babel named the "genre of silence" or, more moderately, Leo Strauss's version of philosophical "writing between the lines", at another juncture, introducing analysis of the role of a philosophical "establishment" by way of Lévi-Strauss's contention that the very phenomenon of writing was originally an instrument of class dominance.

Again: I should argue that to understand the structure of philosophical discourse requires us to address such issues as these, at least to acknowledge them *as* issues. Bu it is also true that these boundary issues enclose the set of more concrete and in some measure independent questions concerning the formal character of philosophical writing which I shall be addressing here. These questions concern the status of philosophical texts specifically as instances of literature, as literary artifacts, and thus as accessible by way of the same critical apparatus that poetic theory has evolved for grasping the artifacts of drama, poetry, the novel—that body of so-called imaginative literature which, given the name, is then commonly assumed to differ essentially from the discourse of history, from that of the natural and social sciences, and not least, of philosophy.

To be sure, given the later prejudice, we cannot merely assume a common status of literary artifact for philosophical writing. Thus, in section 1, which follows, I propose that certain devices of literary theory and criticism do in fact apply, and usefully, to philosophical writing; in other words, that a poetics of philosophical discourse is possible. (I intend *poetics* here to retain the principal feature of its Aristotelian meaning: that its objects issue from poiesis or making, specifically from verbal making. This hypothesis of origins does not exclude the possibility that the same artifacts have other functions— practical, cognitive—as well.) In section 2, I shall be arguing that the possibility of such literary analysis of philosophical discourse is not accidental; that it reflects an intrinsic and thus causal relation between the work of philosophy and its literary appearances—in sum, that a poetics of philosophical discourse is not only possible but necessary. Insofar as these two claims turn out to be warranted, they support the hypothesis that the texts of philosophy need to be viewed not only under the modality of knowledge, but also, perhaps even more fundamentally, under the modality of making. The literary process is obviously not the only mode involved in such production (the phrase itself suggests the relevance of an economic or material mode). But it is an important one, both in itself and for showing in a familiar idiom how categories of making apply to a particular domain of writing which has not often been viewed as subject to those categories at all.

The objections may be raised that in stressing the written texts of philosophy I ignore a major part of philosophical discourse—the spoken word; thus, that I am in a position to make claims for only *one* part of that discourse; that I preclude discussion of the relation between the oral tradition and the written one; even that I assume a questionable priority in general for the written word over the spoken one. But I make no judgment on the latter point (it may well be that the "postliterate" era anticipated by certain contemporary visual arts, like photography and film, announcing the death of some older art forms and the birth of new ones, has surprises in store for philosophy as well) and I have acknowledged the difference which writing as such has made in the past and in the immediate present of philosophy. Indeed, my emphasis assumes no more than is evident in the history of philosophy itself, viewed as a conglomerate historical fact. Obviously much philosophical work has been carried on orally: discussions, lectures, conferences, classes. But it is hard to deny that even taken together, those oral forms, even in their early appearances, owe more to a written than to an oral background: we know something about the important, nonliterate traditions of oral poetry, but little about any like tradition of oral philosophy. If this fact means anything, it suggests that writing has not only made a difference to philosophy in the *species* of its appearances, but that it contributes, beyond that, to the definition of philosophy, to crossing the line between the being and nonbeing of philosophy itself.

1. The Literariness of Philosophical Texts

When the Russian Formalists speak of "literariness," they allude to the characteristics of a text other than its informational or cognitive content, and they tend in fact to speak of texts which as wholes are not primarily informational or cognitive.[4] The originators of this Platonistic neologism thus incline to a dualism of the sort familiar to Anglo-American readers in the dichotomy asserted by numerous philosophers and critics between emotive and cognitive discourse.[5] The two versions in common identify the literary or aesthetic function as noncognitive. Thus the analysis of literariness focuses on textual qualities which, as literary, do not refer beyond the text but exhibit or display themselves or their relations to other literary elements. If there is reference here at all, it is self-reference; even a constellation of such features has the effect mainly of calling attention to itself as a whole. Analysis of this aesthetic or literary function then emphasizes formal variation and complication (as opposed to substantive assertion), emotive or affective appeal (as opposed to verifiable claim), the individual or stylistic distinctiveness of a particular literary object (in contrast to features shared impersonally with other objects).

I do not mean to defend this notion of an exclusively literary or aesthetic function; in section 2, in fact, I shall be objecting that the ascription of literariness to philosophical texts is unintelligible without reference also to a cognitive element that is not specifically literary at all. But my immediate concern is to see whether the features claimed by literariness—precisely *because* that category is defined narrowly—do appear in philosophical texts. Even if they do, of course, we learn nothing from that about the significance of such appearance except that it is an issue. A finding for literariness would be the stronger, the more complete its enumeration of literary features. But it is difficult to know what completeness even means for a poetic theory, and the usefulness of any particular account may be granted, I believe, if the features brought in evidence are important in themselves as representative of other features that could be cited.

1. One aspect of literariness is fundamental to the concept itself and qualifies its other elements as well. This feature is the exhibitive or self-referential or iconic character of the literary work. I attach more to this feature of what I call "expressive identity" than simply the claim that by it a particular text is distinguishable from others (since that in itself can be accomplished by typographical devices or the conventions of bookmaking: title pages, "Conclusions," etc.) The allusion here is not to what is represented discursively by the individual words or statements of the text—their external reference—but to their internal shape, their reference with respect to each other and to the whole of which they are part. If the ideal of referential language can be described as transparency (enabling a reader to see through language to its objects), the expressive identity of a text introduces opacity: an individuated presence—even a persona—that emerges from the relation of the language of the text to itself. Whether that presence affects the directly referential language in a text is arguable (and argued below); my immediate claim is that it accompanies the referential function of language in its literary appearance in philosophical texts and recurs, in fact, in all the elements of that appearance. The paradigm cases of such individuation occur in the visual arts and in music, where the recognition of an individual artist's "hand" may be almost immediate; but readers (of poetry, fiction, and, I am claiming, nonfiction as well) cannot escape the same assertion of an expressive identity. The process of recognition involved in all these cases is more than a matter of identifying or naming a physical object; it cannot be done, for example, by spectroscopy or carbon-dating or even by more specifically textual history (the tracing of

themes, of authorial intention, etc.), although the results of these two processes may be identical in any particular case to those based on the use of expressive identity. In contrast, "nonliterary" texts—as in mathematics and the theoretical or experimental sciences where duplicability is a moral as well as a methodological principle—characteristically deny such individuation or that the texts are in this sense expressive at all. (Whether they make good on this denial is, of course, another question.) The very presence of this iconic character in a verbal artifact is thus, I suggest, a telltale of literariness.

That this feature of expressive identity figures in the reading of philosophial discourse is all the more striking because readers of philosophical texts are often unaware of its effects (the occasional mysteries or disagreements about philosophical authorship would hardly by themselves call attention to it); and because philosophers themselves—especially those who model philosophy after science—have often denied that it is significant for philosophical writing at all. But that it *is* a feature of those texts seems to me undeniable, and how it appears there is clear in the following three passages, all concerned with a single topic, expressing (in these passages at least) consistent views, written by philosophers whose working lives overlapped:

(1)
> I hold, namely, that there is no good reason to suppose either (A) that *every* physical fact is *logically* dependent on some mental fact or (B) that *every* physical fact is *causally* dependent upon some mental fact. In saying this, I am not, of course, saying that there are any physical facts which are wholly independent (i.e., both logically and causally) of mental facts: I do, in fact, believe that there are, but that is not what I am asserting. I am only asserting that there is no good reason to assert the contrary.

(2)
> Given any fact, there is an assertion which expresses the fact. The fact itself is objective, and independent of our thought or opinion about it, but the assertion is something which involves thought, and may be either true or false. An assertion may be positive or negative: we may assert that Charles I was executed, or that he did *not* die in his bed. A negative assertion may be said to be a denial. Given a form of words which must be either true or false, such as "Charles I died in his bed," we may either assert or deny this form of words: in the one case we have a positive assertion, in the other, a negative one. A form of words which must be either true or false I shall call a proposition.

> Here I should say (or admit?) that there is, I think, one important and perhaps obvious difference between 'fact' and say 'event' or 'phenomenon'—a difference which for all I know might qualify as a

(3)

logically fundamental type-difference. But this is very far from making 'facts' to be *not* 'things-in-the-world'. It seems to me, on the
contrary, that to say that something is a fact *is* at least in part precisely to say that it is something in the world: much more that than—
though perhaps also to a minor extent also—to classify it as being
some special kind of something-in-the-world.

Even readers otherwise unacquainted with the work of the authors
of these statements, probably even readers who have not spent much
time with philosophical writing, will recognize that different hands
have shaped these passages; and it would be unusual, I believe, if
anyone familiar with twentieth-century English philosophy could
mistake here the writing (respectively) of G. E. Moore, Bertrand
Russell, and J. L. Austin. It may be objected, to be sure, that these
are unusually distinctive "hands," or that the selections cited are
unusually—atypically—typical, but those points would need to be
argued separately (both seem to me false), and not very much depends on them in any event. For even if we should deny or mistake
the marks of these individual authors, it would be still more unlikely
to mistake the approximate time and place or tradition from which
these writings came (expressive identity need not be the identity of a
single person; this again is evident in the emphasis of stylistic studies
on "schools" or "ages" as stylistic units). And this identification, too, is
not exhausted by historical or "physical" analysis of the texts—the
fact, for example, that certain idioms were in use at a certain time—
but requires also confirmation by the understanding of an expressive
character.

It may be insisted that this process of identification is simply mechanical, whether the reader is aware of it or not; that identification
depends on such quantifiable features, for example, as the "normal"
length of an author's sentences[6]—thus, that there is nothing more
exotic or expressive in such features than there would be in the
fingerprints left by the author on his manuscript. The identifying
"shock of recognition," accordingly, might have psychological or historical interest—for example, in arguing questions of authorship or
dating—but no more. But this is precisely what the exhibitive or
expressive identity of a text is not, since it is the *configuration* of the
elements of the text (themselves referential or not) that constitutes
the expressive identity; although apparently nonexpressive features
(such as sentence length, sentence structure, etc.) *affect* that identity
and its recognition, they do not, simply added together, produce the
equivalent of either.

That the recognition of expressive identity often requires expertise—and even in the simplest cases, training—in no way detracts from the assertion of its occurrence; nor does it make the assertion unfalsifiable (by tempting us to say for any text which defies identification that we only require more expertise). There may well be—there *are*—philosophical texts that are neutral in respect to the identity of a specific author (and this even at a relatively high level of complication; the occurrence of texts which have *no* shape—like texts or other artifacts so unformed as to be *without* style—is a different matter). But that is no more difficult to account for in terms of philosophical writing than it is for other stylistic media.

I do not mean to ascribe the same expressive force or availability for identification to philosophical writing as to painting or poetry. But even a lesser force would be significant for what it precludes: the belief that philosophical discourse is so dominated by a neutral (or even a "natural") purpose, method, and subject matter that those instruments claim nothing for themselves. To be sure, we have not yet asked *how much* of a claim such means make, and the answer to that question is crucial. But my present concern is to suggest that they—the individuality of the text and the features which compose it—do indeed make an appearance; and that as all reading involves a continuing transaction between the expectations or "norms" of the reader, on the one hand, and the capacities or impulses of the text, on the other, the appearance of an expressive identity unavoidably becomes a factor in that transaction. Whatever significance we attach to the emergence of an expressive identity, philosophical discourse *has*—if not invariably, often—a recognizably exhibitive character. The proposals for an ideal and expressively neutral — nonidentifiable—language, as set out by Leibniz or Carnap, themselves attest to the (then-present) situations which they hoped to change. Their own proposals, moreover, were not even alleged by them to have been formulated in the neutral or common language yet to be achieved.

2. Insofar as individuation or self-reference occurs in philosophical writing, this raises a question of its means. Perhaps the single most important such means historically—and not only for philosophical writing— is the theory of genres. The fact that genre theory often makes use of large-scale generic differences—a gross anatomy— argues more for the centrality of that form of criticism than for its lack of discrimination. The claim of centrality is supported, I believe, by the fact that the earliest efforts in what we now refer to as poetics (in Plato and Aristotle, Longinus and Horace) without exception begin their systematic accounts by calling attention to generic differences: between narrative and dramatic poetry, between tragedy and com-

edy, between history and poetry, between the sublime and the "normal." The varieties in these distinctions undoubtedly reflect a shifting interest in specific literary forms, as well as a conventional element in generic criteria. This conventionality has sometimes been offered as a reason for avoiding genre distinctions altogether. But the fact that the distinctions are conventional does not mean that they are arbitrary; it suggests only that they require justification, and in this they hardly differ from the smaller-scale distinctions of poetic theory.

Thus, at a formal level, the problem of identifying genres in philosophical discourse is no greater than it is in locating them for other literary forms.[7] A more positive reason for doing so is that the history of philosophy itself offers prima facie assurance for the usefulness of doing so. I refer here most immediately to the deployment of genre distinctions in the titles of philosophical writing; beyond this—more substantively—in the structural differences among instances of philosophical writing; and finally, in what is explicitly said by philosophers themselves *about* philosophical genres. In the *Poetics*, for example, Aristotle notices the dialogue as a distinctive literary (and by implication, philosophical) form, noting the differences between it and the philosophical poem; it is clear from his references, moreover, that he takes those distinctions to be well established, not of his own making. Admittedly, some evidence for the conscious deployment of genre distinctions in Greek philosophical writing is circumstantial—but hardly more so than for other attributions to that writing. Surely it is a greater jump from the evidence to deny than to agree that when we see Plato writing dialogues against the background of the philosophical poems of Empedocles and Parmenides, the aphorisms of Heraclitus, the treatises of Anaximander and Anaxagoras, we confront there self-conscious choices with respect to literary form, as well as assumptions (tacit or explicit) about the capacity of those forms to carry the weight of philosophical discourse, or at least the weight of their respective authors.

These two features—the choice of literary form and the assumption (conscious or tacit) of a relation between that form and philosophical capacity—are, I should argue, continuous in the history of philosophy. They are evident, for example, in the Hellenistic and medieval meditation and confession, in the medieval commentary and the *summa* (the latter two reflecting both the doctrinal and pedagogic settings in which they took shape); and they continue into modern philosophy, where in conjunction with the growing self-consciousness and possessiveness on the part of *all* makers, philosophical authors too become increasingly deliberate in their contrivance of titles and subtitles. When Descartes includes the stipulation of "Meditations" in one of his titles, "Discourse" in a second, and "Rules" in a third, he not only ratifies visible formal difference in those works, but also calls attention explicitly to the question of what those formal differences amount to. Even if it were shown, moreover, that for any particular juxtaposition, the philosophical difference made by genre differences was slight, the fact that even a literary, allegedly nonphilosophical difference occurs would raise the question of how that difference occurred—and also of how it could occur *without* making a philosophical difference as well.

I propose here as a working hypothesis, a four fold generic distinction in philosophical writing among the *dialogue*, the *meditation* or *essay*, the *commentary*, and the *treatise*. The abruptness of this schema (why not, after all, the *critique*, the *philosophical poem*, the *aphorism?*) calls attention to the central problem of "genre making" that has already been cited: namely, the selection of categories by which the genres are to be distinguished. The model of literary "action" on which the schema above is based has at least the advantage of simplicity; it presupposes only a model of communication as a transaction among speaker (implied or explicit), audience (again, implied or explicit), and the referent of what is said. In its broadest outline, then, the model assumes only that the philosophical text qualifies as an instance of discourse; the very generality of the model suggests that its terms would have to be taken into account, however the model as a whole might have to be refined.

In chapter 2, I shall consider in some detail the role of the author's point of view in philosophical discourse,[8] and I wish here mainly to summarize the differences in textual action for which the speaker-within-the-text may be responsible. In the dialogue—Plato's *Theaetetus*, Hume's *Dialogues Concerning Natural Religion*—the presence of a dominant point of view or of an "implied author" is intrinsically problematic. To be sure, a protagonist may appear in the individual dialogue (Socrates, Philo) who in this role may be taken to represent the actual author. But for the "true" dialogues, the reader makes any such judgment at his peril (in contrast to such pseudo dialogues as Berkeley's *Three Dialogues* or *D'Alembert's Dream* of Diderot; these are variations, in fact, of the treatise); the dialogue itself, as in more purely dramatic representations, undermines any such identification. The protagonist may, for example, use faulty arguments, as Socrates often does; the dialogue itself characteristically ends skeptically or problematically, returning to, rather than resolving the question from which it initially sets out. The several voices of the dialogue speak in a genuine "polyphony"—to borrow Mikhail Bakhtin's term—where the implied author is dominant at most only dramatically and even then in such a way as to undermine that dominance. The action represented in the dialogue is thus not even by inference the action of a single agent; the "conclusions" that the reader draws from the dialogue by a synthesis of its elements represent assertions on the part of the reader himself more than they do assertions of the text. *He,* the reader, then purports to speak in the authorial voice.

The contrast between the dialogue and the meditation or essay (the confession and autobiography are also allied to the latter hybrid form) defines a second authorial role. In the latter (as in Descartes's *Meditations* or Pascal's *Pensées*), the implied author makes an appearance, usually overtly (as an "I") but sometimes less openly, as only a constant and articulated point of view. The implied author is here himself a subject of the text, not only in the sense that *he* is speaking, but also because he is speaking about himself; the work has a narrative thread of which he is a continuing element (perhaps even the elusive "nar-reme" sought by writers on narrative). The experience recounted, the responses to it, the line of inference around which those responses are constituted, are his—available to a reader who may then bring it to bear on his own experiences, but who, if he is truly to test or even to understand the work before him, *has* to duplicate the action represented there. Descartes's *cogito* argument is an example of this type of "first-person" proof—not because of its call for verification by clear and distinct ideas, but because, prior to that, of the "performative" character of the *cogito* itself.[9] Every proof, to be sure, is an action of sorts—but here the action of the proof is itself an action in which the implied author of the text is agent. (The authorial point of view in the essay, as in Montaigne or Bacon, is more open than that in the meditation, more evidently aware of the independence of the reader; but this does not change the basic articulation of the dominant point of view. The autobiography [Vico's, J. S. Mill's] and the confession [Augustine, Rousseau] fall somewhere between the meditation and the essay, mingling the performative emphasis of the former with the emerging independence of the reader.)

Especially with regard to the feature of point of view does the role of the implied author in the treatise differ from the role in the meditation or the essay. For in the treatise (Leibniz's *Monadology*, Hume's *Treatise*, Kant's *Critiques*), the implied author, although present in a recognizable and constant point of view, speaks of experience and evidence which is not distinctively his own even when he uses the first person. His voice is bracketed, neutralized: he speaks not for himself but as an observer, recounting descriptions or facts, the referents to which are quite independent of his own existence. He thus assumes that other observers have reported, or will report, on the objects of his attention as he does, once he has directed their attention to them; in his descriptions, the authorial "we" often replaces the "I"—not out of humility but in order to expand the writer's authority. Thus, Kant: "We may, then, and indeed we must, regard as abortive all attempts hitherto made, to establish a metaphysics dogmatically" (*Critique of Pure Reason* [B], Introduction). Often, first-person pronouns are eliminated altogether in favor of impersonal ones ("It is not so much that there is any special difficulty in conceiving a soul endowed with dispositions as that one can see no logical motive for adding these to the bodily arrangements" [B. Bosanquet, *Principles of Individuality and Value*]) or in favor of the passive voice, which eliminates reference to a subject and by which the implied author claims a position vis-à-vis the objects of discourse identical to that of all possible observers and literally passive: the facts of the matter speak for themselves, undetermined by any action of *his*.

The commentary (Aquinas on Aristotle's *Metaphysics;* Kemp Smith on Kant's *Critique of Pure Reason*) resembles the treatise in respect to the role of a "detachable" implied author, but with an important difference. For here there are two objects to which the implied author refers—more precisely, defers: the one, a primary text; the second the referent of that primary text. The implied author thus places himself in a position of subordination (this is true even where he objects to the primary text, although it would be a rare commentary whose purpose was quite simply to refute the text on which it was commentary). The primary text has an authority which the commentator has in the main accepted; he then proposes to reidentify the evidence for that authority—evidence to which he has access (he believes) in common with the implied author of the primary text. (Some primary works, precisely because of the status of the implied author and his referent, preclude this sharing and thus make commentary impossible, or at most problematic. Aphoristic writing is of this sort, and both the dialogue and the meditation also inhibit the possibility of commentary: one can write treatises *about* these, but not commentaries, since then one would be doing the original work all over again.)

This sketch of the roles of "implied author" in philosophical texts has correlative differences among both the referents and the implied audience of those texts.[10] In the dialogue, for example, the referent is not *described*, as if it were a fact or collection of facts, already given; the referent (of the whole, not of the individual statements within the whole) is no more complete or controlling than is the figure of the implied author, and indeed we assume a direct relation between those two. The reader himself may attempt to constitute such an object; but the text itself warns that such efforts will be provisional, unavoidably incomplete. Thus also, the implied audience is meant to assume the position of implied author: they are not, either of them, in a position to observe a common and determinate object (as they are, each of them, in the treatise). Their object, in fact, is always itself in question—and thus hardly an object at all. It is the process itself of which both they and the object are parts. The characteristic doubts left by the Platonic dialogues, then, are evidence neither of a momentary uncertainty on Plato's part as to where the truth is nor (only) of a desire to emulate Socrates as a gadfly: the justification for the lack of resolution is epistemological—reflecting the same dialectic that Plato alludes to more directly in the *Republic* (bks. 5 and 6).

The factors applied in this brief sketch of philosophical genres have drawn only on literary categories under the rubrics of "implied author" (or "point of view") and "implied reader." (Those concepts are themselves models of epistemic relations, and I speak in section 2 about how such epistemic relations in the *forms* of philosophical texts relate to the explicit epistemic claims that may be made there.) Certainly there are other bases for generic differences, and one central one has also been touched on by the categories cited. It is not easy even for standard literary typologies to specify the formal distinctions between comedy and tragedy, romance and satire—and these difficulties are greater, for obvious reasons, with respect to philosophical texts. But consider, for example, the following definitions of romance and comedy, abbreviated from Northrop Frye's work:[11] romance as a movement of self-assertion and -definition, in which a hero emerges having conquered, and thus having freed himself from, a world of recalcitrant experience, thus the triumph of good over evil; comedy as involving a reconciliation of forces which at first divided (as it turns out, provisionally) groups or individuals in the social or natural world from which comedy sets out. Much more would obviously be needed to support these definitions and the use I make of them—but superficially at least, the distinction between romance and comedy seems exactly to capture an important formal aspect of the difference between Hegel's *Phenomenology* and Leibniz's *Monadology:* the former, a prototype of the *Bildungsroman* in which we follow the trials and education of a character named Spirit on its way to victory, as Absolute; the other in which the ostensive differences and varieties of an often harsh experience are reconciled in the even-handed harmony of the "best of all possible worlds." (Readers have often found the *Monadology* amusing, and they tend to interpret this as a response to a philosophical oddity; but if what I suggest here is correct, they are amused because the *Monadology* is funny.)

Again, such comments mark at most the beginning of a theory of philosophical genres and tropes. But the justification for such a theory appears even with these intimations—since the justification is obliged to demonstrate no more than that distinctions among genres reflect the differences in purpose of the objects among which they are drawn. How substantive that connection is, is also not an a priori question—and the section following this one specifically addresses it. But even now we may anticipate the conclusions likely to emerge by accepting a challenge: to attempt to imagine philosophical works *without* the distinctions of genre—not only without the distinctions proposed by a formal theory, but without the matter-of-fact distinctions which have become "natural" features of philosophical reading (Plato writes dialogues, Locke writes treatises, Nietzsche employs the aphorism), and finally even without the individual and objective features to which those generic distinctions refer. Something, no doubt, would remain if a Demon-philosopher undertook to rewrite all the texts of philosophy within the bounds of a single genre—but it is also true that something would remain if we were to read the repertoire of dramatic tragedy as a form of black comedy (emphasizing, for example, the "happy" reconciliation of Lear, Cordelia, and the play's audience rather than the respective senses of loss). But the fact that something would remain does not mean that the loss, in both cases, would not be considerable. Such reconciliation—to borrow the terms of genre analysis itself—would be tragic, not comic.

2   The Inevitability of Philosophical Style

I have been arguing that certain means of literary criticism apply also to philosophical writing, and although only a few instances of these means have been cited, other examples are readily available. The use of figures of speech (for example, the role of metaphor), the recurrence of irony in philosophical writing (Socratic irony seems only an instance, not an exceptional case of this), the psychological and sociological strategies of philosophical rhetoric—these all revive topics that have been addressed since the first moment of literary theory and that bear directly on the reading of philosophical texts. To be sure, even with the addition of these examples to the ones discussed in section 1, the results need not be philosophically significant: it might well be concluded, for example, that the same critical categories would also apply to the discourse of cookbooks, newspaper advertisements, or road signs. Thus, the argument has still to be made out that the relevance of literary analysis to philosophical writing is more than an accident, that those texts are not merely the chance vehicles in which philosophy happens to travel. And thus in the present section, I hope to show both that and how the substance or work of philosophy is shaped by its appearance as discourse—that in confronting and attempting to grasp the one, we inevitably address the other as well.

I propose to discuss the latter connection under the rubric of "philosophical style." This reference to style does not imply that *all* literary features (either of philosophical or of other literary discourse) are stylistic; but only that the features referred to in section 1 can be viewed as stylistic and that it is useful to examine them from that perspective. I rely for a provisional definition of style itself on the "constant form" referred to by Meyer Schapiro in his much-cited essay.[12] This conception is characteristic of the strong tradition of style analysis which regards as fundamental the distinction between content and form; the difficulties in maintaining this distinction—and thus the need to revise it—are later parts of the present discussion. The "form" in this definition includes the exhibitive and literary features discussed in section 1: those features of an object which are not primarily (or at all) referential and which are allegedly subject to change with no corresponding change in referential meaning. The feature of "constancy" has been anticipated in section 1 in the emphasis there on the expressive identification of individual philosophical texts. For as that recognizability depends on patterns—patterns either of sameness or of transformation around an axis—the key to such recognition is in repetition or constancy. (Schapiro himself mentions instances of style from which this feature of constancy is absent, but these are, even in his own reckoning, exceptional cases.) The crucial point here is that the "occurrence" of style seems linked to the recognition, not only of form, but of the coherence and persistence of that form; that individuality or "signature" marks the object as a whole (in a way that a creator's *literal* signature on his work does not)—and that these elements taken together certify the expressive identity symptomatic of the exhibitive or "literary" character of philosophical discourse (cf. the examples cited above, pp. 25–26).

The issue to be addressed, then, is concisely put as the question of what philosophical style—the "constant form" of an individual text or group of texts—has to do with the substance or content of those same texts and of philosophy more generally. In response to this question I shall be considering two versions of the general thesis that there is in fact a connection between the "constant form" of a philosophical work and its import or content or substance. The weak version of this thesis asserts a corroborative, but finally contingent, relation between these two aspects of philosophical discourse; the strong thesis asserts that this connection is necessary and thus causal. I believe that even the weak version would suffice for a claim of the relevance of a poetics of philosophical discourse to the understanding and assessment of that discourse; that relevance would, of course, be more urgent and more evident if, as I shall also be arguing, the strong version holds.

The weak thesis of a probable but contingent relation between philosophical style and content draws on evidence of two sorts. The first of these is a priori and no more than an application of the principle of noncontradiction. On this principle, insofar as the formal features of philosophical writing can be translated into ideas, the latter would reasonably be expected to meet the same criterion of consistency with respect to the explicit assertions of the work that those explicit assertions observed with respect to each other. Admittedly, it is not always clear whether or how formal features of discourse invite such translation, but the case that at least some of them do so has been made, I believe, in section 1. In the various appearances of implied reader and point of view, for example, we find conceptual commitments not only to the idea of a person but to both his specific capacities for knowledge and a general conception of knowledge as well. In the distinctions among genres, we find conceptions of philosophical method and verification exemplified, and even in such apparently small-scale features as figures of speech, we find patterns—large consistencies—which because they are quite unlikely as accidents, consequently require attention as substantive elements. (Stephen Pepper's ingenious idea of the four "root-metaphors" of philosophical system has this insight at its basis.)

To be sure, there are differences in scope to which stylistic features may call attention. We find differences in personal style, for example, within a generic style (for instance, as among the three writers quoted from earlier); and there are "group" styles of various orders as well, including "schools" (e.g., the middle Academy), time periods (e.g., Renaissance), geographically related groups (e.g., the Marburg School). It may not always be clear—or even be the case—that philosophical commitments are entailed by specific stylistic features of these different orders (as, for example, by Moore's characteristic use of repetition or Ryle's dependence for punctuation on the hyphen). But what this means is only that not all stylistic features are philosophically significant, not that those same features may not be otherwise expressive stylistically, and surely not that *no* stylistic features are philosophically significant.

Writers, furthermore, may not in fact always be consistent in the relation between the stylistic features of their work and the more explicit conceptual claims which appear there—but since inconsistencies also occur *within* each of the two sides of the style-content dichotomy, there is nothing extraordinary about discrepancies *between* those sides. As the ideational content of stylistic features requires translation before it comes clearly into view, those features may be unusually revealing of their authors (in the way that actions, more than words, often reveal intentions); such disclosure is all the more telling for the relation between style and content when the ideas that appear in this way conflict with ideas announced more explicitly. So, for example, the point of view represented in Hume's *Treatise* of a detached and coherent observer is squarely at odds with the conception of personal identity more explicitly proposed in the *Treatise;* and the nonperspectival point of view of the implied author in Nietzsche's *Genealogy of Morals* is, I believe, inconsistent with the criticism of nonperspectival truth that Nietzsche explicitly proposes there. But these instances (examples in philosophical writing of what Stanley Fish has designated, for other texts, "self-consuming artifacts") are notable precisely because more usually—much more usually—we find consistency, not inconsistency. That consistency, indeed, anticipates the second item of evidence for the connection between philosophical style and content, namely, the fact that such connections often *do* occur. Such connections are recognizable as instances of consistency or of aesthetic "fit"; and although the assertion of such relationships is open to the criticism that "objective" criteria are lacking—as they are in virtually all the more standard, aesthetic judgments—they are at least *no more* difficult to identify here than in those others. Thus, it is "fitting" that Plato, given his historical relation to Socrates (which is a literary as well as a historical element in the dialogues), his suspicion of writing, and his conception of dialectic, should—if he wrote at all—use the dialogue form; and it is fitting, given Dewey's account of experience as "funded," accumulated—that his writing should exemplify the same principle: the repetition or funding of a term or concept from one use and context to subsequent ones. (Cf. the migrations of such terms as *experience* itself, *art,* and *nature.*)

Much history is taken for granted in this claim, and, as with any generalization, a question remains whether the evidence collected sufficiently warrants the conclusion drawn—in this case, that philosophical writing has in fact, wittingly or not, been attuned to the relation between style and content. But considerable work *has* been done to support the thesis (almost all writing on philosophical style has emphasized this one aspect of the topic)—enough, certainly, to make the thesis plausible.[13] What is crucial, moreover, is that even on the evidence cited, the contingent relation emerges as probable. If specific stylistic features only corroborate or underscore other features (stylistic or conceptual) of a work, this in itself—given the *necessity* of interpretation for philosophical texts—warrants consideration of philosophical style as a standard element in the reading and—for the same reasons— in the writing of philosophy. (I do not mean to imply with this that all philosophical texts are irresolvably problematic or, as Derrida has suggested, that the reading of one text is never more than the elaboration of another text.[14] But one can stop well short of entering that Heraclitean world and still hold that reading and interpretation are indeed activities invited, even required, by the text.)

The strong version of the thesis being considered is that philosophical style is intrinsically, and thus causally, connected to philosophical content or meaning. This version is more formidable than the other both to prove and then, *were* it proven, in its consequences. For insofar as it holds, not only will the literary features of philosophical writing in general corroborate the content of philosophical texts, but (sometimes if not always) that content cannot even be formulated independently of the stylistic features. This version of the thesis in effect denies the "style-content" distinction that has so far been assumed both in this section and in the references in section 1 to literariness. Thus the two arguments to be considered are also larger than the specific issue of philosophical style; they follow the *via negativa*, through the refutation of consequences of the alternative view.

The first of these arguments considers the alternative in which philosophical content or meaning and philosophical style are alleged to be distinct from each other. For it follows from that contention that there may exist philosophical meanings which have no stylistic features at all, that exist without style. This contention *seems* clear enough—but only, I should claim, if we define style so narrowly as to beg the question of the relation between style and content. Surely the likeliest candidate for an instance of philosophical content which is independent of stylistic predicates is the proposition—that "object of a thought" (Russell) or abstract entity in a "third realm" (Frege) that is so often distinguished from sentences (the particular expression of propositions) and from facts. Just what (or whether) propositions are, has been much disputed in recent philosophical discussion,[15] and these arguments cannot be engaged here except to suggest that beyond the disputes themselves lies the practice of philosophical discourse itself, which has more often than not simply taken the existence of such entities for granted. This practice is followed, for example, in the standard form of histories of philosophy which neutralize the differences among the philosophers included in those histories by summarizing the "arguments" of diverse positions and authors in a single propositional format. And although the strong prima facie evidence that stands behind such efforts is clear—for example, our understanding that sentences or statements in several different languages (e.g., "It is raining" and "Il pleut") yet seem to have the same meaning or content—that evidence is more than balanced, I should claim, by the evidence of the history of the theories of propositions themselves. Russell's criticism of Aristotelian logic turned precisely on the contention that the propositions which were elementary and "standard" in that logic had a problematic shape, one that was not flexible enough to "say" certain things which needed to be said (and were constantly, in ordinary usage, *being* said).[16] To be sure, the tendentiousness of the so-called standard form was not a problem for Aristotle himself since it was *his* metaphysics—specifically his concept of the relation between substance and attribute— that was consistently invoked there. But Russell's criticism has the force of suggesting quite generally that the forms disclosed in the characteristic structures ascribed even to propositions are not context-free. Moreover, even if we credit the subsequent objections to Russell's specific criticism of Aristotle— the objections that more complicated relations, subordinations, and conditional claims can in fact be reduced to Aristotle's standard logical form—this too is reasonably understood as asserting that the standard form is one way of rendering or joining the varieties of assertion. But this, surely, is the language of style, even in the rudimentary sense of "constant form" that I have alluded to before.

Hemingway's deliberate and repeated use of parataxis is perhaps as close as any writer (philosophical or otherwise) has come to bringing the world of Aristotelian (subject-predicate) propositions into view; and however one assesses Hemingway as a stylist or writer, few would dispute the claim that this parataxis is indeed a stylistic feature of his writing. To speak then of the proposition or other possible elements of meaning as both intelligible and distinct from style, is to assert the possibility of a content without a form against the failure of the principal applications of that thesis which have been attempted. If the claim for such a disjunction is made on a priori grounds, it is hardly more interesting than its contradictory; if it is based on empir-

ical grounds, then examples of its occurrence ought to be available—
and they are not. The Platonic appeal to a fundamental difference
between appearance and reality (and surely it is significant that so
many attempts to maintain the autonomy of propositions invoke versions of Platonism: Frege, Meinong, G. E. Moore) hardly serves to
explain why or how reality fails to put in an appearance.

To be sure, even if the argument so far were granted, it would not
yet demonstrate an intrinsic connection between any specific style
and a correspondingly specific content. It finds only that there is no
content without *some* form or style, not that style in any particular
case acts on, or is itself affected by, a content. To make the case for
such an intrinsic connection requires an argument that content does
not act independently of whatever style may characterize it. One
version of the theoretical issue at stake here has been current as the
problem of synonymy. For if we ask whether the same philosophical
content can be rendered in different styles, we are already assuming
that it is at least possible for any two formulations—quite aside from
the question of style—to have the same meaning. This possibility has
been denied by Quine and Goodman, among others;[17] and although
it seems to me that their case on this point has been made—from
which it would follow that no two stylistic contents *could be* identical—the arguments to this effect are hardly settled, and I do not, in
any event, wish to rest too much of the thesis proposed here on it.
For if the thesis is to have consequences for the reading of philosophical texts, it would require not only a small-scale "slippage" in translation, but significant differences.

On the other hand, the arguments against synonymy do converge
with the claims that have been introduced here about the general
relation between style and content. For at the very least, the two
arguments together imply (this is also, I believe, corroborated by the
actual history of interpretation and reading of philosophical texts) that
there is no ground (a priori or empirical) for ruling out of court any
particular feature of a text as stylistic or formal. And insofar as *this* is
the case, it follows that features judged in a particular case to be
purely formal or stylistic (and in this sense, incidental) may in any
other case be cognitively significant. This means, not that there is no
legitimate or recognizable difference, in any particular case, between
philosophical style and philosophical content, but that there is no
general, context-free list of criteria that would enable us to identify in
any particular text the features that fall into one or the other of these
two categories. And this means in turn—what the history of stylistic
analysis has learned mainly by costly experience—that the categories
of style, like many other categories that apply to whatever style is

style *of*, may be distinguished in any particular case only on the basis of evidence from the case itself. In other words, that however many the categories are, they derive from a single source. There is no touchstone on either side; and thus the presumption of a *kind* of philosophical content as prior to or independent of specific philosophical texts is just that—a presumption.

One evident danger in this denial of the style-content distinction was accepted and even celebrated by Croce, who inferred from it a radical incommensurability of the individual objects of art—an aesthetic nominalism.[18] Insofar as form and content are linked, Croce argues, we cannot subsume even quite specific instances under either of those general categories. Generic classifications are, in effect, intrinsically arbitrary and misleading; all that exists is the work of art or the text itself.

But Croce's position on this point contradicts strong prima facie evidence, and it does not, in any event, follow from what I have been saying. If, for example, one asks for a statement of the "argument" of Plato's *Theaetetus* (meaning by that a series of assertions put in "standard" propositional form), the most that one can hope for will be farther from the original text than would be a similar reformulation of an argument by G. E. Moore (and why, we should expect to hear, would anyone want the latter anyway, when the original is exemplary of the same form?). But this fact does not by itself entail that a group of statements based on the *Theaetetus* would be wholly beside the point. Cleanth Brooks introduced the notion of the "heresy of paraphrase" in the literary discussion of the same issue with the claim that to render a poem propositionally was simply to miss the point of the poem. But surely in the case of a poem as well, we can admit—we *should* admit—the difference between a *version* of the original, on the one hand, and the original, on the other, without denying the possible relevance of the one to the other.[19] If the values applied by a particular reader of philosophy—*his* conceptions of philosophy and of truth—are located in propositional assertion, even in that form there will be renderings that are closer or more remote from Plato's text. The fact—what I at least take to be a fact—that none of those renderings, separately or together, will fully capture the import of the text does not mean that the text is simply impermeable.

Thus we understand, too, the fact that a single writer may often present his work in different genres, remaining—we suppose—the same philosopher in using them, and almost certainly claiming to articulate the "same" philosophical position in them all. So Plato, uncharacteristically, is supposed to have delivered a "lecture" on the Good, and Aristotle is supposed to have written dialogues admired by so fine a stylist as Cicero. Berkeley wrote treatises as well as dialogues (as did Hume), and Nietzsche shifts from the form of aphorism to those of the essay and the treatise, sometimes within the bounds of a single work. Let me focus on one difficult example of this phenomenon. I refer above to the several genres which Descartes employs (to the three mentioned, there might be added the "Replies to Objections"), and surely a reasonable question would ask whether the difference in genre makes for a significant philosophical difference in what it is that these several forms express.

The point made immediately before this is pertinent as well to the objection at issue here, namely, that alternate genres may well capture aspects of any particular generic utterance: the denial of synonymy does not imply a denial of approximation. I have, furthermore, also suggested the defeasibility of generic definitions; this means that in any particular instance of discriminating among genres, we may be observing either a crossing of generic boundaries (a mixing), or a shift in the generic scheme itself.

I believe in fact that something like a mixing of genres takes place in Descartes's several versions of his thought, although when this is added to the other qualifications I have entered, the danger appears of so emptying my thesis that the only claim remaining is that genre is one among many accidental features of the philosophical landscape. The case is stronger than this, however, and even the example of Descartes's work seems to me to conform to it. I elaborate below, in chapter 2, the interpretation already alluded to of the authorial point of view represented in the *Meditations*, specifically with respect to the *cogito* argument. That "representation" on Descartes's part seems to me fundamental to both the *Meditations* and the *Discourse*, a motivating force in the other works cited as well. Do they not, though, *all* say the same thing? Well, in part they do, *literally*, say the same thing (e.g., as in specific sentences of the *Discourse* and the *Meditations*). But this means only that the conditions of one genre seem to have been incorporated in a second one—not that the second one (if indeed it is a different genre; this seems questionable as between the earlier *Discourse* and the *Meditations*) has successfully provided its own version of the first.

The point here is that Descartes's argument in at least some of these different appearances has a single structure, in literary terms, of authorial point of view and of the representation of a subject matter. One way of understanding that distinctiveness is in terms set out by generic difference—and this claim would be proved false, I believe, only if the features assigned to a genre (for example, to the meditation), as they appear in a particular example of the genre, were shown to be identical for a second work at both the generic level (as representing a *different* genre) and in its own particular representation. But the role of authorial consciousness, the presentation of evidence, and the concept of method in the *Discourse* and the *Meditations* do not seem to me to argue for such distinctions to any significant degree, whatever the apparent generic dissimilarities between those two works.

The explanation of Descartes's use of the *apparently* different forms must then be sought elsewhere than in the philosophical substance of the works; and indeed we know that the motives of persuasion and defensiveness, of addressing various and quite different audiences and standards, were important in Descartes's own deliberations on the means of philosophical expression. To this extent, Descartes himself acknowledges the derivatively rhetorical character of the various genres he *seems* to employ. Between the *Discourse* and the *Meditations*, I conclude, then, that the case for a generic distinction is weak; it is much stronger for the "Replies to Objections," although Descartes there is in effect writing a commentary on this own work—a complex shift which would require further scrutiny in its own right. Genre, as I have earlier claimed, is not a matter only of apparent form (so the case against Berkeley's *Dialogues* as "true" dialogues), and although undoubtedly not every difference or claim *for* synonymy can be resolved in terms of this distinction between apparent and real forms, enough of them can be to support rather than to weaken the case I have been arguing.

Along the same line: it is surely an intelligible question, to ask for any text what it is "about." If one answers this question, in the case of *King Lear,* that the play is about an aged king who divides his kingdom among his daughters and then, once at their mercy, finds himself badly treated by them—that is certainly to say something true about the play; but it also conveys little of the play's force. Similarly, we may ask questions about *any* text in terms of categories that although intrinsically alien to the text *are* to the point from which the reader starts out. This means no more than that whatever else the style-content distinction is, the principal categories themselves are contextual—the context being in part shaped by the work, in part by the critical apparatus applied to it. There is no certain or obvious way of determining a priori how aptly a particular critical structure will fit any particular work. But this means only what any serious reader quickly learns anyway: that there is no fulcrum from which to move the world of interpretation—for interpreting philosophical or indeed, any other texts. We take a chance when we begin to read; and so far as we *pretend* to eliminate that chance by imposing external categories and then by denying their defeasibility, we falsify both the texts and what we (allegedly) learn from them. Style is not everything in the text, but there is nothing that is not touched by it—and this means that unless we read for style consciously, with the awareness of its role in shaping the process of reading, we shall be reading style anyway, but as nature—our *own* nature. Bacon named a "crime of the mind" the tendency of a mind "to identify its own sense of order with the cosmic order." This is exactly what the presumption of neutrality or stylelessness in philosophical discourse does.

The argument for a poetics of philosophical discourse as set out above is by its own design a programmatic argument, intended to suggest the importance for understanding philosophical texts philosophically, of a poetics which categorizes the literary means of philosophical expression. This does not mean that such analysis will be crucial or decisive in every instance of interpretation—but this same concession would hold, I believe, for virtually any single category of interpretation. What it does mean is that the evidence of philosophical meaning includes the evidence of the literary or stylistic status of the work—and that like the other elements of that meaning in any particular case, this element may make a significant difference. Does it follow from this that once we *have* a poetics of philosophical discourse we can expect radical revisions in the standard readings of philosophy? In philosophy itself? Certainly, if these changes should occur, that would corroborate the thesis advanced here. But it is also important to note that these are not, for every specific text, necessary consequences. If stylistic analysis is one element of philosophical reading among others, at work *with them* to yield an interpretation and understanding, then the consequences of such analysis may or may not be decisive; for any given text, it may in fact make a small difference. But this means no more than that poetics has already, unavoidably, been part of the tacit understanding of philosophy, and this should hardly surprise us. That the standard versions of the history of philosophy are themselves texts is itself an intimation of the textuality of the individual works that comprise that history. Only the philosopher who takes as his goal the ideal of jumping out of his own skin will find anything objectionable—or surprising—in the necessary requirement that philosophy too lives within the text.

Notes

1. *Relatively* little, I suppose I should say. Cf. as examples of general statements: L. W. Beck, "Philosophy as Literature," in B. Lang, ed., *Philosophical Style: An Anthology on the Reading and Writing of Philosophy* (Chicago: Nelson-Hall, 1980); B. Blanshard, *On Philosophical Style* (Manchester: University of Manchester Press, 1954); R. G. Collingwood, "Philosophy as a Branch of Literature," in *An Essay on*

Philosophical Method (Oxford: Oxford University Press, 1933); J. Collins, *Interpreting Modern Philosophy* (Princeton, N. J.: Princeton University Press, 1972); L. Mackey, "On Philosophical Form," *Thought* 40 (1967): 238–60; C. Perelman and L. Olbrechts-Tyteca, *Rhetorique et philosophie* (Paris: Presses universitaire de France, 1952). A seminal work on the literary status of philosophy, although not formulated in literary terms, is S. Pepper, *World Hypotheses* (Berkeley, Calif.: University of California Press, 1942); cf. also R. S. Brumbaugh and N. P. Stallknecht, *The Compass of Philosophy* (New York: Longman, 1954).

I do not mean to suggest that philosophy alone among the "humane sciences" has avoided this question of its own literary status. Works such as H. White's *Metahistory* (Baltimore: Johns Hopkins Press, 1973) and R. Brown's *A Poetic for Sociology* (New York: Cambridge University Press, 1977) have only recently begun to draw attention to that question in other disciplines. Literary criticism and theory have been no more attentive to their literary means—emphasizing even now, mainly the status, not the structure, of criticism vis-à-vis literature. (Cf., e.g., G. Hartman, "Crossing Over: Literary Commentary as Literature," *Comparative Literature* 28 (1976): 257–76; G. Steiner, "'Critic'/'Reader'," *New Literary History* 10 (1979): 423–52.)

2. M. Parry, *The Making of Homeric Verse* (Oxford University Press, 1971); A. Lord, *The Singer of Tales* (Cambridge, Mass.: Harvard University Press, 1960); E. Havelock, *A Preface to Plato* (Cambridge, Mass.: Harvard University Press, 1963).

3. Cf. W. J. Ong, *Interfaces of the Word* (Ithaca, N.Y.: Cornell University Press, 1977).

4. Cf., e.g., B. Eichenbaum, "The Theory of the Formal Method," in L. Matejka and K. Pomoroska, eds., *Readings in Russian Poetics* (Cambridge, Mass.: M.I.T. Press, 1971), and J. Mukarovsky's more restricted version of the same concept in "The Place of the Aesthetic Function among the Other Functions," in *Structure, Sign, and Function* (New Haven, Conn: Yale University Press, 1978).

5. E.g., the standard statements in I. A. Richards, *Science and Poetry* (New York: Norton, 1926); A. J. Ayer, *Language, Truth, and Logic* (London: Gollancz, 1936); C. L. Stevenson, *Ethics and Language* (New Haven, Conn.: Yale University Press, 1944).

6. Cf. Blanshard's comparison of F. H. Bradley and T. H. Green, *On Philosophical Style*, p. 54.

7. For analysis of the systematic problems of genre, cf. P. Hernadi, *Beyond Genre* (Ithaca, N.Y.: Cornell University Press, 1972), and J. P. Strelka, ed.,*Theories of Literary Genre* (University Park, Penn.: Pennsylvania State Press, 1978); and on genres in philosophy, J. Marias, "Literary Genres in Philosophy," in *Philosophy as Dramatic Theory* (University Park, Penn.: Pennsylvania State Press, 1971), and S. H. Daniel, "A Philosophical Theory of Literary Continuity and Change," *Southern Journal of Philosophy* 18 (1980): 275–80.

8. For a general analysis of the concept of point of view, cf. below, ch. 7; and for other applications of the concept to philosophical writing, cf., e.g., J. Klein, *A Commentary on Plato's "Meno"* (Chapel Hill, N.C.: University of North Carolina Press, 1965), and D. Simpson, "Putting One's House in Order: The Career of the Self in Descartes' Method," *New Literary History* 9 (1977): 83–102.

9. Cf. J. Hintikka, "Cogito, Ergo Sum: Inference or Performance?" *Philosophical Review* 71 (1962): 3–32.

10. Cf. W. Iser, *The Implied Reader* (Baltimore, Md.: Johns Hopkins Press, 1974), and *The Act of Reading* (Baltimore, Md.: Johns Hopkins Press, 1978); L. Nelson, Jr., "The Fictive Reader and Literary Self-Reflexiveness," in P. Demetz,

T. Greene, L. Nelson, Jr., eds., *The Discipline of Criticism* (New Haven, Conn.: Yale University Press, 1968); T. Todorov, "La lecture comme constructions," *Poetique* 24 (1975): 417–25; S. R. Suleiman and I. Crosman, eds., *The Reader in the Text* (Princeton, N.J.: Princeton University Press, 1980).

11. As in *Anatomy of Criticism* (Princeton, N.J.: Princeton University Press, 1957).

12. M. Schapiro, "Style," in R. L. Kroeber, ed., *Anthropology Today* (Chicago: University of Chicago Press, 1953). Cf. also for a number of recent statements on the general issues of style (many of them still responding to Schapiro), S. Chatman, ed., *Literary Style* (New York: Oxford University Press, 1971), and B. Lang, ed., *The Concept of Style* (Philadelphia, Pa.: University of Pennsylvania Press, 1979).

13. Cf. for analyses of *particular* philosophical styles that support this general claim, e.g., T. Binkley, *Wittgenstein's Language* (The Hague: Mouton, 1974); A. Donagan, "Victorian Philosophical Prose: J. S. Mill and F. H. Bradley," in S. P. Rosenbaum, ed., *English Literature and British Philosophy* (Chicago: University of Chicago Press, 1971); L. O. Mink (on R. G. Collingwood), *Mind, History, and Dialectic* (Bloomington, Ind.: Indiana University Press, 1969); R. Ross, "Hobbes' Rhetoric," in R. Ross, H. Schneider, and T. Waldman, eds., *Thomas Hobbes in His Time* (Minneapolis, Minn.: University of Minnesota Press, 1974). P. Friedlander, *Plato* (Princeton, N.J.: Princeton University Press, 1970), vol. 1; J. Klein, *A Commentary on Plato's "Meno"*; A. W. Levi, "Philosophy as Literature: The Dialogue," *Philosophy and Rhetoric* 9 (1976).

14. Cf., e.g., *Of Grammatology* (Baltimore, Md.: Johns Hopkins Press, 1977) and also the elliptical exchange (elliptical on all sides) between Derrida and J. Searle in *Glyph*, nos. 1 and 2; cf. also R. Rorty, "Philosophy as a Kind of Writing: An Essay on Derrida," *New Literary History* 10 (1978): 141–60. On Derrida's account, the issue of the relation between philosophical "content" and "form" inevitably begs the question because there *is* no content—a handy way, it seems to me, of concealing the baby in the bathwater.

15. I take the proposition as the readiest instance of the "abstract entity" presupposed in claims for "sameness" of meaning; but obviously it has not been the only candidate (cf. A. Church, "The Need for Abstract Entities in Semantic Analysis," *Proceedings of the American Academy of Arts and Sciences* 80 (1951): 100–112); and efforts have also been made to argue for a functional equivalence of synonymy without abstract entities, for example by invoking truth conditions or linguistic acts (cf. W. V. Quine, " Russell's Ontology," in E. D. Klemke, ed., *Essays on Bertrand Russell* (Urbana, Ill.: University of Illinois Press, 1970), pp. 55–57. The efforts to preserve synonymy but to avoid abstract entities seem to me consistently to beg the question; in any event, the issue discussed here arises just if an abstract entity were invoked in order to argue for synonymy.

16. As in *A History of Western Philosophy* (New York: Simon and Schuster, 1945), pp. 195–196. Cf. also H. Veatch, *Two Logics* (Evanston, Ill.: Northwestern University Press, 1969) for an opposed view of the relation between Aristotelian and post-*Principia* logic.

17. Cf. W. V. Quine, "The Problem of Meaning in Linguistics," in *From a Logical Point of View* (Cambridge, Mass.: Harvard University Press, 1953); *Word and Object* (Cambridge, Mass.: M.I.T. Press, 1964), esp. ch. 2; also N. Goodman, "On Likeness of Meaning," *Analysis* 10 (1949): 1–7; "A World of Individuals," in *The Problem of Universals* (Notre Dame, Ind.: University of Notre Dame Press, 1956); "The Status of Style," *Critical Inquiry* 1 (1975): 799–811.

18. Cf., e.g., B. Croce, *Aesthetic*, trans. D. Ainslee (London: Macmillan, 1922), p. 36.

19. C. Brooks, *The Well-Wrought Urn* (New York: Reynal and Hitchcock, 1947). Cf. also J. Hosper's concept of "true to" in *Meaning and Truth in the Arts* (Chapel Hill, N.C.: University of North Carolina Press, 1946) and L. W. Beck's use of "semantic arrest" in "Judgments of Meaning in Art," *Journal of Philosophy* 41 (1944): 169–78. An interesting twist on this issue is suggested by the title of the current series, "The Arguments of Philosophers," ed. by T. Honderich (Rutledge and Kegan Paul). The implication of the title—and of the volumes that have so far appeared in the series—is that although philosophers may have done other things than argue, those other things either are reducible to argument or are not philosophically significant.

2
Space, Time, and Philosophical Style

The light dove, cleaving the air in her free flight, and feeling its resistance, might imagine that its flight would be still easier in empty space.

> Kant, "Introduction" to
> *Critique of Pure Reason*

My work consists of two parts: the one presented here plus all that I have *not* written.

> Wittgenstein, letter to
> von Ficker, referring to
> the *Tractatus*

It is a continuing irony that in an age of philosophical self-consciousness philosophers have been largely indifferent to questions about their own means of expression. It is as though they had tacitly established a distinction between form and matter, and had also asserted an order of priority between them: the "matter" was what they would deal with—the form of its expression being an accidental feature of the acts of conception and communication. To be sure, there is a method, or at least a dogma, behind this inclination. If one assumes that philosophical discourse cloaks the outline of a natural propositional logic, then the mode of discourse would indeed be arbitrarily related to its substance; at most, the medium of discourse would reflect an aesthetic decision—where "aesthetic" is meant to suggest a matter of taste, and "taste" in turn, a noncognitive ground. However one first put the utterance, it could be translated into a single proposition of standard form which would be either true or false.

But this presumption at once concedes too much to the grasp of logical structure and too little to the contingencies of philosophical truth. At all events it *is* a dogma, and if not the first or largest in the line of "scandals to philosophy," it yet warrants attention, specifically to the question of how the kernel of truth from which it grew finally turned against itself. The issue thus raised need not be prejudged by

47

us either; thus the question at stake here is still, in the end, whether there *is* a connection between the form and the substance of philosophical expression, or again, of what in that same source has acted in so many accounts to render the connection invisible. I shall be suggesting that the link between the form and the content of philosophical writing is more fundamental even conceptually than the distinction between them; and that a program for the analysis of philosophical style follows from the recognition of this connection—a program which then bears directly on the practice, or "doing," of philosophy itself.[1]

1. Literary Points of View

Recent literary theory has fruitfully employed the concept of the author's "point of view."[2] That concept refers to the way in which the author of the literary work or, more precisely, the author's persona in the work affects the pattern of literary action. The possible variety of these appearances, once the principle is indicated, is evident. The author may, for example, act openly as a "teller," explicitly directing the reader's attention, asking questions, passing judgment on the events of the literary process as or after or before they occur. He may otherwise, under a superficial cover, establish his presence through one of the characters of the work, by means of the authorial "I," or by such emphasis or autobiographical fidelity that the identification becomes unmistakable. Again, he may act less overtly, as the concealed narrator who reports a sequence of events under the semblance of a bystander's neutrality. Here, too, variations occur. The more fully the author is informed on private events—feelings, thoughts—in the lives of his characters, the more the author, however concealed, asserts himself as omnipotent controller and thus principal of the narration: to know all, where the knower is also creator, is to be accountable for everything. At the other extreme, the fullest attempt at self-effacement will occur as the very notion of a sequence of narrated events is place in doubt—where, as in the "New Novel" of Sarraute and Robbe-Grillet, the figure of the author is submerged in an express reluctance even to impose continuity on the events of the narration. (It is important to note the limits to this extreme: the author will be with us in *some* form unless, *per impossibile*, the events described and also their descriptions are fully random.)

Analysis of these variations on the author's point of view affords a useful means of stylistic discrimination: its common categories have served to make intelligible the procedural differences among such

diverse authors as Sterne, Dickens, and James—and also among the
works of a single author (as Van Meter Ames did for Conrad).[3] These
concrete stylistic differences also subtend more abstract features, like
the generic status of the individual works. The lyric poem, for example, involves a distinctive appearance of the author's persona: the "I"
usually figures as both "subject" and "substance" (to cite Dewey's
distinction) of the poem—related in both those aspects to a single and
personal moment of experience. A ready contrast to this generic feature marks the epic poem, where the author's persona is transper-
sonal or intersubjective—to the extent that Lukács, in *The Theory of
the Novel*, argues that the point of view which shapes the epic is not
that of the individual author but of the author's society as a whole.

These distinctions are crucial for a grasp of the significance of individual works, of their kinds, and finally of the medium of the literary
art as such: the questions of what the import is of individual literary
structures, of genres, and of literature in general, what ends they
realize and what the conditions are which enable them to do this,
would be problematic without these and related distinctions, even if
the distinctions by themselves do not fully answer those questions.
What we accomplish by such conceptual clarification may be only a
ground from which speculation sets out—but that ground, it seems,
comprises a sine qua non.

I shall be suggesting that a similar method of analysis is fruitful in
uncovering the structural intentions, and finally the meanings, of
philosophical texts. Prima facie, of course, substantial differences
separate philosophical discourse and the forms of writing conventionally labeled literature—fiction, drama, poetry; thus, the pertinence of
similar analytic techniques remains to be established. But at least one
item in the cluster of superficial differences between the two forms
suggests that the issue of the author's point of view will be still more
decisive in its bearing on the philosophical work than it is with respect to poetry or to fictional prose. The question "What is literature?" is not a necessary concern, even tacitly, of the literary author;
the point of view which he asserts as author imputes no general
character to literature. "What is literature?" in other words, is not
itself a literary question. The philosopher's position differs markedly
from this. "Philosophy," Simmel writes, "is the first of its own problems"; and one could hardly be accused of hyberbole in finding that
for the history of philosophical writing this has been its *only* problem.
The variety of points of view embodied in philosophical writing represents a claim about the character of philosophy as a project if only
because there is no way of dissociating those points of view from that
project. Few philosophers have conceived of their writings as belong-

ing to one of several possible media or genres; and although I have suggested in chapter 1 that there is good reason for speaking explicitly of philosophical genres, this traditional reticence on the part of philosophers themselves is something more than only a symptom of parochialism. It indicates, rather, the more dominant end of philosophical truth toward which the philosopher has traditionally moved and to which he had tended to subordinate all discussion of the discursive or literary means. (*That* means, in any event, has not been treated as an end.) But this single-mindedness of purpose also has an interesting consequence for applications of the concept of point of view: it is precisely such intentionality that makes point of view significant in the literary understanding.

2. The Structures of Philosophical Point of View

In the following discussion, then, I attempt to derive or "deduce" a typology of philosophical writing from the category of the author's point of view. Because of its intended breadth, the typology will be rough both in definition and in the applications to be cited. Yet the distinctions marked even in this approximation are, I should argue, real enough; they can, or at least ought, to make a difference in the reading—and perhaps, at some remote end, in the writing—of philosophy. Those prospective differences provide, in any event, a criterion of confirmation for the account.

The main distinction proposed here delineates three modes of philosophical writing: the "expository," the "performative," and the "reflexive" modes. The differences among these modes, again, are centered in the role asserted in the work by the author or the author's conception of the audience addressed; the boundaries of the subject matter of which the point of view is a view; and the purpose which that view is meant to accomplish. The author, I shall be arguing, speaks tacitly of each of these through the medium of the point of view; the three modes differ from each other in one or more of these respects.

The expository mode refllects the literal force of the term *exposition* as we understand it to suggest a putting or laying out. The preeminent feature of this mode is the static and independent character of each of its points of reference: the author, his audience, the subject of the exposition, and the exposition itself. The relations among these, and thus the act of communication in which they are actualized, are accidental; the process makes little difference to any of them. The author may be named in the body of the work, designated by an editorial "we" or the less formal "I"; but he need not introduce himself at all, and the difference between the works in which he does and does not do so is irrevelant to the mode. The philosopher conceives the subject of his writing as an intelligible "given" whose status is independent of anything he says about it and a fortiori of the fact that the writer, or anybody else, addresses it. In other words, he *exposes* a subject matter for philosophical analysis; his writing is an attempt to mirror or to represent that subject matter. He may hope that this representation will be original insofar as it makes identifications which previously had not been, or had been insufficiently, remarked—but even if he succeeds in this, his act is one of discovery rather than of invention; he articulates what had otherwise been indistinct.

In this manner of address, the expository mode also assigns a character to the author himself. Specifically, it supposes that as his subject matter is fully formed and open to analysis, he, the philosopher, is also complete, at least in the sense that what it is he is examining and the results to which that examination may lead neither affect nor are significantly affected by him. He appears as a detached observer who possesses a power of comprehension corresponding in elements of its process to elements in the object to which the process is directed. The object, as it happens, is intelligible—and he, also as it happens, has the capacity for penetrating that intelligibility.

Related features distinguish the audience addressed in the expository mode. These differ from the elements of the answer to the merely psychological question of *why* the philospher writes—a question which could evoke a multiplicity of reasons including the claim that finally he writes for his own pleasure, indifferent to whether anyone will ever read, let alone agree with, what he says. Even in such an extreme case, he will have built into his work a conception of what the reader *would* be who *did* read and work—and it follows reasonably, if not inevitably, that the image of the conjectured reader closely approximates the same ideal of detachment assumed by the writer himself: independent of the subject matter being examined and also of the author's representation of it, yet capable—like the author—of grasping that representation and of recognizing its relation to the subject matter from which it has been abstracted. The reader is thus held to be essentially identical with the writer; the accidental fact that he is *not* the writer is in effect amended when the reader has understood what the writer has written. The reader then has in *his* head the same thing that the author had,—and this, it seems, represents success on both sides of the venture.

So far the portrait is an abstraction, and, as with any portrait,

references to the sitter in the flesh may not by themselves demonstrate its aptness. But consider, for example, the opening lines of
Hume's *Treatise*, that paradigm of analytic method which "falling
still-born from the press," still continues to beget descendants in the
philosophical literature: "All the perceptions of the human mind resolve themselves into two distinct kinds, which I shall call *impressions* and *ideas*. The difference betwixt these consists in the degree of
force and liveliness, with which they strike upon the mind, and make
their way into our thought or consciousness. . . . I believe it will not
be very necessary to employ many words in explaining this distinction."[4]

The essayist in these lines injects himself into his prose, and one
may find in this fact the intimation of a less impersonal manner of
philosophical writing than that referred to above as the expository
mode. But counterevidence appears even in the brief passage cited,
and that counterevidence is dominant in the *Treatise* as a whole. In
his reference to the "human mind," it seems clear, Hume also includes the Humean mind: he looks on himself no less than on others
as an object of experience, and the difficulties he has in *finding* such
objects, in himself or any other self, do not detract from the intention); his own self, he asks his reader's warrant, is a typical or characteristic self—most certainly, if the work as a whole is to make an
impression, also the reader's self. The latter, too, will recognize the
division of quality which separates impressions from ideas; he, too,
will acknowledge that all perceptions are subsumable under one or
the other category; and he, too, will come to see, as the *Treatise*
expands its range of analysis to include such topics as substance,
abstract ideas, space and time, causality, that they are indeed aspects
of perception reducible in accordance with the principle asserted in
Hume's opening lines.

A portrait is thus defined by the point of view shaping the *Treatise*
of an author who is addressing what James later named a "block
universe"—a conglomerate "given," which is all the philosopher or
any observer can start from and conclude with. If impressions and
ideas do not constitute a world identical to that of which the more
traditional realist would speak, it is only because the realist's world is
for Hume quite beyond either speech or comprehension. Impressions and ideas comprise all the world to which we have access, and
there is nothing problematic either about it or about the way its
inhabitants inhabit it. This is a model of knowing, if we seek parallels,
to which "normal" science and the normative scientist, since the seventeenth century at least, have been committed. There exists, on the
one hand, a public, or at least a common, subject matter; on the other
hand, addressing it, an investigator. The assertions of the latter are

open to inspection by an audience that stands in the same position before its source as does the philosopher. It is not to the immediate point, although it is very much to another point, that in the example cited the image projected by the author's point of view is quite at odds with the conception both of the self and its relations which the author *purports* to be bringing into view. The former is a feature *of* the writing which in this case, it seems, differs from what emerges *in* the writing. How such discrepancy is to be interpreted is a separate issue, however, from the fact that the author's point of view on his subject matter, on his own work, and finally, on his audience is firmly lodged in his written words, even if those words say nothing explicitly about any of them. It will be evident, furthermore, how traditionally philosophical in character the implied assertions thus ascribed to the expository style are; they include claims about both human nature and the reality of which that nature is a part—claims which, if they were expressed more overtly, would certainly not go without saying and which may, in the event, not go even with the saying.

Consider next two other familiar passages from the philosophical literature, one written in the seventeenth century, the other in the twentieth. These are instances of what I shall be calling, using John Austin's term,[5] the *performative* mode. The first of these selections appears in part 4 of Descartes's *Discourse on Method:*

> Thus, on the ground that our senses sometimes deceive us, I was prepared to suppose that no existing thing is such as the senses make us image it to be; and because in respect even of the very simplest geometrical questions some men err in reasoning and commit paralogisms, I therefore rejected as false (recognizing myself to be no less fallible than others) all the reasonings I have previously accepted as demonstrations; and finally, when I considered that all the thoughts we have when awake can come to us in sleep (none of the latter being then true), I resolved to feign that all the things which had entered my mind were no more true than the illusions of my dreams. But I immediately became aware that while I was thus disposed to think that all was false, it was absolutely necessary that I who thus thought should be somewhat; and noting that this truth *I think, therefore I am*, was so steadfast and so assured that the suppositions of the skeptics, to whatever extreme they might all be carried, could not avail to shake it, I concluded that I might without scruple accept it as being the first principle of the philosophy I was seeking.[6]

The second appears in G. E. Moore's essay "Proof of an External World":

> It seems to me that, so far from its being true, as Kant declares to be his opinion, that there is only one possible proof of the existence of things outside of . . . I can now give a large number of different proofs, each of

which is a perfectly rigorous proof; and that at many other times I have been in a position to give many others. I can prove now, for instance, that two human hands exist. How? By holding up my two hands, and saying, as I make a certain gesture with the right hand, "Here is one hand," and adding, as I make a certain gesture with the left, "and here is another." And if, by doing this, I have proved *ipso facto* the existence of external things, you will all see that I can also do it in a number of other ways: there is no need to multiply examples.[7]

It has been argued by Hintikka that Descartes's statement of the *cogito* satisfies (and gains its force from this fact) the criteria laid down by Austin for peformative utterance.[8] I suggest here a related but broader point: that certain features of the statements by Descartes and Moore define a characteristic—performative—mode of expression recognizably different from that identified in the passage from Hume.

The first of these features concerns the way in which the authorial "I" literally *shapes* the philosophical structure. In their statements, Descartes and Moore (in contrast to Hume) are referring not to a general or common self, but specifically to the individual who is making the statement and performing whatever other actions accompany the saying itself. Descartes himself wrote in part 1 of the *Discourse:* "My present design is not to teach a method which every one ought to follow for the right conduct of his reason, but only to show in what manner I have endeavoured to conduct my own." And even if we hear in these words a nuance of ritual modesty, the longer quotation cited from Descartes testifies to the presence of other elements as well. Both Descartes and Moore present themselves as selves engaged in an action; they are not speaking of independent facts or a world they never made. To be sure, what they uncover in their discourse has a life of its own and is independent of the work of philosophy: Moore's hands (if his account is correct) *are* there, and were there quite apart from his proof (that is, in the main, what he claims to have proven). Descartes's self (if his argument stands) demonstrably exists. But the view from which Descartes and Moore as philosophers write of this is a view—if we take them at their words— of contingency, of a state of affairs which might or might not obtain, not because contingency is itself in question, but because the identities of philosophy and the philosopher themselves are initially regarded as contingent. The shift here has moved from a detached view of the philosopher's "I" as an object both like the objects of its scrutiny and causally independent of them, to an assertion of the "I" as a subject affecting and being affected by that assertion.

The same point might be put in terms of Russell's distinction: the "I" of the author is not only "mentioned" in the passages quoted, it is also "used." The author's persona is in balance in the work itself and thus dependent on its conclusions, not in the hypothetical sense that we would all of us be different if the force of gravity on the earth's surface were ten times greater than it is, but insofar as what he says or does at certain junctures in his work makes a difference at once in him as philosopher and in the philosophical work, if not quite in the subject matter of his analysis. The process of philosophical discourse unfolds not as an image or reflection of a given state of affairs but as a construction or performance of both the state of affairs and the philosopher himself; one hears something of this simply in the rhetorical emphasis on the authorial "I". An intelligible or "given" reality is perhaps being asserted by the two statements—but that status as defined philosophically remains a function of the involvement of the authors in the statements.

The requirement which such presentation imposes on the reader is correspondingly different from that encountered in the expository mode, where the attention of the reader—like that of the writer—is directed to an external reality for which his own presence is a matter of indifference. Here, too, he is invited to duplicate the writer, but not in the sense that if he simply opens his eyes, or his mind's eye, and reads, a faculty of his will find itself joined by affinity to an object—and that even if he does not, the object will be essentially unchanged. Rather, *if* the reader chooses to reenact what the author has done, if he follows the procedure indicated by the latter, he may establish for himself what the writer has established; it is that personal and individual construction, a constitution of the philosophical self, which is the prospect offered by the writer. The reader *need* not accept; neither the procedure nor the question to which it is directed is a "fact." The author thus *wills* the shape of the assertion—and perhaps, as that will persists, the shape of the reader as well.

The claim is admittedly vague that the writer in the performative mode takes the concept of a person more seriously than is the case in the expository mode; but it is no accidental appreciation of their work that Descartes is so often linked to the beginnings of "modern" thought, with its divergent emphasis from that of the medieval tradition on the status of the individual thinker; or that Moore appeared to his Bloomsbury followers to have struck a blow for individual as well as for philosophical freedom from the cumbersome apparatus of Idealism. The figure of the writer appears in this mode, then, not simply as a rhetorical image (although it is also that), but because the writer finds it conceptually impossible to take the self and its objects—even his own self and *its* objects—for granted. The contrast here with the expository mode is not meant to imply that experiment or the process of verification is irrelevant to the latter, but that the questions on which such procedures bear are posterior in the expository mode to the philosophical starting point. The performative mode, on the other hand, attempts to start with the reader at the beginning of philosophy as well as at the beginning of the individual problems admitted by philosophy; and whether or not it successfully reaches back to that first self-conscious point, this suggests a different sense of purpose from the one we have previously seen in the expository mode, according to which the writer, the reader, and the world of which they are part are all comfortably settled before the owl of Minerva takes wing. It is some further evidence of this emphasis on the origin and person of the philosopher that in Descartes the problem of "other minds"—of how the individual knowing himself can know anybody else—enters philosophy; and that in Moore and the tradition that follows him, this same question and one parallel to it, concerning the possibility of a private language, appear so vividly. Persons pose a problem here, given the beginning of reflection from an inside, which they could not for Hume, who had rejected to begin with the formal distinction between insides and outsides. Moore's suggestion in his autobiography that he would probably never have been engaged by philosophical problems were it not for the foolish things that other people had said about them speaks more concisely to the same point: starting with the self, occupied with it, one first discovers the possibility of philosophical discourse not by the contemplation of some variation on Hume's matters of fact but by the personification of those matters of fact in language.

The reflexive mode appears as a mediating point between the other two modes. We have noted thus far the author in his role as an external observer or agent, acting to represent a given subject matter; and we have seen, on the other hand, the author setting out from his starting place as author, internal to the questions of philosophy, governing their resolution only insofar as he establishes his own place with respect to them. In the reflexive mode, the point of view of the author attempts to transcend the exclusivity of these two points of view by affecting a characteristic and deliberate ambivalence in the form of presentation. This ambivalence or shifting between an external and an internal center is the most striking stylistic feature, for example, of Plato's dialogues and of Kierkegaard's pseudonymous writings. The reader can never be free, in his encounter with these works, of the search for the author's persona. What, we continually (and finally) ask ourselves, is Plato *asserting*—about the soul, about knowledge, about the philosophical life? The same opacity persists in subtler form when, even as we close in on what we take to be the doctrine of the author (and surely we do this, whatever the obstructions, for both Plato and Kierkegaard), we find ourselves moved, not by a redirection of perception to an object which the author has seen, or by an invitation to perform an action first completed by the author, but by a lure which would involve us, *together with the author*, in a process which promises only that it will continue to take us as seriously (and long) as we take it—perhaps, finally, to a common point of realization.

Consider as an example of this mode the short Platonic dialogue *Euthyphro*, in which the course of action follows a regular and consistent pattern. Euthyphro has brought criminal charges against his father for the killing of a slave. Socrates encounters him in court before the trial, and after the two have agreed that bringing such charges raises the issue of filial piety, Socrates asked Euthyphro to explain to him the standard of holiness which justifies his suit. Euthyphro first begs the question by replying that what he is doing is holy; pressed by Socrates, he offers a definition of the holy as that which is pleasing to the gods. But Socrates, after pointing out that the gods often disagree among themselves, raises the subtler question of whether what is holy pleases the gods. Euthyphro takes this question seriously (or as seriously as he can) only to find that, however he answers it, he is still begging the initial question: either one of the alternatives presupposes a general conception of holiness. Socrates tries again by inquiring after the relation between holiness and other virtues, such as justice; holiness, according to Euthyphro, is part of justice, the other part having to do with the service performed by mankind. By such services, it turns out, Euthyphro also means holiness—that is, a commerce between man and the gods which gives the gods what they desire. But how can man give the gods anything which they lack? Or how can the gods lack anything? "And so we must go back again," Socrates concludes, "and start from the beginning to find out what the holy is." Euthyphro, however, discovers that he is in a hurry: "Another time, then, Socrates. . . ."

Socrates' own impending trial serves as a background to the developing confusion in which this dialogue ends. The conclusion suggests that Euthyphro knows no more what he is about in bringing his own father to trial than do his friends who have brought the charges against Socrates. But the dialogue is more than a period piece. It raises even for the reader ignorant of the historical context an abstract question about the nature of virtue; but for him, as for Euthyphro, it provides a series of apparently false starts in place of an answer.

Where, the reader asks, is Plato the writer in this? To be so adroit in uncovering what virtue is not *seems* to presuppose a grasp of what it is—and yet the reader is apparently to be allowed no share of this. It might be held, of course, that the dialogue is the historical record of an actual conversation; in this case the question of the author's point of view would be hermeneutically if not historically an irrelevance. But if we accept the external and internal evidence that this is not the case for *any* of Plato's dialogues, the original questions remain: What can we make of the author's persona? Does he have one? And if so, what relation is meant to be asserted between the persona and his audience?

The evidence that there *are* answers to these questions is compelling: Plato's Socrates may be neither the historical Socrates nor the historical Plato, but he is, nonetheless, the dominant figure in this dialogue as in nearly all of the others. The questions raised in the dialogue remain unanswered; but the force of the questions and of the method by which they are addressed is only intelligible in terms of an object to be realized—an object which, however, makes no obvious appearance in the dialogue. Enough has been said about the substantive role of the dialogue form in Plato's writing to suggest how fundamental that role is; I deal here only, and rather sketchily, with the topic of the author's point of view that we have been following. The articulation of that point of view in the *Euthyphro* is, it seems, twofold—emerging both within the dialogue (insofar as Socrates is evidently the dominant figure) and from outside the dialogue, in the sense that the sequence of discussion comprising the work, however inconclusive, nonetheless defines a pattern for the whole separable from the statements of even the dominant figure.[9] The discourse internal to the dialogue, in other words, is aimed at a goal which stands beyond it; as this is the case, both the participants in the dialogue and the reader who follows them are also intended to reach beyond it. This does not mean that the *process* initiated in the dialogue is ultimate—that Plato is intimating, as has sometimes been supposed, that philosophy is no more than a method. For the method disclosed in the structure of the dialogue is only intelligible as it is understood to reach toward a substantive end. The question of what virtue is, and the elements which compose that question, are real enough. There is then for philosophy a subject matter—but one for which the process by which it will be comprehended is intrinsic to the comprehension and inseparable from the persons of both the reader and the writer. The point at which the reader enters the dialectic will vary according to the place he is in to begin with; the author himself is at one such point. Like the author acting both within the work and in his control of the structure as a whole, the reader is incomplete—to be realized, as a first step, through the process of the work. Like the author who has shaped the dialogue, the reader who commits himself to the process *commits* himself also to the presumption of completion or fulfillment: the drive of Eros, Plato suggests in the *Symposium*, is itself sufficient evidence of an object.

The presumption of the existence of an object for philosophy constrains both the object and the role of the reader. The object is for Plato quite real—but it is not a "given" which the reader can expect to fit into a prefabricated framework. Both the individual dialogues and philosophy as a project are intended to uncover the ground on which such frameworks are constructed—and this, too, we understand from the indirection of the dialogue form. There is no "thing" to be communicated or transferred from writer to reader. The end for philosophical discourse is in the comprehension of that point from which the specific questions of the dialogues devolve—knowledge which requires a merging or identification between the object and the knower (whether he be writer or reader). Euthyphro, hurrying away from the conversation to continue his suit, may obliterate in his own mind the seed of doubt planted by Socrates' refutations; the reader who observes that doubt planted has less excuse for ignoring it himself. So far as he admits the doubt, he will, like Socrates, continue to search for its resolution, or finally attempt *to become* its resolution.

3. Point of View and the Poetics of Philosophy

The conceptual possibility of the typology outlined or of another like it would exist, it seems, only insofar as questions directed to style as an aspect of the philosophical surface were embedded in the deeper structure of philosophical mattter—if, that is, in asking after the author's point of view, we acknowledged a bond between that apparently rhetorical appearance and the philosophically systematic assertions whose appearance it is. The anatomy so far given here of that bond, even with the work of the preceding chapter, has been gross; the possibilities of refining the anatomy are implicit, however, and return us, after some indirection, to the title of *this* chapter.

The stylistic concept of point of view is a visual metaphor and, even within the limits of the metaphor, cites a single item in a complex transaction. But the elements of the metaphor, the perspectival field of space and time which composes a point of view, are not merely symbolic. As philosophers have written about the fundamental character of space and time, so *in* their writings, we may locate those same categories or parameters. They serve at that level as something more than either a manner of speaking or a merely theoretical answer to a traditional problem of metaphysics; they articulate the philosopher's world—more precisely, the world of his work. The persona of the philosopher appears as a moment or unit of force on that space-time grid—and the question left over by *every* philosophical work is whether and to what extent the analogous framework from within which the reader reads, which defines *his* point of view, can be linked to that other framework. The distinctions among the alternate modes cited above thus appear as variations in the action and place of a unit traced internally by means of the categories of space and time.

In the expository mode, the interior space and time of the written work define a structure of stable dimensions; by his motion across them, the author serves as a pointer, focusing the attention of the reader on objects located in the matrix. Contingency is excluded from the movement of the effective unit of force, if only because it is excluded from the dimensions themselves; at most, the movement may bring to light unpredicted, but not unpredictable, occurrences. The grid as a whole underwrites a neutrality of impulse and a governing disinterest to which any activity taking place subordinates itself: the interior time and space of the written work permit no alternative. There is thus nothing originative—with respect either to itself or to the objects it encounters—in the motion of the unit of force. That unit may assume various guises, but whether it assumes the role of a bundle of impressions and ideas or of mind contemplating a particular event under the aegis of Spinoza's third level of knowledge, its formal identity is constant: the activity, its viewer is made to understand, is for the sake of circumscribing an object and is quite indifferent to the results of that discrimination. The system may in some sense be self-reflective; according to information returned in its process, the process as a whole may become more or less active—or free, as Spinoza would designate this possibility. But even this variation will make no essential difference to the discursive structure, as structure, or to the movement that takes place within it. The image presented is finally that of a Newtonian universe in which space and time are autonomous elements and for which the only intelligible motion is that of physical bodies, themselves defined in terms of those elements. The formal work of philosophy on this model, as it is seen clearly and to its end, converges on the work of physics.

In the performative mode, the interior space and time of the work are not laid out *for* the activity which takes place; they are defined *by* it. This contingency, which turns on the proximity of the author's point of view to the structure which emerges as his philosophical

"world," involves the viewer as well. The contingency of interior
space and time is shared; those features and the structure which
depends on them appear *in* the act of constitution. There are alternative directions in which that process may move, and because of this,
the structure that finally emerges seems almost to have *chosen* its
form, conferring the mark of individuality which such choice conveys.

The openness does not deny the reality or efficacy of the originative
point of view—but only that the philosophical space represented in
that point of view comes into existence *with it*. It may seem odd that
the figures cited in connection with this mode—Descartes and
Moore—should thus be identified with a formulation that otherwise
resembles the pattern of traditional Idealism. But there is a historical
point here: that Idealism, however it ends (as for Hegel) by the
subordination of the individual to logical form, at least thinks to have
derived that subordination from the character of the individual himself. And there is a systematic point here as well: that the persona that
speaks from within the philosophical work may (like the rest of us)
sometimes speak more or less than it has in mind to speak and even,
at times, against itself. Here, too, intentions are revealed not only by
what is said about them but, more largely, by what is done with or
through them.

The interior space and time of writing in the reflexive mode are
located initially on the two sides of Appearance and Reality; the purpose of the author is to overcome the *apparent* discrepancy between
those modes of being. (He has similar designs on the future of the
reader.) Kierkegaard's aesthetic man takes himself as seriously as he
feels anyone should; for him the ethical and religious lives are aberra-
tions, exaggerations that fail to heed evident boundaries. But the
limits of space and time that circumscribe the aesthetic life are there
shown—from within, driven by the despair that serves for Kierkegaard as a fundamental motive—to be arbitrary, as illusory in their
restrictions as is the "moving image of eternity" by which Plato labels
the time of the apparent world. The problem for the agent in the
reflexive mode is how to span the two frameworks, how to lead himself and the viewer from the structure of appearance to that of reality
without begging the question of how to account for the existence of
either one of them. In humility before the problem—since it is *his*
problem no less than the reader's, the problem which set him to
writing in the first place—the agent conceals himself in his work, with
his anticipation of an object beyond it; only the process that he in-
itiates, if anything at all, can overcome the bifurcation. Even to explain the *fact* of that bifurcation requires concealment: thus Plato
finds refuge in the "likely story" of the *Timaeus*, and thus Kier-

kegaard's dialectice consists always of leaps forward, never (as we might sometimes wish, and not only out of nostalgia) backward.

This triadic schematism of philosophical writing is, it seems, orthodoxly philosophical in the claims it ascribes to philosophical texts. It finds in the work, on behalf of the author, a presentation of self together with a conception of the process of philosophical discourse; few philosophical writers can be named who, if they have not examined their own manner of expression for such themes, have not spoken about those same themes in the abstract as items of philosophical importance. It may be a version of humility that philosophers have commonly refrained from seeing in their own figures or manners of expression a rendering of the character of philosophy; it is more likely that this failure reflects a lack—deliberate or naive—of self-consciousness.

If the interior forms described are not equivalent, in their implied discourse, to the author's written words, they nonetheless project assertive images of the persona of the philosophical author. We do not know—we for whom a mass of images have come to constitute the elements of our own selves—how that incorporation takes place; and this is due in part to the variety of selves. But the child in every man, of whom Plato speaks in the *Phaedo* and Aristotle in the *Poetics*, who never quite escapes his original impulses, begins life, Plato and Aristotle attest, as an imitator; as this is so, in greater or lesser measure, we may expect the interior life of the philosophical work to produce echoes in the interior of those who encounter it. The medium of expression, if it is not all of the message, is nothing apart from it either; also the form of philosophy has a philosophical texture.

The implication of these distinctions, in contrast to the distinctions themselves, is not, then, primarily formal. Even the question of consistency between the author's point of view and his explicit assertions soon leads, I have claimed, to issues of philosophical substance. The distinctions drawn thus comprise a background to the philosophical text as a whole, and this is no less the case for the reader who turns first to more specific elements in the philosophical thesis being argued. Within the overarching question "What is philosophy?" other, limited questions occur; it would be foolhardy to insist that the broader question be settled or even that it be addressed before the others are taken up. And yet, of course, the larger question is never far away. "What is justice?" (as an example) remains a constant and urgent concern, one which, if the philosopher ignores it, is not likely to be acknowledged by anyone else. But it depends for sense as a question as much on the philosophically systematic context in which it holds a place as on the political or moral conflict which undoubtedly suggested originally that it should have a place. The philosopher who addresses the limited question will thus at one and the same time be speaking about the nature both of that question and of philosophical questions (and answers) in general—of what he expects to gain from them and of what he or anyone else can contribute to them. Such peripheral stipulations often remain unspoken, but this does not mean that they do not affect what is explicitly stated; even the narrowest philosophical question can hardly avoid being asked and answered from *some* point of view. Nietzsche lays about him with a broad brush when he castigates the "ascetic ideal" of traditional philosophy, that standard of scholarly detachment or disinterest which the philosopher thought to honor by rising out of or above himself. But the moral of the attack in *The Genealogy of Morals* on that ideal is one which the philosopher, finally, *cannot* escape: that it is *he* who is asserting what is asserted—and that his writing will involuntarily, if not by design, reveal its own biography. The expository mode as described above purports to escape the force of this claim or at least to defy it. But that attitude (or point of view) is itself subject to the weight of Nietzsche's criticism—a critique which is also formulated, more gently but to the same effect, in the epigraph from Kant cited at the beginning of this essay: the author, try as he may, cannot leave himself out. As an expressionless face is still to be interpreted as having an expression, so the most covert or self-denying style will remain a style.

A number of summary comments may be attached to (in some ways, against) the foregoing account. For one thing, I have suggested that the modes of expression through which an author speaks may be mixed—the author shifting his vantage point within a single work, and still more probably among his several works. The conflicts reflected in such shifts provide data as well as problems for interpretation. Why, we will be concerned to find out, do the changes occur? Again, the typology outlined seems only to mark the beginning of an analysis whose applications remain to be determined. Can we derive from it, as has been done at the same point for literary works, the pattern of philosophical genres of which I began to speak in the preceding chapter? The lyric poem and the novel, the comic and the tragic modes, accomplish various ends in expression. It is unlikely that the same generic distinctions will hold for philosophical writing; but the differences to which the typology outlined extends, as between, for example, the presentation of self in Augustine's *Confessions* and the universal reason which writes (and underwrites) Leibniz's *Monadology*, between Spinoza's geometry and the Hegelian dialectic, suggest that analogous distinctions are there to be made. The encompassing question also remains of what, given such formal distinctions as are described here, *accounts* for the linkage between them and the substantive assertions of philosophical discourse. The suspicion, even the fact, of that connection does not by itself reveal its source.

The need is thus indicated for a "poetics" of philosophical composition—a need, it turns out, which affects the philosopher as philosopher, and not simply as stylist or rhetorician. I have not claimed for the schematism outlined here priority over alternative analyses of philosophical style, still less that it could be useful only with their exclusion. My emphasis has been quite openly formal; even within the limits of this approach, other possibilities extend beyond or around the elements of the author's point of view. I have not alluded, for example, to the analysis of philosophical language; and it seems probable that such analysis, of the choice of philosophical metaphor and still more basically of the syntactic composition of individual sentences—the ontological status of subjects and predicates, after all, is a long-standing philosophical problem—would further illuminate the individual philosophical project.

It will be evident, moreover, that these same issues are also open to consideration which is less strictly formal. The appearances of philosophical writing, for example, will unavoidably figure as social devices or instruments. Whether the social reality be defined as class struggle or harmonious individualism, there is no reason for locating the work of philosophy outside of that definition; we should thus expect to find that style as a social mechanism, reflecting and opposing specific values and interests, operates also in the philosophical text. An analogous point might be made with respect to the influence of psychological forces acting on an author as he builds a systematic structure the shape of which reflects characteristic dominances and modulations, distinctions, and conjunctions. Simply to mention these possibilities is at once, it seems evident, to suggest the past indifference to them of writers on the history of philosophy and the benefits in comprehension which their study would afford. At least one of the features disclosed in the preceding discussion, however, seems to me to define a necessary theoretical ground for any such future analysis of philosophical style. A long tradition in the study of style, including philosophical style, has regarded style as an adverbial concept that represents only the "how" of an action—an action which could, by implication, have been effected as readily by some other means. Style, on this account, is at most a symptom—the outside of an internal process where it is the internal process which finally is at issue.

Nothing I have said, I believe, would preclude this manner of *speaking* about the concept of style—but everything I have said supports the more fundamental thesis that the symptoms of style, finally, are integral to the phenomenon itself. The outside of the written work, in other words, is no more—because it *cannot* be more—than the inside looking out.

Notes

1. The first step here, of course, is in recognizing that philosophy *is* a form of practice and thus that philosophical writing is itself a type of action. The historiography of philosophy, largely under the influence of nineteenth-century Idealist writers, has been almost exclusively formalistic in its view of history; thus the sociology of knowledge has yet barely touched the reflections of philosophy on itself. Gellner's *Words and Things* (Boston: Beacon Press, 1959) is still an unusual book in this respect, although see also Ree, Ayers, and Westoby, *Philosophy and Its Past* (London: Harvester, 1978).

2. See below, chapter 7, and the bibliographical references in notes 1 and 2 there.

3. Van Meter Amers, *Aesthetics of the Novel* (Chicago: University of Chicago Press, 1928), pp. 177–93.

4. David Hume, *A Treatise of Human Nature*, bk. 1, pt. 1, sec. 1.

5. As, e.g., in "Performative Utterances," in *Philosophical Papers* (Oxford: Oxford University Press, 1961).

6. *Descartes: Philosophical Writings*, trans. N. Kemp Smith (New York: Macmillan, 1958), pp. 118–19.

7. *Philosophical Papers* (London, 1959), p. 144.

8. J. Hintikka, "*Cogito, Ergo Sum:* Inference or Performance?" *Philosophical Review* (1962) 71: 3–32.

9. Note the difference in this respect between the Platonic dialogue and, e.g., Berkeley's *Dialogues between Hylas and Philonous*. The point at issue then bears not on the dialogue "form"—but precisely on the representation of the author's point of view. In Berkeley's dialogues, the actual and implied authors are one and the same; the dialogue form itself is thus accidental to the primarily expository mode of his writing. Compare on this point, and for the more sustained distinction in Plato, ch. 4 below.

3

Philosophical Humors

All men who are outstanding in philosophy, poetry or the arts are melancholic, and some to such an extent that they are infected by diseases arising from black bile.

Aristotle

If laughter, or their reputations as philosophers, depended on the jokes that philosophers tell, we should pretty quickly reach the end of both. So, for example, the magisterial Kant, who like a number of other Enlightenment figures had a soft spot for ethnic jokes, uses the American Indian to demonstrate—he thinks—how obviously mistaken and funny it is for anyone to suppose that aesthetic pleasure is identical to the pleasure we gain by the satisfaction of an appetite: "[It would be] like that Iroquois Sachem who was pleased in Paris by nothing more than the restaurants." And then the spiritual Bergson, writing about laughter in his book by that name and arguing that it is the mechanization of nature which produces it, appeals for proof to the lady "whom Cassini, the astronomer, had invited to see an eclipse of the moon. Arriving too late, she said, 'M. de Cassini, I know, will have the goodness to begin it over again, to please me.'"

Some greater appreciation may attach to the jokes of which philosophers themselves are the subject. However we may distrust Diogenes Laertius, for example, we are still reluctant to forgo his portrait of Thales, in which Thales, laboring to earn his future title as the First Philosopher, stuns his tough-minded contemporaries with the declaration that the diversity of solid and earthly things that they saw, or thought they saw, were really, underneath it all, water—and then, one evening, his eyes fixed on the stars (no doubt attempting to strong-arm them too into his thesis about water), tumbles into a well.

But then, such jokes are in the eye of the beholder— and often, we might suspect, in his mind as well. "Which way was I walking when I stopped to talk to you?" asks the practical Dewey, standing on Broadway (or perhaps it was the clerical Whitehead on Massachusetts Ave-

66

nue). "That way," replies the puzzled graduate student, pointing in the direction of Columbia (or perhaps in the direction of the Widener). "Ah, then I've had my lunch," the philosopher (Dewey or Whitehead, or perhaps even Thales) replies. And our interest in such anecdotes is in reassuring ourselves that the mighty are sometimes fallen, not in recalling that (or how) they are also sometimes great philosophers.

Is there anything more to be said about philosophical humor—something to demonstrate that, whatever the advantages of brevity, longevity, that evidently necessary condition of philosophers as well as of philosophy, is no barrier to wit? This is, I believe, a serious and unsmiling question, the answer to which—an anatomy of philosophical humor—turns out also, I believe, to be serious and unsmiling. But if talk about humor had a special obligation to be funny, talk about tragedy would in fairness have to be unusually tragic, about love, amorous, about truth, truthful. And it is clear that we should do what we can to avoid such invidious criteria.

I shall then be arguing, or at least exhibiting, two theses, one of which is so conventional as to pass without notice, the second of which is unlikely enough to be questionable even with notice—although it is the second one that would, if true, be of special interest. Thus:

> Thesis I: Irony is the characteristic literary form or trope of philosophical humor.
>
> Thesis II: Irony is the characteristic literary form or trope of philosophy as such.

First, Thesis I.

Humor or the comic may finally be indivisible, but provisional distinctions are obviously useful, and I shall be depending here on a traditional distinction among four types of humor: *irony, satire, romance,* and *farce*. The points of difference among these comic forms—what seems finally to control all generic or subgenre distinctions in literature—are differences in the types of action that they characteristically represent. So, for example, it is essential to farce that it should leave things (and people) at the end of the farce exactly where they were at its beginning (the possibility of repetition which this suggests being a large part of its attraction); romance brings a transforming resolution and harmony (often in the form of marriage or reconciliation) to the scene of a conflict; the satire is aimed to produce conflict or separation, and irony both incites conflict and discloses the subordination of one side to the other in that conflict without, however, reconciling them.

Or again, in terms of the types of power that motivate these actions, irony contrasts with the other forms in the kind of efficacy which it embodies; namely, the power of seeing or knowledge. The original character of the *"eiron"*—the stock character in Greek comedy from whom the term *irony* is taken—assumed a role of weakness and self-deprecation. But that weakness was also allied with awareness and a strength of consciousness—on this point Socrates' role as *eiron* remains a paradigm, and not only for philosophy—and the same balance of power appears in different combinations in the other comic forms: in Satire, for example, where the end to be realized is practical rather than conceptual; in farce, with its emphasis on the physical use of power (as in slapstick); in romance where the power that acts is the power of hope or expectation that follows reconcilation.

The feature of irony which is central to this very rough map of contrasts is its peculiar doubling effect, the combination of apparent surface and more real depth, initial weakness and eventual strength, affirmation and subsequent denial—all held together in the single view of the ironist. There is something of this bifocal effect, to be sure, also in the other comic forms, and there may be no general theory of the comic in which a version of the doubling and then reversal of consciousness does not play a role. The distinctiveness of irony is that the doubling is forced on the viewer with its two parts as cotemporal or synchronic; that we also, at the *same* time, recognize that they are not equals, that one of them—the part which is unspoken—is a base or ground. At no moment in irony is the agent or his audience permitted to lose sight of the immediate object of irony or, on the other side, of the ground by whose presence the object is put at a distance, made into an object. It is this sense of juxtaposition that is emphasized in the common definition of irony as "the use of a word to express its antonym" (Ducrot and Todorov, *Encyclopedic Dictionary of the Sciences of Language*). What is essential in this definition is the reference to opposition, where an opposed and stronger truth is clearly present even in absence, in the restraint of what *is* said, so much so that it need not be expressed directly—indeed, where if it *were* expressed directly, it would be *less* present.[1]

The field of vision in irony—again, for both the agent and his reader—is thus literally binocular in a way that the other comic forms do not require or match. Irony is, moreover, disclosed in a single view—much as physically binocular vision brings together the independent perceptions of the two eyes. To put this in terms of the literary concept of point of view: the perspective of the ironist is unified and constant, to such an extent that the ironist himself seems detachable from the view. The latter feature is significant in explaining the unusual intersubjectivity of irony, the fact that the reader or audience of irony takes up exactly the position of the ironist himself. "Beautiful day," I say, as we drive together in a torrential rain—and there's little chance that you will quarrel with the implied opposite: we see the same rain; we were going on the same picnic; we know equally well that it is *not* a beautiful day. There is even less room here for dissonance or for "creative interpretation" on the part of the audience than occurs in other forms of humor—and humor is altogether less a creature of criticism than are other literary appearances. Perhaps the only thing more difficult than teaching or arguing someone into laughter is teaching or arguing someone out of it. In virtually all literary genres or figures, some correlation is indicated between the roles of implied author and implied reader, but irony seems the clearest case in which those roles are directly superimposed one on the other.

Such comments only anticipate a theory of irony, but they serve to frame the evidence for the thesis that irony is the principal form of humor to be found in philosophical discourse. Socratic irony is, again, the source from which the career of philosophical irony sets out, although I mean with this first thesis to refer not only to philosophers whose work is comprehensively ironic but also to the many more local and isolated appearances of irony which populate philosophical texts.

Thus, there is nothing startling in adding a claim here for the strongly ironical character of the writings of Kierkegaard and Nietzsche to the one more usually made for Plato; and one common aspect of the work of these three figures in particular affords a useful entrance to certain of the intentions of philosophical irony. For as these authors are among the most self-conscious writers in the history of philosophy, the most constant object of their irony, it turns out, is the history of philosophical discourse itself. So for example, Nietzsche launches himself against the tradition: "[Philosophy's] systematic form attempts to evade the necessity of death in the life of the mind as of the body; it has immortal longings on it, and so it remains dead. The rigor is rigor mortis; systems are wooden crosses, Procrustean beds on which the living mind is primed. Aphorism [in contrast] is the form of death and resurrection, the form of eternity." Or again, Kierkegaard, also on the attack: "What the philosophers say about Reality is often as disappointing as a sign you see in a shop window, which reads: Pressing Done Here. If you brought your clothes to be pressed, you would be fooled; for it is only the sign that is for sale." And in Plato we find this irony turned not only against the conventions of philosophical writing, but against writing as such and surely against his own writing as well: "No intelligent man," the author of the Platonic dialogues writes, "will ever be so bold as to put into language those things which his reason has contemplated, especially not into a form which is unalterable—which must be the case with what is expressed in written symbols."

The ironic reversals invited by these writers are not, to be sure, directed only at past history. They are more explicitly pointed at their respective conceptions of what the work of philosophy is; and the key function here, I believe, is displacement—that same displacement by which, at the level of individual statement, an ironic assertion is in effect the assertion of its opposite. Socrates in this sense does not only practice irony—he *is* irony, combining in his own person in fact the two stock figures of Greek comedy—the *eiron* and the *alazon*—the self-deprecator and the impostor. "I do not know," Socrates repeats to the politicians, the poets, the generals, the Sophists whom he confronts—although he also acknowledges that he does at least know *that*. With this confession, he discloses his imposture, his strength, and the ideal of knowledge that, as a final cause, continually feeds the Platonic irony: the assertion of ignorance implies its opposite, knowledge. Socrates' own person, it may thus be said, represents the literary figure of irony, implying *its* opposite, motivating the tensions in the dialogues between Appearance and Reality and the dialectic which is intended continually to unmask the one to the other. Not to know is to start from where we are, as we are. That place is the world as given and apparent, where politicians make laws, generals give commands, Sophists sell their knackeries. Is there anything beyond or more real than those practices? Well, let the practitioners drive themselves to the denial which is indeed more real than the practices are. So Thrasymachus, in the *Republic,* plunges into a discussion about the nature of justice, shouting at Socrates that he (Socrates) is blind where even fools can see—that justice is nothing other than power. "Even when those who have power make mistakes?" Socrates asks—and Thrasymachus shows how power can make mistakes by making one, at least in the sense that he contradicts himself: "Of course not, Socrates; only when they do not make mistakes." Is Socrates unfair to take advantage of Thrasymachus's blunder? Not if we understand the irony which the blunder makes possible, and the fact that the ironist then uses it to displace one piece of the apparent world with a patch of the real one. Thrasymachus himself also implies his opposite—and Plato adds Platonic irony to the Socratic variety. So we understand, too, something more about that peculiar doctrine of anamnesis—knowledge as recollection which is, after all, always and everywhere available. Error and ignorance thus can never justly claim for themselves that they are the best their possessor can do, whoever he is and however incorrigible or invincible his mistakes may seem. The dialogues move through the disclosure by appearance itself of a reality behind it; the *eiron*—Socrates—provides the motive force by upholding the possibility of knowledge itself—the innate and thus truly constant possibility by means of which ignorance may and in some sense must become its opposite, knowledge. Even where it is not actual, irony is always possible; the truth is always present, lurking, waiting for the reversal that will disclose it.

Kierkegaard speaks more explicitly about his use of ironical method in *The Point of View for My Work as an Author:* "An illusion can never be destroyed directly," he writes there—thus justifying the systematically oblique attacks in his other works on the aesthete, the ethicist, the normal Christian—each of whom is, must be, driven from within, by *his own* works, to the reversal based on despair. The author's view here is twofold, and not only as the writer who is in control of his characters, but as consciousness itself. "In order to help another effectively," Kierkegaard writes, "I must understand more than he—yet first of all surely I must understand what he understands." The philosopher then, Kierkegaard as writer, will start not from where *he* is but from where his audience is; his task is the task of subversion, of showing to its holder from the terms of that starting point both its own inadequacy and its implication of an opposite— what we saw before to be conditions for the definition of irony. The person at the median stages of life's way affirms its opposite (in this sense consciousness itself is ironical)—and so we come back to that twofold division by which individuals may yet go beyond themselves and which Kierkegaard as author attempts to infuse in both his writings and his readers. Why did Kierkegaard sign his pseudonymous works pseudonymously? The author too must be aligned with his creation, not apart from it; it is the means by which the reader is made to feel so at home that he will not doubt his own later discovery of the inadequacy of that identity—as he undoubtedly would if the author Kierkegaard simply told him that that was the case. Even at this last point, moreover, where the leap of faith takes over, Kierkegaard does not stop being an ironist; without that leap, the irony itself would lose its power to mere skepticism which is, for Kierkegaard, a feature of the aesthetic life, itself a cause for despair.

The claim for the importance of irony in the work of these several writers is hardly novel, and as I have mentioned, my first thesis is directed not only to such broad examples, but to the appearances of philosophy at the level of individual statement as well.[2] Here too, in fact, we find ready and many examples, an insistent use. One would not, for example, usually think first of Aristotle as an ironist, although that surely has something to do with the sheer bulk of his work: what, we ask, did he leave out to see double with? But this, nonetheless, is the case, certainly in individual statements or arguments. The concept of the mean, for example, is central for Aristotle to the science of ethics. By it, we learn, reason enters practice; striking between the extremes, the moral agent finds in the mean the right act for the right occasion. But, the reader is asked to consider, is the mean *always* to be consulted? Consider, Aristotle suggests, the actions of robbery, or of adultery. Would the doctrine of the mean commit us to adultery "at the right time, at the right place, with the right woman?" And so we are driven ourselves in the opposite direction, to see how misleading the mean is on that occasion.

Again, the medieval tradition takes seriously the role of the philosopher as educator, and nowhere is this more evident than in Maimonides' *Guide of the Perplexed* where irony, again, turns out to be a principal one of the educator's devices. Anthropomorphism, Maimonides recognizes, is a threat to the idea as well as to the ideal of monotheism. This danger includes, of course, the ascription to God of emotions; and after recalling for the reader that the anthropomorphic features of anger or jealousy are attributed to God in the Bible only where he reacts to idolatry, Maimonides concludes: "Know accordingly that when you believe in the doctrine of the corporeality of God or believe that one of the states of the body belongs to him, you provoke his jealousy and anger" (pt. I, ch. 36). God does not become anthropomorphically jealous—except as idolaters conceive of Him as becoming angry or jealous.

And so, also—skipping rapidly forward—the stern and unforgiving Kant, sometimes represented as so far separating morality from pleasure as to leave them not only distinct but opposed—Kant himself yet takes pleasure in ironies at once ornate and deep. "The light dove, cleaving the air in free flight, and feeling its resistance, might imagine that its flight would be still easier in empty space," he writes in the Introduction to the first Critique; and we see in that turn a capsule history of the philosophical dogmatism which the Critique as a whole is intended to subvert: the claim for an unmediated or immaculate grasp of reality—the makers of which claim, like the dove if *it* acted on its beliefs, fall, Kant believes, flat on their faces.

Or again, consider Gilbert Ryle's use of travesty, those imagined examples with respect to which Ryle invites his readers to supply from their own world the more cogent counterexamples. Arguing in *Dilemmas* against reductionism, for example, Ryle confronts a hypothetical undergraduate with a hypothetical college auditor who explains to the undergraduate that "all the activities of the college are represented in these [the auditor's] columns" of financial assets and debits. Should not the undergraduate be persuaded, then, Ryle writes, "that this expert's way [is] perhaps, the right way in which to think of the life of the college . . .?" That *that* is what the college is? This imaginary proposal gains its power from the reader's recognition both that it is false and that it is not imaginary at all. The irony here forces its way through, leaving scientific reductionism more real an object—and more objectionable—as the reader himself supplies a refutation for its economic analogy.

Such examples could be multiplied, but short of gathering them *all*, of course, there is no way of showing that they do outnumber other types or instances of philosophical humor. Indeed, although I have been claiming that this *is* the case, it should be clear that the philosophical comic *in general* is a recognizable phenomenon and that it also includes the other parts of the fourfold distinction I have cited.

More's *Utopia*, for example, is inconsistent in various ways, including that of its form, but certainly one of its basic impulses is to satirize the society that was not nowhere but immediately present. So, in political relations with other countries, the Utopians, we learn, never make treaties:

> In their part of the world, which is diametrically opposed to ours . . . you can't rely on treaties at all. The more solemnly they're made, the sooner they're violated, by the simple process of discovering some loophole in the wording. . . . That, as I was saying, is presumably why Utopians make no treaties. Perhaps if they lived in Europe, they'd change their mind.

There seems, in fact, a natural, or at least literary, affinity between many of the great futurist visions of philosophers and an impulse for satire. Certainly we miss much of the vividness (and some of the argument) in Plato's *Republic* if we do not see that he wrote with one eye, mocking, constantly on the Athens whose citizens had become so accustomed to life in their caves that they would take the shadows cast on the wall before them for creatures of the real world; who chose their political leaders on the basis of favors done or promised, rather than on favors bestowed by nature; who accepted as literal models for their own actions the poets' descriptions of the gods lying to (or with) each other.

The romantic comedy, too, has a place, although its characteristic "green world" comes in rather mottled hues.[3] Readers have often found Leibniz's *Monadology* amusing, but they have usually understood this amusement simply as a reaction to what is, on any reading, a philosophical oddity. But as we watch Leibniz's transformation of the fragmented and disjointed world of common experience, mixed as it is with wrongdoing, evil, and incoherence, into a harmonious collective of monads each one of them both realizing its own nature and mirroring and supporting every other one, we do well to recall the standard version of romance in which conflict is transformed to reveal affinities, reconciliation, marriage, and pleasure as natural. The *Monadology*, we may well conclude, amuses not, or not mainly, because it is odd, but because it is, in the manner of romance, funny.

A more serious if more literal-minded version of the romance appears in the classical statements in political philosophy of the Social Contract Theory. Admittedly, if that theory is understood as designating a single historical moment at which the social contract was signed, one moment which then irreversibly shapes the political future of the members of a society, the dramatic impulse in such accounts will be viewed rather as tragic than as comic: a falling off from origins which evokes inevitably frustrated efforts to recapture that first moment of reason and compliance. But if on the other hand, the social contract is seen as a- or trans-historical (and there is evidence for such interpretation even in Hobbes and Locke), then we have the prospect not only of a single eventual moment of resolution, but of reconciliation and communal celebration at *every* moment of apparent disharmony or conflict. That citizens should think of themselves, whatever their reservations, as continuously giving "tacit consent" (Locke's phrase) to both the policies and authority of the government, is surely, from the points of view of the government and even of the citizen, an idyllic figure. (Insofar as democracy presupposes a social contract theory, it shows, we infer, how romantic comedy extends to political practice as well as to its theory.)

Farce, with its characteristic emphasis on physical and nonverbal mechanisms (typified by the literal "slap-stick"), is a rarer form in philosophical discourse than the others, but even here instances are available—predictably in the genre of the philosophical dialogue where the individual voices of distinguishable characters inject a bodily presence. Diderot's *D'Alembert's Dream* and *Rameau's Nephew* have strong elements of slapstick and farce; the same elements are notable in a number of the Platonic dialogues—for example, with Alcibiades' riotous entrance to the *Symposium* (in which we have already heard Aristophanes' explanation of love as the longing of our half-bodies—all that we have left—for the other halves from which they have been carved); or in the opening of the *Protagoras* where Socrates, dragged from sleep at the crack of dawn by a young friend to listen to the master Sophist—arrives at the appointed house only to have the door slammed in his face; and then, grudgingly admitted, discovers Protagoras already pacing and holding forth in the portico, a line of luminaries flanking him, a band of lesser lights behind: "As I looked at the party," Socrates reports, "I was delighted to notice what special care they took never to get in Protagoras's way. When he turned round to walk back, the listeners divided in perfect order, and circling round took their place each time in the rear. It was beautiful." Beautiful enough, we recognize, to be repeated later, many times and to good effect, by the Marx Brothers.

Such examples, however, do not, I believe, tip the balance; the main part of philosophical humor is still and nonetheless ironic, even though the counting required to make good that claim is here left incomplete. And the question then, if we are unwilling—as we ought to be—to conclude simply that the occurrence is accidental or arbitrary, is why this should be the case. It is in response to this question that my second thesis becomes pertinent—and even before addressing that thesis head-on, we can see something of the direction it takes from the notion of philosophical system itself and the clear disposition in favor of systematic thought in the history of philosophy, even from the history of very different philosophies. For irony, I suggest, is not only compatible with a formal adherence to system, but requires it—in the sense mentioned before, that the doubling vision with which the ironist sees is not a doubling of equals. There is nothing ironical in the duck/rabbit example of "seeing as" which Wittgenstein borrowed from the Viennese "funny papers," and the reason for this is that nothing in the figure itself suggests priority for either the duck or the rabbit (although the figure *as a whole* suggests a priority for a world in which ducks do not appear as rabbits or vice versa). Such equality is clearly absent from the instances already cited of philosophical irony; the binocular vision represented there has in each case one eye fixed on a ground that Kierkegaard himself, in *The Concept of Irony*, names an *Urgrund*, and it is only because of this ground that what is then seen by the other eye—the appearance—becomes exchangeable or problematic and is shown, i.e., demonstrated, to be so. Irony, in other words, is at odds with skepticism (here I am at odds myself with other accounts of irony, for example, that of Paul de Man)[4]—and at least some of its own force comes from the possibility of a system that skepticism, for example, would preclude. It is precisely the ground that system provides which irony requires in order to demonstrate that the incongruities, gaps, or extraneous items of appearance—the first side of the twofold vision—can be overcome, ironized. Lukács refers to its role in the novel when he describes irony as "the highest freedom that one can attain in a world without God." Even when the philosopher admits God to his world, and certainly when he does not, that world is also the world of the philosopher's making, one in which *he* is the Prime Mover and where *he* realizes that "highest freedom" of irony.

Thesis II: Irony is the characteristic trope of philosophy. The very dimensions of this claim may seem strained. The thesis requires first that we think of philosophy and philosophers as a single whole, without setting up fiats of exclusion and inclusion. It requires, secondly, that we think of philosophy as a unified or at least familiar set of literary artifacts, subject to analysis of the kind applied to standard examples of "imaginative" literature like fictional prose. Neither of these premises will pass easily through the eye of the philosopher's needle, but I have argued for them in the preceding chapters, and for the moment, in any event, they can be viewed through the filter of the willing suspension of disbelief. My own way here is motivated by Hayden White's proposal in *Metahistory*, that the writing of history is hardly the straightforward compounding of events and facts, that in fact the individual structures of written history—his examples are the works of nineteenth-century historians: Michelet, Ranke, Tocqueville, Burckhardt—disclose significant connections with one or another of the four main literary tropes distinguished in medieval rhetoric and later, more substantively, by Vico: metaphor, metonymy, synecdoche, irony. Against this background, the possibility presents itself of moving up a level—advancing from varieties *within* historical writing, for example, to varieties of writing of which the writing of history *as a whole* would then be one. Is it possible to draw analogous distinctions *there*, to view entire disciplines or areas of study as modeled on the literary tropes? If the tropes are more than just techniques or accidental devices, would they not represent systematic modes of thought?

I recognize at least some of the difficulties which such questions must surmount before they can win conviction. The tropes themselves, even historically, have been problematic in form and even in number. On another side, the fields of discourse are vague at the perimeters and unruly within them. Is there, for example, a formal distinction between history and the study of literature? Between history as such and the history of literature? Are such differences proportionate to the differences between philosophy and social science? If philosophy is, as a whole, trop-ic, are these other disciplines as well? And if so, what figures do *they* embody?

The latter two questions in particular are crucial for any general theory in which the thesis argued here would have to find a place, and I have only a preliminary view of what might constitute such a theory: the physical sciences, for example, as a sustained version of synecdoche and then of the romance, as they look ceaselessly for a least and common unit (the atom, the gene) which would then neutralize the many more apparent natural differences; the writing of history, with its metonymic particularity—the single events standing in for the whole—as tragic, irretrievable (unless, as Marx suggests, history should in fact repeat itself—when we would be back, as he himself adds, to farce). But it would be more than enough if something useful could be said along these lines only about philosophy and the claim that philosophy is natively, characteristically ironical; that it is this trope that fundamentally shapes the literary form and whatever else that substantively implies of the philosophical text.

This proposal depends once again on the concept of doubling and reversal that I have referred to in the examples already given of philosophical irony. Those examples came mainly from *within* philosophical texts, where the philosopher draws a circle around single items to be seen through; I am suggesting now that the frequency in philosophy of such examples is not accidental, that irony is not only a manner of speaking for philosophy, but a manner of being; that what individual ironies attempt piecemeal—disclosing by way of a single affirmation its opposite—philosophical systems characteristically do as corporate wholes, the surface of experience serving the philosopher as a foil for deeper intelligibility. This is, simply put, a claim that the Appearance-Reality distinction is as essential to philosophy as it is to irony—that as irony posits a state of affairs the more sharply to emphasize the opposed truth, so philosophy characteristically posits a surface "given" (given by reason or experience or the philosophical tradition and more likely a combination of all of these) which is then taken to disclose the less apparent reality. Heraclitus finds in the apparent instances of stasis evidence of motion, as Parmenides finds in apparent plurality and motion evidence of the One, which has neither of those qualities. Those examples are clearly opposed to each other in *what* they say, but they are much alike in the saying itself; and the formulations of that saying are recurrent in the history of philosophy, in the voices of the individual philosophers: "You (or others, or the tradition) ascribe to appearance *this* character—but if you look harder, admit the evidence that the appearance itself provides, you will see that the reality is the other way round." The dualism here is not between falsehood and truth or between inadequacy and adequacy, but rather an opposition in which the second term is implied by the first, as reality is implied by appearance in the many specific moments from which the philosophical systems that most openly name those concepts.

F. H. Bradley's heavily ironical *Appearance and Reality* is the most forthright recent confrontation of the distinction celebrated in its title; but we understand something more in the character even of that work, and of the distinction more generally, when we place them both against the background of Hegel, who lays fair claim to title as the supreme philosophical ironist. It was Hegel, after all, who argued that the least likely of texts, an encyclopedia, could also be ironical. Look, he suggests there, at the pieces of world history: Egyptian painting, the Chinese invention of gunpowder, the rise of monarchy in Europe, the Indian Upanishads, the shape of the human figure. At first blush, one might be inclined to say that such diverse items must be unrelated, that they *could* have nothing to do with each other, in themselves or historically. But at second blush, they turn out to represent not only an order, but a necessary order—in the single and tightly woven plot of world history in which a protagonist named Absolute Spirit struggles past an array of obstacles, diversions, and temptations until finally, whipping them all into one shape, he (it?) triumphs. Was there ever, we ask ourselves, reflecting on these adventures, a *Bildungsroman*, the triumph of consciousness over experience, that was *not* ironical? "The logic called dialectical," Loewenberg writes about Hegel's method, "is the logic of comedy par excellence." It is no *deus ex machina* that here discloses the reality behind the appearance; the machine of appearance *itself* does so, always pointing out the fragmentary or partial character of what had gone before. "In Hegel," Kierkegaard concludes, "each moment contains within itself the seeds of its own dissolution."

Even where the Appearance-Reality distinction is less openly cited, moreover, the tension between concepts that feed into them is often unmistakable—and this in a broad range of philosophical accounts that may otherwise seem to share almost nothing more than this common subversion of appearance. This is, quite clearly, a strong factor in the heady career of Hume's scandalous claim that causes and effects are, *in reality*, no more than what they *seem* to be (a double irony, in the terms I have been proposing)—namely, constant conjunctions; it surely is the only way we can account for the fact that G. E. Moore's otherwise quite unremarkable two hands remain joined in philosophical memory to the existence of an external world.

Point Two: In these varied instances, it is not only the Appearance-Reality distinction that gives a shape to the arguments—the Appearance being addressed first, the Reality then allegedly forcing its own way out of the Appearance—but the overcoming is a function of mind or vision; it is always a domination by understanding, not by action, not by feeling or taste, only provisionally even by experience, since for empiricism, too, it is understanding that gives a name and shape to experience. This again, as I have suggested, is native to the figure of irony, where first the ironist and then his audience see or understand their way through the appearances at the same time that they hold them in view *as* appearances. This claim is not diminished, I believe, even by the classical ideal—Plato's for example—of philosophy, as the *love* of wisdom rather than as an abstracted seeing that we might associate with *theoria*, for the love in Plato's *philosophia* is the love of mind for itself. Nor is the claim constrained even by Marx's attempt to turn Hegel right side up. For there too—"Philosophers have only interpreted the world in various ways; the point, however, is to change it"—the action is the action of praxis in which the mind is conceived as instrumental, where thinking takes place in the hand not less than in the head. Indeed, Marx honors that same confidence in the rationality of history that was represented by Hegel, the same keen eye—albeit with a different lens—for finding reason in the dispersion of historical event: "The truth is always present," Marx notes, "but not always in truthful form"—as fundamental a faith in the power of irony as has ever been openly (i.e., nonironically) professed. In each of these instances, the philosophical starting point at once reveals its own inadequacies and at the same time poses the corrective that would make for adequacy; it implies—or at least is *alleged* to imply—its opposite.

It may be objected that the ironical elements I have been pointing to are hardly peculiar to philosophy; that there is perhaps no organized intellectual discipline from which such elements are absent; that described in this way, irony itself is so equitably distributed—in the projects of history, sociology, or even physics—that if *that* is what is supposed to be distinctive about philosophy, philosophy (as numerous detractors and even some proponents have claimed) has no character of its own, is nothing apart from any of them. But there are differences here, I believe, that nonetheless warrant the claim for the distinction. The writing of history, for example, takes the reality of its own discourse for granted; moreover, as it reorders or makes sense of events or objects, it moves only from one sequence to another—from Appearance, in effect, to Appearance, leaving the way always open to historical revision. But philosophy benefits from neither of these vantage points: Appearance for it is radically in question—in the first instance, its own Appearance, since the nature of philosophy is itself one, even the principal one, of its own questions. And this is the more heavily underscored because that Appearance contrasts not with another Appearance but with a putative Reality to which the Appearance attests even if it does so negatively, offering "one word to express its antonym." That is, ironically.

Does this emphasis on the trope of irony mean that the other tropes do not "figure" in philosophical texts? The obvious answer to that question is no—that as there are plentiful examples in philosophy of comic forms other than irony, so the tropes other than irony also affect philosophical writing. Metaphor, for example, as analyzed in the history of philosophy by such writers as Stephen Pepper or Richard McKeon, is demonstrably an important factor in shaping philosophical texts, even in writers like Locke or Hobbes who explicitly criticize the use of metaphorical figures. Thus, my contention is not that the other tropes do not affect philosophical writing, but that their roles are subordinate to the more basic turn of irony—that they begin (and indeed take their specific content) at a source that irony provides.

But what, it may be objected to this general claim, of philosophical writers who seem not in the slightest ironical, even in the perhaps too generous sense of that term I have been using? Here a distinction might be made between philosophers whose work is deliberately and openly directed against the partial or bifocal vision essential to irony, and those philosophers who escape irony because they never, perhaps even to themselves, acknowledge it as a possibility. About the latter—the naive realists and naive skeptics, in their assorted contemporary guises: positivists, ordinary-language philosophers, those phenomenologists whose only act is to bracket reality, the deconstructionists, even, I suppose, Richard Rorty's "conversationalists"— there is little to be said that they do not say themselves. They eschew irony in effect only to become its objects, incongruously split in the view of any onlooker more willing than they are themselves to notice the difference between what they say and what they do. The image that comes to mind here is again the figure of Protagoras (through a surrogate, Theaetetus), this time pursued by Socrates for his doctrine that knowledge is perception.

> Soc. Can a person know something and also not know that which he knows?
> Theae. It is impossible, I suppose.
> Soc. Not if you say that seeing is knowing. . . . Consider: a gentleman puts his hand over one of your eyes and asks you whether you see his coat, etc., etc. . . .

The other case is stronger and more difficult, bringing out again the fact that although irony is not only in the eye of the beholder, there is no irony without that eye—and that the eye itself, for the reader of philosophy as well as for the philosopher, may have various impulses. It might be conceded, for example, that Aristotle sometimes wrote or spoke ironically, but it could still be asked how with a project that sets itself to the study of being qua being, we are to find irony in such a system? So, Aristotle opens the *Metaphysics* by asserting that "All men by nature desire to know"; and we can even appreciate the ironical reflection—half an objection—by which a recent commentator (John Herman Randall, Jr.) reacts to that assertion: "Aristotle never had the privilege of teaching in an American university." But what, we ask, of Aristotle's initial statement itself?

I can only return here to the general form of the argument so far presented, suggesting in fact that if Randall's objection were taken as ground rather than figure, then it is Aristotle's original statement (against the backdrop, to be sure, of students or faculty in Athenian, not American universities) that represents the ironic turn I have been speaking about; certainly one would have had to look well, and vigorously, beyond the political and social *appearances* of even fifth-century B.C. Athens to discover that the common impulse of its entrepreneurs, soldiers, politicians, courtesans, and Sophists was indeed toward knowledge. It is not, here, Aristotle's single statement (or the immediate context of which it is part) that is ironical (that implies its opposite); it is the evidence that speaks through the philosopher and which his statement then consummates. In this sense the irony is at one remove, mediated—but the remove does not itself affect the ironic turn that continues to be represented. The point here is that even with being qua being as his object, the role of the philosopher is that of disclosing, of unveiling, of catching his reader looking in one direction or at one set of surfaces when it is in another direction, toward another set of surfaces, that the reader is in fact committed, whether he knows it or (more likely) not. I cannot, again, show this to be the case for all the instances that might be brought up—and so I close with what seems to me a very unlikely instance, and thus a likelier piece of evidence.

There is, we would be inclined to say, nothing funny about the *ordo geometricus* or Spinoza's application of it: not irony, not satire, not farce, not even, as far as I have been able to discover, a solitary or accidental joke that slipped past the author's passion for regularity and order—a *single* order. Spinoza, the most conscientious of monists, would never, could *never*, see double; that is in fact what the method is intended, not only to reflect, but to demonstrate. Well, perhaps. For he only succeeds in this to the extent that we accept him— that "gottertrunkenes Mensch"—as indeed part of his own system, as living within it as well as talking about it. But can we, his readers, do that? Perhaps we could if he did so himself—but there, it seems, is the rub. So Spinoza writes in the *Ethics:* "I will analyze the actions and appetites of men as if it were a question of lines, of planes, and of solids." That "I," we recognize, his or his reader's, is not itself a line or a plane, not even, geometrically speaking, a solid—and the disparity here, the wedge through which irony pushes its way, is framed for the ages in an epic misreading which Spinoza, we may reasonably conclude, invited. "I would call attention," the respectful and supportive Henry Oldenburg, Secretary of the British Royal Society, writes to Spinoza, "to the ambiguities in your treatment of God and Nature: a great many people think you have confused one with the other."[5] Spinoza, of course, had wanted to do nothing else; Oldenburg reports the sort of mistake that invites laughter not just because pratfalls are funny, but because when it is a missed irony that causes the pratfall, the sound of the thud is especially loud. What Oldenburg reports as confusion not only was deliberate but was the most forceful turn that Spinoza had intended to give to the view of reality he was proposing—a turn which Oldenburg's statement also discloses as ironical. For irony asks us to see double; when we do not understand that request, we do not see even once.

Notes

1. Fowler, in *Modern English Usage,* anthropomorphizes this doubling effect into a requirement for irony of an audience of two persons: "one party that hearing shall hear and not understand, and another party that, when more is meant that meets the ear, is aware both of that more and of the outsider's incomprehension." But although irony may often be thus used as a weapon, the more fundamental—and philosophical—account it means to settle is with the audience of a Single One.

2. I refer here to the claim that irony is methodological only (as in the alleged interchangeability of Socratic Irony and Socratic Method); that finally, at the point where Plato or Kierkegaard open their systems to an element which is non ironical (as in the theory of forms or in the leap of faith), they leave their roles as ironists. This is, I should argue, a confusion of irony with skepticism. Since irony only occurs as a figure only so far as one part of its double vision serves as a base, this is also true for the trope of irony as a whole.

3. Northrop Frye discusses the place of a "green world" in the geography of New Comedy in "The Argument of Comedy," in D. A. Robertson, Jr., ed., *English Institute Essays, 1948* (New York: Columbia University Press, 1949).

4. P. de Man, "The Rhetoric of Temporality," in C. Singleton, ed., *Interpretation* (Baltimore, Md.: Johns Hopkins University Press, 1969). Irony is also, I believe, at odds with allegory which has sometimes been held to be one of its forms; the difference there is that allegory begins when the dialectic of irony ends.

5. Letter from Oldenburg to Spinoza, 15 November 1675.

4

Presentation and Representation in Plato's Dialogues

> I have a notion that when the mind is thinking, it is simply talking to itself
>
> Socrates, in the *Theaetetus*

Recent commentators have been more sensitive to the importance of the rhetorical structure of Plato's dialogues than at any time in their critical history.[1] This attentiveness has produced advances in the understanding both of individual dialogues and of the substantive issues which run through them—in the last account, of Plato's conception of philosophy. It promises as well a growing comprehension of the connection between form and matter in philosophical writing— the central concern of a philosophical hermeneutics *if* it existed.[2] I propose here to consider a structural feature of the dialogues with implications for both of these issues. This feature is the recurrence in Plato's writing of two modes of expression which I shall be calling *presentation* and *representation:* "presentation" as the assertive statement of a state of affairs; "representation" as an image or iconic sign. Unlike much philosophical writing, Plato's work makes deliberate use of both of these modes of expression. The tension which the dialogues set in motion at the intersection of these forms (so my claim goes) is an important and frequent device of Plato the dramatist: it determines the aesthetic point of individual moments in the dialogues and, as those moments are seen to expand, it reflects Plato's intentions for the genre of the dialogue as well. It also speaks substantively both about and to the philosophical enterprise, and is thus an instrument of Plato the philosopher. It represents in itself, then, an argument for the connection in Plato's work of those two roles. That claim is hardly startling; but the way is still open for understanding the technique involved in effecting such a connection—its manner—and for seeing why Plato took this project as seriously as he did.

1. Two Modes of Discourse

In defining *presentation* and *representation* I do not move far from the ordinary usage of those terms; what is at issue, in any event, are the phenomena they are designed to mark. By presentation, I mean the assertive or discursive force of a proposition, the quality of its claim that something is or is not the case. Proofs or arguments involving connectives and a set of propositions may also be said to "present" a claim or assertion. To this extent, inference (either inductive or deductive) is presentational.

Representation is an exhibiting or portrayal. By it, an object or state of affairs is shown, held up to view. It may thus afford the intimation of a reference; but if the viewer decides on an implied assertion, he does so with only nominal direction from the representation itself. A representation possesses unity or coherence, the implication of each element with every other, in a measure denied to presentational assertion by virtue of the latter's predicative structure. The representation may be itself composed of assertions. Where it is, the presentational force of those individual assertions is submerged in the quality of a whole; the conglomerate of assertions have a "look" to them. Presentation may be roughly said to argue the relation between a subject and a predicate; representation does not assume, certainly it does not assert, that distinction. The difference, in this respect, is between mediacy and immediacy.

So, for examples: the statement "A tree has fallen in the quadrangle outside"—a presentational formulation—asserts the existence of a state of affairs. It is true or false, and although the speaker may not be able immediately to demonstrate his understanding of its claims or to determine its truth value, the possibility of doing both is presupposed in the form of the assertion. A kindred example of representation would be a photograph, perhaps of a tree fallen in the quadrangle. In contrast to the other, this mode of expression makes no formal assertion and has no truth value. We do not call for evidence in order to evaluate its "claims" (unless it is already part of a claim): We see it as a representation, as a "picture-of-something"—or perhaps we don't, but the seeing (or at least the sight) is in either event nondiscursive.

It may be quickly objected that the forms of these two modes of expression are more complex than has been stated. But much ink has been spilled on the status of representation (pictorial or otherwise) as well as on the status of propositions (for example, of whether propositions are not themselves representations or pictures), and to deal with those issues here would preclude dealing with anything else. In partial compensation, I at least make explicit the following disclaimers:

(1) The proposed distinction between presentation and representation does not mean that their objects could not be roughly translated from one framework to another. Where this is done, however, it occurs always with greater "slippage" than would be the case for a translation between instances of one or the other forms. (2) One thing which the difference between the two is *not*, is the difference between two equally discursive forms. For even if a pictorial representation may be translated into *some* propositions, no set of propositions will duplicate the immediate nuance or the tension of design in the original. Precisely what this remainder is may be disputed; something more will be said about what Plato took it to be, but for the moment I am assuming at least that it exists. (Without it, for example, could one account for the fact that forgeries in art criticism are more common than forgeries in the arts themselves?)

The reading of Plato's work to which I call attention can, then, be formulated as follows: that the dialogues characteristically employ both presentation and representation as modes of expression; that there is a typical conjunction in the dialogues in the occurrence of those modes; that the reasons for the conjunction are not only stylistic or rhetorical, but are embedded in Plato's epistemology; and finally that the dialectic set in motion by this connection bears a strong resemblance to the dialectical form ascribed by Plato to the process of philosophy itself.

Examples of the conjunction of these modes of expression extend in some cases over a recognizable section of a dialogue; elsewhere it may appear in a single statement. Such variations, although they make for difficulties in forming a pattern of explication, are not themselves significant. If anything, they underwrite the possibility that the dialogues as larger wholes, even perhaps Plato's "system" as system, may yield to the same analysis. The following are a number of characteristic examples of this conjunction.

In the *Cratylus* (384a–390c), Hermogenes proposes the thesis to Socrates that names are conventions. Socrates' predictable concern is that Hermogenes understands his thesis to mean that not only names but the defining properties of the objects name are also matters of convention. And so Socrates pursues Hermogenes across a field of carpenters, smiths, and weavers, arguing that for the distinctions on which their crafts are based, mere convention could hardly suffice. Even the crafts or the craftsmen themselves should not be identified merely as matters of convention. But how to show this? Well, think perhaps of the craft of giving names.

Thus we hear (the passage has been compressed):

> Soc. And who uses the work of the lyre maker? Will not he be the man who knows how to direct what is being done and who will also know whether the work is being well done or not?
> Hermogenes. Certainly.
> S. And who is he?
> H. The player of the lyre.
> S. And who will direct the shipwright?
> H. The pilot. . . .
> S. And him who knows how to ask and answer the questions of legislator, the director of the legislator if all these names are to be rightly given, you would call a dialectician?
> H. Yes, that would be his name. . . .

If the man who gives names is by virtue of his skill himself assigned a name, then the names which he dispenses will embody that skill. The argument at the presentational level has concerned only the latter; the appearance of a name for the namer which in effect confirms the argument is not itself part of it but an exhibition of what the argument asserts.

Two concrete and familiar examples of the phenomenon I am speaking about appear in the *Theaetetus* and in the *Republic* respectively. Theaetetus is introduced by Theodorus as resembling Socrates in appearance: snub-nosed and homely. But this is, it turns out, no disadvantage to Theaetetus's ability to follow Socrates' argument against the hypothesis suggested by Theaetetus himself that knowledge is perception. There must be, Socrates points out from an unending number of directions, something more than perception or the grasp of appearances to account for knowledge.

> Soc. Through what perceptual organs do we perceive such concepts as difference or unity or existence?
> Theaetetus. Really, Socrates, I could not say except that I think there is no special organ at all for these things. . . . It is clear to me that the mind in itself is its own instrument for contemplating the common terms that apply to everything.
> Soc. In fact, Theaetetus, you are handsome, not ugly as Theodorus said you were.

Theaetetus's own person, it turns out, belies the claim that knowledge is perception.

We find a similar example in book 1 of the *Republic* and the extended encounter between Socrates and Thrasymachus. Look first at Thrasymachus's entrance (in Socrates' description):

Gathering himself up like a wild beast, Thrasymachus hurled himself upon us as if he would tear us to pieces. And Polemarchus and I were frightened and fluttered apart. He bawled out into our midst, what balderdash is this that you have been talking, and why do you Simple Simons truckle and give way to one another?

And then look at his exit (again compressed):

> *Soc.* Then it is the wise man who is just and happy, and the unjust miserable?
> *Thras.* So be it.
> *Soc.* But it surely does not pay to be miserable.
> *Thras.* Of course not.
> *Soc.* Never then, most worshipful Thrasymachus, can injustice be more profitable than justice.
> *Thras.* Let this complete your entertainment, Socrates.

What is at stake in the arguments that lead from Thrasymachus's entrance to his exit is, of course, whether justice is the interest of the stronger, whether force by itself suffices to determine advantage. Thrasymachus is presented by Socrates with a sequence of argument which controverts that thesis. But this sequence, in addition to its asserted claims, also has a form which *represents* Thrasymachus's passage from lion to lamb, a journey which no lion would make except under duress. There is something more to determining advantage or right than its mere assertion; and what could put a finer point on this thesis than the disadvantage of Thrasymachus himself?

A more heavily ironical example of the relation between presentation and representation appears in the *Parmenides* (127e ff.): Socrates asks Zeno to reread the first hypothesis of the first argument of Zeno's treatise which has been offered in support of Parmenides' arguments on the One. On the surface, Socrates' request simply rephrases the hypothesis that plurality is impossible, and Zeno accepts Socrates' reformulation. But Zeno had been too quick in explaining away the reality of the Many; he had in effect begged the question—and this is sharply represented in Socrates' presentation of the hypothesis:

> *Soc.* What does this statement mean, Zeno?"If things are many," you say, "they must be both like and unlike. But that is impossible; unlike things cannot be like, nor like things unlike." That is what you say, isn't it?
> Yes, replied Zeno.
> *Soc.* And so, if unlike things cannot be like or like things unlike, it is also impossible that things should be a plurality; if many things did exist, they would have impossible attributes. Is this the precise purpose of

your arguments—to maintain, against *everything* that is commonly said, that things are not a plurality? Do you regard *every one of your arguments* as evidence of exactly that conclusion, and so hold that, in *each argument* in your treatise, you are giving just *one more proof* that a plurality does not exist? Is that what *you* mean, or am *I* understanding you wrongly? . . . [Emphasis added]

The reader is given a portrait of plurality—in the form of Zeno's many arguments, even in the difference in persons between Zeno and Socrates themselves—at the same time that the presentation is said to deny it. This representation, as matters turn out, is a prelude to the presentational defense of the theory of forms as a means of reconciling the One and the Many which comprises the larger part of the dialogue.

A version of the relation between presentation and representation shaped rather differently from these others appears in the *Sophist*. In the first of that dialogue's two major sections (216a–236d), the Stranger traces a lengthy series of distinctions into the figure of the Sophist: acquisitive, pugnacious, a money-making practitioner of eristic, etc.—finally, something less than either a likeness- or a semblance-maker (the former imitates an original; the latter captures the look of the object). The persuasiveness of this representation of the Sophist is due to the recognizable view it offers; there is little argument or presentation in the whole of this section. The second part of the dialogue on the other hand, sketches what the reader has already *seen* as a representation. The argument in it reacts against the sophistic thesis that since error implies reference to nonbeing, error itself could not exist. Plato thus attempts to show that error is real enough—by demonstrating the possibility of the existence of the Sophist, a possibility which is no idle exercise in dialectic so long as the representation of the Sophist serves as preface. We search for the possibility of error governed by the view of its actuality.

The formulations in each of these series of interchanges work at two levels—the one, a sequence of discourse, of thesis and counter argument, in which the predicative structure, if not always sound, is at least evident. On the second level, stepping back from the first, we find that presentation has an appearance as well, that with its assertions seen now as objects, it also represents or portrays an aspect of what has been at issue in the presentation.

Admittedly, these have been scattered examples, and it may seem extravagant to ask them to bear much of the burden of a general account of the dialogues. But other examples might be cited—and more important than any argument from numbers is the fact that the structure of the examples reveals a common motif supported and completed, as we shall yet see, in other facets of the design of Plato's work.

2. The Grounds of Interpretation

Certain methodological questions and possible objections to what has been said need to be considered. One such question would ask for assurance that the interpretations reported are more than the results of a fanciful reading—for example, that what I have claimed to be going on between Zeno and Socrates is in fact taking place. An analogous question could be raised, of course, with respect to *any* instance of interpretation, and I make no special plea for the readings given here. One point, however, is worth mentioning which distinguishes the examples cited. It would be unfair to impose the criteria for presentational formulation on the appearances of representation—that is, if the reader refused to acknowledge the latter because the passages themselves did not *assert* that they were representational. That is, of course, precisely what representation by its nature will not do—and while the absence of such statements is obviously no evidence *for* the presence of representation, it is more important that their absence should not be construed as counter evidence.

A second, more decisive question, unfortunately not much apart from the first, is whether the supposed conjunction of presentation and representation appears *at all* in the dialogues. For if *that* could be established, then so to interpret any particular instance would be at least formally respectable. But again: The fact that there is no hard or knockdown proof even of one such instance is surely not peculiar to the case argued. Interpretation assumes a set of instruments which serve as a medium for grasping the object interpreted, what Kenneth Burke speaks of as an "index" of interpretation. As it turns out, the terms of that index, the categories it applies to the object, are to an important extent determined by the object itself: one doesn't spin a critical apparatus out of whole cloth if one wants it to fit. But even as this circularity is pointed out, the *fact* of interpretation—that it works, more or less—remains. One has finally then to measure the congruities cited by the interpreter against the improbability (which I would claim here) that they could be fortuitous.

The principal substantive question about the convergence of presentation and representation in the dialogues remains. What is the significance of that conjunction? What role do the two forms of expression have? This role is almost certainly various—although finally the variety is fruitfully viewed as a related series of accounts, nesting within each other. One could, for example, build an explanation simply on the claim that the convergence of presentation and representation is but another expression of the irony or wit commonly acknowledged in Plato. And surely this is part of the account. It would be a mistake, furthermore, to be patronizing in this acknowledgement, to assume that "Plato playing" has little in common with "Plato philosophizing." We have, for one thing, the warning of the last words in the *Symposium* of how what is comic and what is serious are bound to each other. More important, we have the examples of wit themselves and their evident concern with issues central to Plato's philosophical reckoning: the relation of knowledge to virtue, of the One to the Many. The possibility is worth considering beyond this, that the connection between presentation and representation may itself qualify as a representation. That connection becomes evident only as the reader shifts his attention from one scheme of expression to another, as he acknowledges that the object of attention at one moment appears in the following moment in a different and unexpected light. This theme is recognizable in otherwise variant general theories of the comic (for example, in Bergson's or in Freud's) which agree on the way in which expectation suddenly comes undone, how an apparently solid and predictable structure is unmasked as neither solid nor predictable; so, for example, the pratfalls of vaudeville. The phrase that things are not (or not only) what they seem is trite enough, but it is Plato himself who so constantly reiterates the distinction between Appearance and Reality, playing with the consequences of its denial: to Socrates' friends; with a sharper point, to the Sophists; even (with a Pickwickian twist) to the Eleatics.

Still, this explanation bears on the occurrence of wit as such, and furthermore, both inside and outside the dialogues: we learn nothing about presentation and representation in particular from it. A second possibility might then be summoned—namely, that presentation and representation are two devices called on by Plato to express a single thread of argument, that finally they link up in a single structure as duplicate statements. A limited number of themes, after all, recur in the dialogues; this could then be one form which that duplication takes. And again, there almost certainly is *some*thing to this bald statement—but something else, also, which needs to be added. For this account might be understood to suggest that Plato in using the two modes of expression is doing the *same* thing twice, but by different means—as if the means were incidental to the "thing"; and this, I would argue, is a mistake. The grounds for the latter claim are not only that Plato would hardly expect the mere repetition of a thesis to make an impression where a single statement had failed; the reasons are more substantially philosophical. One of these reasons, itself of several parts, derives from Plato's theory of learning; a second is embedded in the epistemology which is the more general source of that theory.

With respect to the former of these: Plato in a number of places in the dialogues refers explicitly to discrepancies in levels and modes of comprehension, to the different capacities displayed both *among* individuals and by different sides of a single individual. Thus, the Divided Line in the *Republic* distinguishes different levels of comprehension; and the Allegory of the Cave, which follows immediately after it, in the beginning of Book 7, suggests more strongly that those levels do not exist only in specific individuals, but in *every* individual. The object of the Allegory is a reiteration of the process laid out in Books 2 through 5, through which all men would pass if they were able. Thus, Socrates introduces the Allegory (514a, emphasis added): "Next, said I, compare *our nature* in respect of education and its lack, to such an experience as this." And there follows the description of the cave.

The point here, so far as concerns the practice of philosophy, is twofold. First, that in what might be called the ontogeny of knowledge, different individuals will at different moments in their development both require and only be able to comprehend different modes of formulation. The stages of knowledge are stages on a way which is not itself composed of disparate parts. Those parts are integrally related, the later ones presupposing the earlier ones, and the earlier ones foreshadowing the later ones—materially, if not formally implying each other. Correspondingly, the process of learning or "understanding" in each of the stages assumes distinctive shapes bent to conform to the capacity of the student.

This feature of Plato's theory of learning is explicitly applied by Plato in the writing of the dialogues themselves. One of its appearances is in the fact that the arguments which Socrates offers are consistently pitched to the level of his interlocutors. In other words, he never speaks outside a context that is defined for him at one limit by the capacities of the speakers whom he is addressing and by the place in which he encounters them. He wants a great deal from his interlocutors, of course—but expects much less, and not because of any overriding cynicism. This is the reason, it seems, why some of the arguments in the dialogues, out of context, are weak on the face of it. I do not mean to claim that *no* faulty arguments can be ascribed to Plato. But when the reader encounters the elementary fallacies of composition or amphiboly, it is a matter less of piety than of prudence that he should assume that Plato could also recognize those fallacies; and thus that they—the arguments and fallacies together—serve a function in the context. This is one case in the analysis of philosophical argument where the more obvious the blunder, the more certainly it reflects deliberation.[3] And there are numerous instances of this. So, for example, in the discussion betwen Socrates and Thrasymachus referred to above, we encounter Socrates' argument that (in a paraphrase) "since experts in music or medicine try to 'outdo' only those who are less expert, the unjust man who tried to 'do' everyone 'out' of whatever he can shows a lack of expertise which would argue that injustice could not be profitable (as Thrasymachus claimed) after all." This equivocation on the word *outdo* (πλεονέκτειν), Cross and Woozley in their Commentary describe as "embarrassingly bad." "We wonder," they write, "whether Plato is being intellectually dishonest, or whether he is unaware of his own inconsistency."[4] And as regards an argument taken by itself, their objection is surely warranted. But if we recall that the statement is addressed to Thrasymachus, and that the issue which Socrates is forcing is not what a good argument is, but whether Thrasymachus can be led to recognize that there is such a thing *as* argument (other than force), then its presence becomes less problematic. Admittedly, such a qualification, once included in the index of interpretation, must make it difficult to know precisely which—if any—arguments in the dialogues Plato is committed to beyond the immediate and literal context in which they appear. But because this is difficult does not mean that it is impossible; the difficulty, quite simply, exists.

The second item based on the theory of learning and the importance to Plato of the variety of modes of comprehension is his use of the myth. This is not the place to add to the numerous accounts that have been given of that function—except to enter the stipulation that together with all such speculation, indeed prior to it, one must recognize that Plato himself has a *theory* of myth, intimations of which we find explicitly in the *Republic* and the *Phaedrus*, as well as in the context of the myths themselves (for example, in the *Meno* and the *Gorgias*); and that this theory refers specifically to the myth as the object of a form or level of understanding. The myths, then, are neither evasions of the philosophical points which Plato is making nor simply repetitions of the same points he has otherwise made; they have their own integrity. This is evident, for example, in the *Phaedo*, where a myth appears at the end of a series of increasingly abstract arguments on the immortality of the soul. Those arguments represent a battle—the dialogue as a whole has the form of an "agon"—between Socrates and his friends. Socrates is not persuaded even finally that the acquiescence of his friends signifies understanding, and of course this doubt is justified. "Where shall we bury you, Socrates?" Crito asks, after Socrates has spent the last hour of his life trying to show Crito that there is no way that they *can* bury him. "Catch me if you can," Socrates replies. The myth which precedes this interchange is Socrates' bequest to those who have failed to catch him—or the argument—at the level of discursive or presentational argument.

The general epistemic consideration underlying this emphasis on the variety of levels and techniques of comprehension is no less pertinent. This is the intimation often given by Plato that the stages on the way to knowledge are not over and done with, once transited, but rather make persistent demands on each individual even if on balance he has gone beyond them. This may seem to contravert the conception traditionally ascribed to Plato of the philosopher who has freed himself of the bonds that tie him to the senses—a conception of the autonomy of reason. But it is worth noting that (with some exceptions) such emancipation is not formulated by Plato in terms of a flat denial or elimination of the senses or appetites, but rather of their subordination. The appetites, in the chariot metaphor of the *Phaedrus*, must be held in check; and it appears that this is a constant requirement for anyone less than the gods themselves. This constancy is clearly a feature of the most fully developed reference to the soul, which appears in the *Republic*. In the terms of that analysis, we infer that although reason is meant to govern, its rule is obliged to give to each one of its constituents what it ought to have, *not* to coerce them into being something they are not. Cebes, in the *Phaedo*, after listening to Socrates' first two rounds of arguments on the immortality of the soul, tells him that still, the arguments notwithstanding, there is a little boy in him who is not persuaded—and won't Socrates speak to him? That little boy, it seems, would never be *quite* charmed away.

3. Setting the Dialogues in Motion

The process has been circuitous; but the possibility of accounting for the conjunction of presentation and representation may emerge from this indirection if we can once locate those two modes of expression in Plato's own formulation of them. The structural difference claimed between presentation and representation suggests, in broadest terms, the difference between an assertion or argument on the one hand, and a portrait or depiction, on the other. Those terms of themselves recall elements of the Platonic metaphysics and in particular the ranking which Plato himself assigns to various modes of expression: as he speaks in the *Ion* and the *Republic* (books 2 and 10), for example, about the representations of the rhapsode or the artist, or as in the Seventh Letter where he contrasts images with the discourse of understanding. This particular order is in fact both constant and consistent wherever the distinction itself is referred to: discourse or presentation is active in a measure of which no representation is capable; representation acts at the level of images. The implication of this point, then, for the copresence of presentation and representation can be stated simply: that they respond to different requirements and capacities in the levels of understanding, the one discursive, the other nondiscursive—the two focused now on at least rhetorically equivocal objects of knowledge. Plato, as R. S. Brumbaugh has shown against the traditional portrait of a feckless aristocrat, had a keen eye for practice and its instruments. And so as well, it seems, for what he understood to be the practice of his audience—Socrates' interlocutors within the dialogues, the listeners or readers outside of them. Understanding itself, as he conceives it, asks for harmony among its parts, the conforming of emotion as well as the articulation of reason.

This is not yet the whole or even the heart of the matter, however, for what has been said would argue only for the *copresence* in the dialogues of presentation and representation, not for the convergence or distinctive tension that I have suggested marks their relation. They are not just *there*, they occur in a configuration in which one is constantly played off against the other, in which when we think we have settled on the significance defined by the one, the other obtrudes to unsettle it by directing the viewer to a different perspective. There is, it seems, something more basic than either art or rhetoric which is at work here; and a clue to what that is may be forthcoming if we build further on the detail of the hierarchy in levels of understanding referred to above. What is important in this notion is that the elements of the hierarchy, as rhetorical elements, but also as ontological elements, are interdependent; they evoke each other. It is especially clear, for example, that the sharp line drawn before this between representation and presentation is crude as measured by Plato's own reckoning; the force ascribed to Presentation as discourse *simpliciter* is just that—too simple. Remember again that we are speaking of presentation *in the dialogues*, that the occurrences of presentation are not, then, in Plato's own estimation instances *of* discourse—as spoken—but, so it might be put, instances *as* discourse. What appears as presentation—fragments or even chains of argument—is written or more precisely, since they may be spoken, fixed. And it is thus subject to the essential strictures which Plato imposes on all such discourse. His reservations with respect to his own writing are most forcefully stated in the Letters, but one comment in the *Phaedrus* is more pertinent to the distinction on which the discussion here has focused. So, Socrates:

> The painter's products stand before us as though they were alive, but if you question them, they maintain a most majestic silence. It is the same with written words; they seem intelligent, but if you ask them anything about what they say, from a desire to be instructed, they go on telling you the same thing forever. (257d)

The claim is entered by this statement that what I have been calling presentational discourse, once it is frozen into the immobility of a written formulation, shares an essential feature with representation. It too, at that point, takes on a nondiscursive character, which if it is not representational in the strict sense, is similarly constrained in force: it loses the articulation in its initial design in favor of what may be a lifelike, but is finally an inert description of a state of affairs. We may ask of it as we may ask of the representation just what it *is* asserting or why, but we cannot, more than for the other, expect an answer; and this, Plato seems to suggest, means that even at best it achieves something less than knowledge after all. Articulation of the rough division which I have referred to between subjects and predicates vanishes—not apparently, but in the final analysis. Presentation, then, even as one extracts or conjures it from the text of Plato's own dialogues, will not suffice for knowledge, for the consummation of the philosophical process. It always also has an appearance, a representational character that projects an image, dragging its assertiveness back, impeding its process.

This will sound as if Plato, finally, has written himself into a box—and not Pandora's box of possibilities, either. If representation is to be distrusted, and if presentation turns out to be linked dialectically to representation, what then can be made, not only of the instances in the dialogues where those two forms of expression are most evident, but of anything that Plato says which employs them even tacitly—that is, of anything that Plato says or writes at all? There can be little doubt that we must proceed here gingerly, allowing for the probability that Plato indeed did not mean the dialogues to be taken as marking his final position—if there was one—on the subjects which they touch.[5] But if they are not his last word, it is reasonable to suppose that they would not *contradict* that word, and perhaps that they might even provide a hint of what it would be. In other words, one might expect that Plato's wariness of the written word would somehow be built into his writing itself. It is obvious enough that this wariness is a general factor in the use of the dialogue form: we are informed, just by that fact, that the face value of what is asserted also has a face. And we are in a position now, in reflecting on the relation between presentation and representation, to see how that relation also qualifies the structure constituted by the dialogues as entities. Plato's skepticism of any fully formed expression is conceptual, not simply prudential; it is no surprise, then, that we should be able to discern in it the convex side of an image of the philosophical process itself.

What I have been arguing so far seems finally to come to this: that the tension between the modes of expression of presentation and representation sets in motion a form of dialectic which approximates closely the process of philosophical dialectic—not a presentation or a representation of the process, but as involving the listener or reader of the dialogues in the process itself: *he* is meant to be set in motion. This thesis reflects two specific implications of the earlier discussion of presentation and representation. The first of these is that each of the two modes of expression implies the other. That is to say, presentation on its side yields, if it does not simply become, representation: assertions also have a "look" to them. Representation, on the other side, requires the explication of presentation: it does not and cannot speak by itself about what it represents. The second implication is that, as man goes about the business of knowing, each of the pair is required; that is, not only *would* they be bound together *if* either one or the other had reason for occurring—but there is a reason why each should occur. The process does in fact get started.

It follows from these conditions that as presentation and representation make their appearances in the dialogue, the written word itself and even perhaps the spoken word will not—because of the mutations to which words by their nature are subject—put the final period or full stop to what is written or, more important, thought. Not only can words themselves not complete that process, they virtually insist that the progression continue even when the ostensive elements of the dialogues—*their* words and speeches—are exhausted, over and done with. For however we conceive of the force of any specific moment in the dialogues, whether in the terms of presentation or of representation, any combination of those elements posits the requirement of a mutation—and the reader can hardly do less than follow (so long, of course, as he is following at all). The so-called elenchic dialogues, which conclude in an explicit contraversion or puzzle, like the *Euthyphro* or the *Laches,* underscore this point: the reader is *made* to know that a question remains, that the philosophical process has but reached another starting point. But that is something of which he would properly be aware even if it were not exposed in this fashion; the same impulse is embodied in the later, more subtle and superficially nonelenchic dialogues.

The conception of the work of philosophy manifested in this structural phenomenon has the appearance of an endless process, an infinite progress, if not regress; and this *is*, I take it, both a structural ingredient of the dialogues and an implication to be drawn from them—that as Socrates demonstrates more explicitly in the *Phaedo*, there is no end either to philosophers or to philosophizing. Such a claim is not, it is important to note, a version of the claim that philosophy, like the sciences, is perpetually open to emendation because of new or revised findings. The contention here bears on the substantive character of the dialectical process, not on the accidental probability that the process, at any given point, will be inadequate or incomplete; philosophy *is* a process, not by external necessity, but by nature.

This fundamental commitment, embodied in the dialogues as a whole, does not mean that there is no consummation beyond or even within the philosophical process, no moments of illumination in which the process realizes itself, although there *is* some indication that Plato reserves such possibilities as limiting or boundary concepts. The conditions for such consummation, in any event, can be seen in the relation between presentation and representation: we should be at that magical point where they meet, leaving nothing over, where discourse completes a full circle of analysis; no questions are left to answer; the representation is one with the objects represented. It is this sense of an ending which is indicated, I think, in the apparently inconclusive resolution of the *Theaetetus*, as the conclusion to that dialogue's search for a definition of knowledge. The three major hypotheses entertained there form an interesting pattern. The problem with the first two of them, that knowledge is perception and that knowledge is true judgment (respectively), is that neither provides a fulcrum in terms of which knowledge can be measured or asserted. The third hypothesis, that knowledge is true judgment with an "account," supplies such a fulcrum—the account or "logos"—but *still* fails: the fulcrum provided is external to the judgment and may thus be supposed to be the source of an infinite regress, requiring another fulcrum by which the first could be assessed. The implication thus emerges that the fulcrum for knowledge which distinguishes it both from perception and from true judgment will be located within knowledge itself. Knowledge must finally, it seems, not only *be* knowledge, but must also reveal itself *as* knowledge.

Like the *logos* in the last of those three hypotheses, presentation and representation each, by themselves, leave something over, which, in order for their process to be concluded, requires integration into a larger whole. Their means, then, are fragmentary and partial, not *as it happens*, but essentially. This constitutes the burden which the dialogues slip onto the reader's back, which he is meant to carry beyond them. If he succeeds in carrying that burden, the end may be quite different—the unity, perhaps, reflected in Plato's image in the Seventh Letter, where, in the blaze of knowledge, what is being consumed and what is doing the consuming are one. But the dialogues themselves or in their parts do not purport to reach this point. Quite the contrary: they insistently stop short. It is as though they offer the reader an invitation to become one of the *dramatis personae*, in order that *he* should see and do as the *personae* see and do. It does not matter, indeed, which of the *personae* he becomes. He is almost certain to find *some* member of the cast whose role he fits; and as he outgrows one role, it will only be to assume the dimensions of another. The process itself literally "comprehends" him once he enters. To respond to the invitation of this process does not itself produce the unity of knowledge to which Plato directs the enterprise of philosophy; it promises no more than a unity between the reader and the dialogues themselves. But that is a stage from which the other unity may yet be reached. The dialogues, then, are only a beginning.

Notes

1. Cf., e.g., P. Friedländer's classical work, *Plato*, first published in 1928 (2nd edition 1954, trans. by R. Manheim, Princeton, N.J.: Princeton University Press, 1958); H.-G. Gadamer, *Platos Dialektisches Ethik* (Hamburg: Felix Mèurer, 1968); and *Wahrheit und Methode* (Tübingen: J. B. Mohr, 1960); J. Klein, *A Commentary on Plato's Meno* (Chapel Hill, N.C.: University of North Carolina Press, 1965); B. Rosen, *Plato's Symposium* (New Haven, Conn.: Yale University Press, 1968).

2. I refer, of course, to the lack of hermeneutics *of* philosophy—not to Heidegger's conception, for example, of philosophy *as* hermeneutics.

3. Cf. the development of this point in R. K. Sprague, *Plato's Use of Fallacy* (London: Routledge and Kegan Paul, 1962).

4. R. C. Cross and A. D. Woozley, *Plato's Republic* (London: Macmillan, 1964), pp. 52–54.

5. General critical skepticism introduced by this qualification aside, it is clear that certain moments in the dialogues come closer than others to defining Plato's own commitments. What is implied, then, by these conflicting tendencies is the need for a program of interpretation on the philosophical level analogous to the program which various commentators (like Campbell) have carried out on the formal or stylistic level. There is a large number of tell tale disclaimers which Plato employs, from the explicit qualifications he almost invariably attaches to the myths, to the subtler gradations in Socrates' descriptions of his own epistemic commitments in various contexts. These remain only straws in the wind, and they don't come to much aside from the general outline of a theory of interpretation—but given Plato's economies with language, they afford a possibility. In any event, the only possibility.

5

Philosophy and the Manners of Art

The question of what philosophy is—more precisely, what it ought to be—has understandably been an item of philosophical concern: philosophy must itself devise a lever by which to move its world. As it happens, most of the answers given the question turn out to be personal representations—the writer himself writ large—and this too is predictable: the philosopher faces the question inside his own work, where he is already doing philosophy, evidently as he thinks it should be done. It might well be argued in fact that this self-portraiture in philosophical wrtiting is no less a virtue than a necessity: the reader of philosophy who can say with the reader (or writer) of poetry that whoever "touches this book touches a man" surely has found a source of the power in great philosophical writing.

Still, the question of what philosophy has been in fact can be distinguished from the question, as individual philosophers have addressed it, of what philosophy really is—and it is the former topic rather than the latter that I shall be discussing here. In addition to the history of what philosophers have said that philosophy is, there is a history of what philosophy has been; and *that* history, I hope to show, is in certain ways more revealing than the other of what they are both, in the end, histories of.

One means of confronting the collected works of philosophy as a single historical object is by comparing that object with others that have been similarly compressesd. In drawing such a comparison, I suggest that on a spectrum extending from the abstractions of science at one end to the concrete appearances of art at the other, philosophy comes closer to possessing the manners of art than those of science—so close in fact that it becomes a pressing question as to how philosophy and art differ at all, as well as to how the incongruity between philosophy and science could ever have been, as it often has, mistaken for a likeness. In outlining five points of comparison, I make certain judgments about the characters of art and science as well as of philosophy; if those judgments are not always argued, they are explicit enough to be arguable.

1. The Concept of Progress

The concept of progress presupposes a "final cause"—an end toward which an advance is made. Thus, the goal of medicine historically has been a combination of prevention and healing—and there can be little disagreement that current practice is closer to that end than earlier practice was. The criteria here are at least superficially objective: life expectancy, incidence of disease, capacitis of surgical technique and medical technology—and the contrast is obvious, that no analogous criteria are available for marking philosophical progress. The "goal" of philosophy itself continues to be a subject of dispute; and even if we recall that the efforts of philosophy have historically converged on one or several common ends—linguistic analysis, for example, or conceptual mapping, or even wisdom—there, too, we find symptoms of inconclusiveness. Philosophers often claim that they do what they do more effectively than their predecessors—but this is not because of the lapse of time: they make the same claim with respect to their contemporaries. The fact that a twentieth-century philosopher has access to the thinking of 2,400 years with which Aristotle was unacquainted makes it no more likely that the former will do even what the latter failed to do, let alone to improve on what he did. The starting point from which the two set out seems in this sense to have remained constant. Hegel's suggestion of a goal toward which philosophy moves and which the history of philosophy itseslf determines implies that philosophy not only starts by picking itself up by its bootstraps, but manages to jump again and again in mid-air—and even if we wished for philosophy this career as an acrobat, we could hardly assume success until we saw how, or even *that*, it had landed.

Philosophers have consistently found in their predeccessors an interest that was more than archaeological and less than honorific. A physician, informed and competent by the standards of 1981, may have studied Galen, although this is unlikely; it is much more unlikely, however that a modern philosopher will *not* have read Plato or Aristotle. The great figures of philosophy often appear no less alive to later readers than do their actual contemporaries—and occasionally more so, if only in the way that certain of one's own contemporaries will appear more alive to him than others. Philosophical texts, then, compose a library "without walls"; they are historically pertinent for understanding why philosophy has become what it is, but they are also pertinent with respect to the present, as a categorical framework applicable at an earlier time turns out to make sense of a later moment as well. This does not imply a single perennial tradition of philosophical thought, nor does it preclude criticism among philosophical systems; it suggests only that the history of philosophy does not move linearly, that the fact that a philosopher may be willing to place himself with respect to the part of philosophy does not mean at all that he has outstripped that past.

Originality is unmistakably a philosophical virtue, but it is never, for philosophy, a matter of spinning out of whole cloth. This may seem only a renewed claim for progress, philosophy building on the advances of its history—but it is the features of a recurrent present rather than an evolving past that serve here as the occasion. There is repetition in the history of philosophy—in Kant, of the Stoics, for example, in Whitehead, of Plato—a repetition, however, which does not detract from the interest of either the earlier or the later figures. It serves, in fact, to explicate both of them; the similarities between Locke and Hume, for instance, are—in either direction—as illuminating as are their differences for understanding the empiricist's conception of mind (as well as the empiricist's own mind). Even as an ideal, then, the issues on which the past of philosophy has focused do not point to single (future) moments of resolution, as do the problem-settings and solvings of scientific analysis.

There is, futhermore, a second, reductive side to the concept of progress—and here too we note a difference for philosophy. A feature commonly ascribed to an evolutionary process is the shedding of excess structure: as the direction of a line becomes more explicit, the vagaries or diversions in its shape are pared away. Progress toward a future is in this sense made by being rid of a past—by working free of problems that have been solved and are no longer alive, by the removal of topics that have been reassigned elsewhere. It may seem that especially the latter reductions have occurred in philosophy—for example, as the "natural philosophy" of the seventeenth and eighteenty centuries turns into modern physics and chemistry, or as the social sciences spin off from "moral philosophy." But the assumption in many of the interpretations of this history—which sometimes, as for Comte, anticipate a point at which philosophy will be left with nothing at all to call its own—is that these offspring of philosophy come to do well what philosophy itself had been willing to do badly. And surely a fair alternate description would be that even if philosophers had sometime attempted to do what one or some of the sciences now do, this was because they anticipated the importance of the results for philosophy, not because producing the results was itself philosophy. The spinoff, then, may represent progress—but not necessarily for the philosopher.[1]

The resemblance is thus suggested between the status of progress in this history of philosophy and the role of progress in the history of art; for in the latter, too, what is accomplished or realized is a function of time in its individual moments rather than as a single process of development. The audiences of the various arts take account of the periods in which Homer or Bernini or Mahler worked, but as a means of explaining, not of explaining away, the artist's work; later authors and readers hardly discard Homer, or even much lesser writers, on grounds of obsolescence. Thus, whatever the purpose or end of art (the extent of disagreement here corresponds to disagreement about the end of philosophy), we do not assume that because art has the failures and accomplishments of the past behind it, its present (or future) will even probably, let alone necessarily, improve on them. It is true that claims are often made for stylistic development in the arts; for example, that the stages of Renaissance painting occur in a progressive and even a necessary order. But such claims are most plausible in reference to short periods of time—and even there we could hardly predict the form they would take if we did not know, for example, as a matter of historical fact, that Raphael worked in Perugino's studio rather than the other way round. Thus for art, too, there is a constant present, a museum "without walls" in which changes and differences reveal no single line or direction. To be sure, historians of art have often claimed *retrospectively* to detect historical patterns with a beginning in the past and a provisional end in the present or future—but the more unified the pattern, the more clearly do those findings seem to represent coherence in seeing rather than coherent making. "Take any three dots," Leibniz suggests, "and you can find a pattern."

2. The Creative Process

Even less that is useful has been said about the way philosophy is made than about the creation of art or science, but certain historical features are evident. For one thing, philosophical authorship has been associated with individuals, not with groups. Neo-Platonists and Kantians may be linked retrospectively by a school tie, but not because they ever enrolled as members of a corporation. Plato did not have that relationship to Socrates either—and the dialogues come as close as does any sustained philosophical writing to supporting a claim of joint authorship. Admittedly, a similar pattern has held for the past of science; even with the recent phenomenon of "teams," individual names stand out. But the possibility of corporate effort that is alive in science is alien to philosophy. And in art, too, the work has characteristically been the work of a single person. The discrimination of artistic style comes close, in fact, to the way we recognize individual persons: a good likeness of somebody else's style is a forgery, not a portrait. Whether or not this emphasis on recognition or individuality has been an intention of the artist, it has come to be seen as his accomplishment.

A second aspect of the making of philosophy, related to the individuality of authorship, is the uniqueness of what is made. The question of attribution or precedence has become so urgent in science that, like miners, scientists often stake out claims, publishing descriptions of what they *mean* to work on; it is enough that the boundaries should be clear to potential trespassers. Little pressure of this kind is felt in either philosophy or in art—not because their creators lack ambition but because (we infer) of a sense that their accomplishment will be theirs whenever it occurs: the problem is in the doing, not in the dating. The claim is plausible for even the most important scientific achievements that if they had not been accomplished when they were, they would almost certainly have been anyway, although perhaps later, by others. Such contentions are largely irrelevant for the work of philosophy; in this respect again, a Kant or a Hegel stands closer to the role of the artist than to that of the scientist. There have been great writers and painters since Shakespeare and Rembrandt— but not anyone about whom it would be said that if they (Shakespeare and Rembrandt) had not done what they did, other artists could have or would have. As with art as well, furthermore, there is an implied criticism in the judgment that a piece of philosophical work so closely resembles others that authorial attribution or identification is difficult; for important achievements in art or philosophy, in fact, such judgments are rarely even at issue. They may well arise, however, with respect to scientific work, and if not in praise, at least with no sense of derogation. All that will be said about a later "discovery" identical to an earlier one is that precedence rules. A student of mathematics who by himself hits on the Pythagorean Theorem is neither a magician nor a forger, although, on the other hand, he gains no credit (at least not Pythagoras's credit) for doing so. Somewhat differently, the work of science that presents a new and original finding *could*, from its form, have been the work of any of a number of investigators. There is nothing in this against its scientific standing: the intelligence of science is not expected to have personality. Thus, scientific attribution is rarely possible on the basis of the work itself, although it is certainly possible as a reading of the chronological place of the work in the history of a problem. For philosophy (and art), precisely the reverse is the case: individual attribution speaks, and the determinations of history are muted.

A last aspect pertinent to the making of philosophy is the relation between the philosophical work and other contemporary accomplishments of speculation or creation. One need not argue for a *Zeitgeist* fully grown to admit the sometime occurrence of a common expressive form in several media—not only among the arts (for example, as in "baroque" architecture and music), but in other cultural institutions as well. This more than chronological connection appears in the designations of "Renaissance" or "Enlightenment" philosophy; imprecise as the terms are, they are no more vague when applied to philosophy than to literature or the visual arts. Nobody can *prove* that the geometric methods of Spinoza and Jan Vermeer have more in common than the fact that both their creators were born in 1632 not far from each other—but neither do we have to believe that parallel lines meet, to allow for the association. And here again, a proportionate contrast occurs with respect to science: science obviously has a history insofar as individual events or discoveries presuppose others—but it is primarily the rate at which science moves (and sometimes not even that) that is affected by other contemporary representational forms. A vertical rather than horizontal reference shapes the endeavors of science at any specific time. The kinds of its questions and the methods it employs seem largely independent of the other cultural expressions alongside it—more so, certainly, than for art, and more so, as I have been arguing, than for philosophy.

3. Evaluation and Verification

Interest in systems that can be judged as either true or false often turns specifically on whether they *are* true or false—and however philosophical systems are evaluated, this does not seem to be the way. The prima facie evidence here is strong. There are large differences between Plato and Aristotle and probably larger ones between either of them and Kant or Hegel—but few philosophical critics would write off any of these figures even if there could be agreement that, on a specific point of contention, he was "wrong." The continuing criticism of a philosophical position itself testifies to at least the relative plausibility of what is criticized: Why otherwise would one bother to refute an argument that was centuries old and had been (simply) invalid when first made? If we continue to review Aristotle's objections to Plato's theory of Forms, this is hardly because one or the other will be discarded when the assessment is complete. St. Thomas and Kant refute the ontological argument as it appears in Anselm or Descartes—and somehow all four, the arguments and the refutations, have managed to survive. Thus, we understand the varieties of philosophical appreciation and also its unlikely conjunctions: Thomas and Kierkegaard, Plato and Hobbes, Aristotle and Wittgenstein. The burden of argument is on anyone who finds inconsistency in such combinations, who sees in them diminished claims for the coherence or applicability of philosophy itself.

This does not mean that for philosophy anything goes; contradiction, qualification, or (a stronger reaction still) indifference frequently marks the pattern of response. The fact that the process of evaluation in philosophy is related to the individual context of what is being evaluated does not make the evaluation any less stringent than it would with the application of criteria of truth or falsity; it means only that there are no general rules of exclusion and inclusion—and this again draws the analogy close to the process of art where we find no sufficient or necessary conditions for judgments of approval and condemnation. With philosophy, as with art and in contrast to other forms of discourse in which criteria *rule*, evaluation is a function of seeing what the object evaluated does to us, not what we can do to it.

What is it in philosophy, then, that we hesitate to judge as true or false but that goes beyond the flat, indisputable lines of mere taste? In the microcosms of art, as, for example, with Dickens or Brueghel, members of an audience gain an opening they would not otherwise have, on a world they would otherwise not have known. The opening comes as perception; as in a multifaceted eye, there is no more disagreement or inconsistency among the facets than there is between the right hand and the left. It may be that the separate facets make a whole—or it may be that the only whole we ever recognize is one that consists of facets: either of these conditions would still leave room to claim a view of alternate realities.

That strains or incompatibilities occur among philosophical systems only underscores the possibility of an evaluative pluralism. Philosophical methods differ because it is inescapable that every philosophical system should propose a method, and differences then become inevitable. Philosophical subject matter, its medium, also varies, since what philosophy is *about* is linked to the question of what philosophy hopes or expects to do *to* what it is about. Where a structure has indefinite boundaries, whatever is asserted about it becomes itself part of the boundary, taking on an exhibitive quality. The analogy between philosophy and art is sustained with these examples as well, since for art, too, method and subject matter start with the artist himself: a good part of his art is spent in making *them*—before and aside from what he makes *of* them. For neither philosophy nor art, furthermore, does the continual revision or re-creation of method and medium produce dissonance, either within a single work or within the history of many works. There is room, perhaps even a need, for such variety—and this could hardly be the case if the only legitimate "variety" available to the work of philosophy were the alternatives of being true or being false.

When we speak of the person of the philosopher, we find similar parallels. A "good" automobile mechanic sees the problems in an engine and knows what to do about them. If no such problems ever occurred, he might still be a good mechanic, but he would have no work. Philosophers and artists also need to be technicians, but only because they are first something more as well: the questions they ask need them more than the other way round. There is no evident "job of work" for which the philosopher applies. So a "good" philosopher is only in part what he will be as philosopher; it is a step on the way to being a *philosopher*—as a "good" triangle seems to have moved to the verge of being just that, a triangle.

4. Teaching and Learning

Plato argues (in the *Meno*, for example) that whatever else learning is, it is not a process in which a teacher transmits units of knowledge to a student. At most, the teacher provides his student with an occasion, a point of departure. Much teaching, in practice, pretends otherwise—that the teacher is a purveyor, literally putting what is in his head into the heads of others. So, on this model, the apprentice lawyer learns cases of precedence together with various rules of classification—what to do, when; and the physicist learns all that is known of a certain particle about which he will himself then say more. Neither the methods nor the objects here are problematic; they constitute a space that the student continues to fill in or up, and that he then transmits, slightly enlarged, to others who have replaced him as student and who will later replace him as teacher. The units of knowledge accumulate, and the progressive specialization of scientific learning is an inevitable consequence. In the domain of practice as well—driving a car, cooking, building a bridge—there is evidently teaching and learning, giving and taking: knowing where to put your hands, what to put *in* your hands, dangers to avoid. Of course, practice here (not mere knowledge) makes perfect—but the practice, too, has a structure that experience or learning has disclosed to the teacher and that he then puts at the disposal of his students.

But what, we ask, either from history or practice, do we find that the apprentice philosopher or the apprentice artist learns from *his* masters? In the end, the transactions come to little more than this: two writing tables or easels side by side, and two people working at them who occasionally look at each other's work. What can the master give his student here? What can the student take? Only the opportunity to look, and the talk that may follow, the recognition, in retrospect, that what was done was important to have done—and perhaps that more will be. The student may himself become a master, but the process is much like growing older: it happens as it happens. The only difference is that, for the student, it does not always happen.

The student, to be sure, is confronted by a crowded past, filled with labels. But if they capture him, then the object of philosophy has become history, and its project becomes mere repetition, at most resurrection. As both the method and subject matter of philosophy are live contingencies in the philosopher's work, then the past, which has no patience with possibilities, can easily be misleading. There is no way to learn from the past what contingencies look like, no way to anticipate them: like generals, all that philosophers can learn by rehearsing philosophical experience is how to fight the last war. Faithfulness to the textbook of a hundred literary plots provides no assurance to a writer that *his* plot will be worth reading; if he does not go beyond the rules, he goes no place at all. And the student-philosopher is no better off. Neither he nor his teacher has bargained for his job; in a sense, they have not even decided to do what they do. The questions the student raises have to be of his own asking; if he borrows them, he might as well borrow the answers too. The teacher of philosophy can exhibit philosophical work, his own or others'—and there is in fact little more he can do; if he had a framing device more dramatic than book covers, the analogy with the settings of art—the walls of a museum, the stage of a concert hall—would be quite clear.

5. The Illusion of Finality

Artists step beyond the past when they face the blank canvas or paper before them, and they challenge the future when they fill it in. This, where they are, is where, as they see it at that moment, art culminates; the claim is rarely made in so many words, but mainly because the artist has so few words to spare. For the scientist, such a manner would be hypocrisy: since he first comes to life by progress, by the death of his predecessors, how could he then refuse to die in turn? In contrast, there is nothing provisional in the philosopher's assertions about what there is. If the later history of philosophy displaces a particular moment, this is the cathartic push of non-philosophical history at work, not the author himself. Thus, philosophical writing in the prefaces and introductions to so many works in its history—for Descartes, Locke, Kant—first rejects the past, and then shows how the past makes the author's present, this new beginning, both possible and necessary. If future obsolescence were foreseen here, the present could hardly be so hopeful. They represent illusions of course, these claims for a true (and new) beginning, for the beginning of the end, the last word. The same artist, the same philosopher will make the same claim in his next work—and he will mean it then no less than he meant it before. This is not arbitrary or mere egotism, a pretense to have settled matters because the creator is who he is; the illusion of finality appears because philosophy is what it is, because the hope it expresses of a new beginning, a fresh start, and perhaps even an end, is the hope which philosophy has historically been commissioned to provide. Again and again.

The objection may be made that in citing these points of analogy as historical description I have given weight to what *some* philosophers have said about their work but not to the opinions of others—in effect that my opening claim for philosophical neutrality in this discussion was misleading. Certainly what I have said conflicts with the not uncommon representation of philosophy as a variety of science and thus as progressive (usually with that progress either beginning or ending with the philosopher who makes the claim). Certain philosophers, furthermore (often the same ones), have challenged the very concept of a history of philosophy invoked here as evidence— and if that history does not exist, neither, of course, does the evidence. But disagreement on this point, it seems to me, is itself historical—not primarily theoretical or philosophical, and still less a matter of will or desire. It may be that the work of philosophy will one day be complete, and that the only work left for subsequent reflections on philosophy, like histories of the dinosaur, will be to arrange the events that came between its beginning and its end (the two histories probably involving the same issues: disproportion of body to brain, predatorial competition, inability to adapt). Seen from the outside, the narrative history of philosophy undoubtedly has the form of a fiction—but in this sense of making or contrivance, it is like any other narrative. Thus, in placing philosophers within a history I have been trying only to take the history at its one word, not the philosophers at their several ones. It is not an unusual phenomenon, I have suggested, that individual philosophers should view their work as a conclusion to the whole; but such claims have not yet brought an end to the history of philosophy, which continues to exhibit a hearty appetite. And here as elsewhere, it is difficult to argue against history, because we hardly know what to argue against it with.

Two other objections to ascribing the manners of art to philosophy cut in different directions: first, that whatever the likeness between them, philosophy still is not yet art (and vice versa). But we can admit this and still agree that there will be other times and reasons for marking the differences: philosophy can be *like* art without *being* art. Secondly—that since the argument here has assumed the external history of philosophy as a given, the claims made are only as good or long as that history. And surely, then, we cannot know that the history of philosophy does not progress (for example) until we have seen the whole of the history, that is, until it is over. As a counsel of prudence, of course, this is unexceptionable: like the anatomist, the historian works most easily with corpses. But such counsel obviously asks a longer time for the naming of philosophy than the philosopher or anyone else has to wait; in the long run, we know, the prudent too are as dead as if they had not been. What I have proposed is a small argument, then, for daring to run ahead of philosophy in order to get a glimpse of its face—as we do always with art. As we do, in fact, when we are most in the midst of it.

Note

1. If the concept of scientific progress cited here seems to conflict with the concepts recently argued by Kuhn, Feyerabend, et al., it remains the case—without arguing one way or the other between them—that (a) the "linear" model has been part of an influential paradigm; and (b) philosophers who have sought in their own work to imitate science have been imitating *that* paradigm rather than any other.

PART II

Poetics and Persons

6

Style as Instrument, Style as Person

The voice is the voice of Jacob, but the hands are the hands of Esau.

> Isaac, blind and puzzled—Genesis 27:22

When Augustine writes in the *Confessions* that "if he is not asked what time is, he knows; if he is asked, he knows not," we recognize something more searching than a design for paradox and broader than a reflection only about time. It is as though Augustine would inform us that the more closely we approach the center of distinctively human phenomena—the organ of vision or understanding itself—the less clearly can we resolve the elements of that center as objects. The converse of this may not always be true—that where analysis becomes opaque, we can infer that we are looking at the human face, mainly our own—but I suggest that the two sides of this prospect have been true, *are* true, for the attempt to grasp what style is: the sense of both presence and elusiveness which Augustine finds for time, and a source for that complementarity in the relation between style and the defining features of the self.

In examining this relation I do not mean to contest or even to say much about the apparent, if grudging, consensus in the body of recent work which addresses the *fact* of style. That consensus, it seems to me, has been shaped by an interest which, although pertinent to the question of what style is, left to itself begs the question. To define style as a "regularity,"[1] "frequency distribution,"[2] or "deviation from a norm"[3] is not so much to give an account of style as to isolate symptoms of what such accounts ought to be accounting for: the immediacy of recognition and of understanding which even the glimpse of a drawing or of a line of poetry—like the look on a face—may convey. The reasons for this immediacy will emerge only as the question of what style is, is projected onto a different axis, and I shall be attempting that translation here into a Kantian or transcendental framework

113

within which the question becomes how style is possible—what, in other words, is necessary in order that style (and thus, later, stylistic analysis or appreciation) should exist.

The answers to such questions, Kant proposes, have the force of principles, assertions with a different function and type of necessity than the occasions which set the questions in motion. In response to these requirements, I shall be arguing toward a principle of style which originates in a redescription of the evidence—proposing that the vocabulary of stylistics is a vocabulary of human or physiognomic expression—and which then argues from that reformulation and the evidence underlying it that the phenomenon of style—what stylistic categories categorize—is made possible by a protocol of "repetition" that confirms style as a mode of personification and an end in itself, rather than, as has more often been held to be the case, an instrumentality supposed to act on, or on behalf of, some other purpose. Not then, in Buffon's words, as he distinguishes between the individual manners of style and the determinate stuff of style's content, that "the style is the man himself"—meaning by that his idiosyncracies—but differently and in the end contradictorily, that style represents the assertion of content—and thus *most certainly* the man himself.[4]

The history of the concept of style is the history of a metonymy. The stylus or instrument for incising letters on a tablet comes in its Latinate and again in its English history to designate a quality of what is written, and then, more generally, the manner in which any job of work is executed. What I am proposing—not recommending, but finding in the logic of this development—is a formal conclusion to the metonymy: an extended reference beyond the work and then beyond the quality of the work to the person of the worker himself. But we have to follow a contrast between two conceptual models of style that differ in principle, and in the practice that derives from it, before this extension becomes plausible.

1. Style as Noun and Adverb

The question "How is style possible?" assumes the existence of style, and the most obvious evidence for this presupposition, as well as for determining what it means, appears in the talk about style, the deployment of stylistic categories. That talk extends in common usage to such attenuated references as styles in dress, styles of social exchange, life-styles. To limit the discussion, I speak here primarily of artistic style, but it will be clear that the ramifications of the argument extend beyond the arts, indeed beyond style as well.

On this line of inference, the practical question of what the use or function of stylistic analysis is plays a controlling role, in effect setting a dialectic in motion. For if there is a stopping short in the first—adverbal or instrumental—model of style, and an amending completeness in the second, verbal or transitive, model, that difference starts from their respective conceptions of the function which stylistic analysis, and finally style itself, serve. It is important, then, to keep the question of function in mind; that question serves in fact as a mediating link between the appearance of style and the discourse about it, on the one hand, and the final question of how style is possible, on the other. The two models of style to be described differ explicitly on the last of these points, and they differ at least tacitly in their conception of the mediating link: the question of the function or use of style. Those differences in turn make a practical difference even in the immediate description of particular styles.

Consider the following two examples of stylistic criticism which serve as points of reference—the first from Samuel Johnson's *Lives of the English Poets*, the second from Heinrich Wölfflin's *Principles of Art History:*

> The metaphysical poets were men of learning, and to shew their learning was their whole endeavor; but unluckily resolving to shew it in rhyme, instead of writing poetry they wrote only verse, and very often such verses as stood the trial of the finger better than of the ear; for the modulation was so imperfect that they were only found to be verses by counting the syllables. . . . Wit, abstracted from its effects upon the hearer, may be more rigorously and philosophically considered as a kind of discordia concors; a combination of dissimilar images, or discovery of occult resemblances in things apparently unlike. Of wit thus defined, they have more than enough.[5]

> The development from the linear to the painterly [styles involves] the development of line as the path of vision and guide of the eye, and the gradual depreciation of line: in more general terms, the perception of the object by its tangible character—in outline and surfaces—on the one hand, and on the other, a perception which is by way of surrendering itself to the mere visual appearance and abandoning "tangible" design. In the former case the stress is laid on the limits of things; in the other the work tends to look limitless. Seeing by volume and outlines isolates objects; for the painterly eye, they merge.[6]

In the contexts from which these descriptions are taken, it could be shown that the two accounts reflect different conceptions of what style is. But for the moment, the passages are at the reader's mercy, fragments out of context; thus abstracted, it is what they have in common which is more accessible (if hardly startling)—specifically, to begin with, the function of classification. The concepts of metaphysical poetry and the linear-painterly distinction define categories which may apply beyond the examples actually cited for them (as Eliot showed, for instance, in extending the concept of metaphysical poetry as a generic term), but which even in their original formulations provide lines of organization whose further use we might well not question. With the advantage of Johnson's notion of the metaphysical in poetry, we make more manageable, set our mark on, an otherwise heterogeneous (let us suppose) collection of English poets; Wölfflin's discrimination of the linear and painterly styles, with the other four stylistic pairs that he notices, contributes to a distinction otherwise marked by the unwieldy and (for art) arbitrary line between the sixteenth and seventeenth centuries. At this minimal level, then, the categories serve a naming function. They answer to a version of the Linnaean ideal of classification which originates in what may be claimed as a source of language itself: the fact that without it, we are restricted to pointing at the individual members of a class—the class itself, of course, being undiscerned; that once we had left their presence, we could say, perhaps even remember, nothing at all about the individuals themselves.

This function appears, in the caricatured history of grammar from which I derive the two models of style, as that of the noun, and a minimal "nominative" function is thus ascribed to the models of style discussed here. This nominative function, moreover, is not only a condition of the other functions disclosed in the model of style. Although few *theories* of style see this first function as exhausting the possibilities of stylistic discourse, stylistic *practice* often goes no further—content only to attach to an object or to its parts the names of a creator, school, period, genre, figure of speech. The act of naming, in such cases, seems an end in itself.

The mediating question of use or function, however, is not resolved by this limit. It is evident that most systems and instances of classification—including many that classify only tacitly—reflect broader purposes than that of naming. Classification, although usually a matter of convention, is rarely arbitrary, and one has only to note as an example of this the varieties of purpose assembled in the literary genres of encyclopedias or cookbooks to recognize how such differences in purpose, reflecting both origins and goals, shape the lines of classification. The instrumental and transitive models of style share also this second-level function; their later divergence reflects what they do, or do not do, with it.

By the concept of style as instrument or, grammatically, as adverb,

I refer to the use of stylistic categories in characterizing the "how" or the means by which the object that exhibits a stylistic imprint is articulated. This usage presumes on the first one mentioned, of classification: there is some *thing* prior to or independent of the manner, and the manner or instrumentality qualifying the "thing" then becomes the focus of stylistic analysis. When Johnson, for example, speaks of the versification of the metaphysical poets, he draws attention to a manner which sets that process off from the poetic process in other writers; it is no less clear from Wölfflin's distinction that, at the least, he is speaking about two different ways in which lines can be drawn. What is represented in these distinctions, then, is a version of modality or instrumentality: if we want to understand the effect produced by particular poets or painters, we must look to their means, their instruments. And at first glance, even at second (certainly after we have had them pointed out to us), the instruments or devices employed seem readily distinguishable from the process itself.

This pattern of discrimination between an object and its means is superficially plausible. It moves the reader closer to an apparent intention of the important analyses of style quoted above (important in themselves and influential as examples); in doing this, it seems also to bring him closer to the works and artists referred to in those analyses. But this apparent innocence in the view of style as instrument is deceptive. For this model, and so also the dominant tradition in rhetoric and poetics that incorporates it, are made possible by a conceptual basis whose own warrant is questionable. It is a fact, in any event, that in most of the early writings on style—for example, in surviving citations from the Sophist Gorgias[7] and, more fully, in Aristotle's work—style is represented as an instrumentality by which another more basic process is realized. Thus, in the *Rhetoric*, for instance, Aristotle carries on the battle between sons and fathers as he acknowledges—sounding like Plato—that it is *easier* to formulate a statement in defense of a true thesis than in defense of a false one; but—against Plato—the contrast is held to be manageable, Aristotle implying that the difficulty with respect to the defense of falsehood is tactical only—*not* that an adequate means is not to be found.[8] Again, Aristotle suggests that "it is not enough to know *what* we ought to say; we must also say it *as* we ought":[9] a distinction here between the "what" and the "as" is assumed. The structure of style in this account is separable from whatever style is the style of: *that* (apparently) is neutral, independent of stylistic affect.

A commonsensical way of understanding this conception of style and its evolution in critical theory into the dichotomy between form and content is suggested by the analogy between the making or ap-

preciation of art, on the one hand, and the articulation of more ordinary actions, on the other. Many individual actions, for example, can
be performed in various ways without altering the actions themselves. I walk across the room quickly or slowly, unconsciously or
deliberately: the manner does not alter the fact that in each case I
have walked across the room. The same pattern of analysis is readily
transposed onto the practice of rhetoric, which gives rise historically
(as for Gorgias and Aristotle) to the study of style. For the "action"
that marks the occasion of rhetoric is evident: persuasion. And the
variables which then prescribe alternative versions of an individual
rhetorical act—the audience to be persuaded, the probable objections to be overcome—are hardly less distinctive. We understand,
moreover, how the required extension might take place from rhetoric
to art, especially in that central tradition of aesthetics which conceives
of art as imitation, and in particular, within *that* tradition, as Aristotle
himself identifies action as the principle element of poetic imitation.
Here again, the implication goes, a single action may be articulated in
several ways. The act of performance for the work of art does not
differ significantly, then, from those that yield more commonplace
products; the content of an action or group of actions in an individual
work thus becomes a constant to be distinguished from its particular
appearances. The manner of the action or work is individual and
contingent; it may vary, and we thus infer the possibility of variation
in the patterns of style—style itself then appearing as the adornment
or ornament of a central theme that could otherwise be made evident
without it. Style, to locate it in spatial terms, plays the outside to
content's inside.

If we look for the basis in Aristotle's own principles which underlies
this instrumental or adverbal conception, the relation to certain logical and metaphysical doctrines is unmistakable: the parallel and independently consequential lines of rhetoric and metaphysics meet. Two
formulations in particular mark this convergence: the subject-
predicate distinction on the basis of which Aristotle structures the
logic of discourse, and the related distinction, developed mainly in
the *Metaphysics* and *Physics*,[10] between essence and accidental predicates. According to those distinctions, for every natural entity (by
analogy, for all entities), there is an essential property of which the
other qualities of the entity are said to be predicated: Socrates was,
but need not have been, snub-nosed, to cite one of Aristotle's favorite
examples of accidental predication; what Socrates *really* was, i.e., an
individuated capacity for reason (which thus counts as his essence),
could have had a nose that was shaped differently and indeed, if we
push this a bit, no nose at all. As Aristotle relies on this account in the
general analysis of entities or relations, we should not be surprised

that it recurs when he is speaking about rhetorical structures, or that the common formula should persist, by way of Aristotle's influence, both in the history of metaphysics and in the later migrations of the instrumental conception of style.

The connections among these several levels, beginning with the conventional practice of stylistic language, moving to the theory of style and, more broadly, to a principle of style, constitute what I earlier alluded to as a conceptual model of style. On this model, the adverbal categories of stylistic distinction are related asymmetrically to their objects: they qualify something that does not reciprocally qualify them. They serve, furthermore, to classify artists or their works in the interest primarily of showing how distinctions of manner are made; they thus represent the means or instruments used for realizing an assumed end—not for exhibiting the end or for defining the relation between it and the means. Style here is an external feature; by implication a range of alternate styles and even, at a logical extreme, no style at all might be fitted to a single object without changing it essentially. Johnson's description of what makes for metaphysical poetry appears in his work titled *Lives of the English Poet*, and the conjunction in that title of biography and poetry is significant. The lives of the poets, in Johnson's own terms, "*have*" certain characteristics, one among which is the making of poetry. There is more than a tacit indication in this manner of speaking of a distinction also between two manners of being: the one, a ground that is determinate in the poet himself; the other, as in the varieties of poetic expression and convention, contingent and occasional.

In terms of influence, it is clear that this conception of style has been and remains dominant in the history of criticism, poetics, and aesthetics. it figures, after Aristotle, in such classical authors as Quintilian and Demetrius, and persistently after that as well—for instance, with the critical concerns of the eighteenth century, in such writers as Lord Kames, Buffon, and Cuvier. It recurs, furthermore, in many contemporary writers who address the problem of style from an otherwise diverse range of perspectives: in linguists like Enkvist, Rifaterre, and Ullmann; in writers on poetics, including the structuralists (among them Lévi-Strauss and to some extent Jakobson); and in a multitude, almost certainly the majority, of practicing critics.[11]

2. Style as Transitive

The durability of the tradition in which it figures is itself evidence that the instrumental model of style must be taken seriously, that whether we finally accept that model or not, we have to take account of the impulse that underlies it. But I shall also be claiming here that finally the model itself is inadequate from the point of view both of internal coherence and of applicability—to such a degree, in fact, that an alternative conception is suggested by its own formulation. These defects become evident through the mediating question of function, as we ask of the instrumental or adverbal categories applied to style what use *they* have. For although style conceived adverbally provides a way of "handling" works of art, when we press the question of what that handling is *for*, a break occurs in the argument. We ask what the instrumentality leads *to*, what its means are predicated *of*—and although there is always the *presumption* of an underlying content or center, neither conceptually nor in the practical discourse about style is that center evident. Either the object of which the means are predicated becomes so neutral or ineffectual as to be aesthetically vacuous ("*King Lear* is a play about suffering"), or as a consequence of the abstraction of all predicates, it vanishes entirely. We must, it seems, add to the grammatical syntax of style that so far has relied on nouns and adverbs; and I suggest that this be done in a "verbal" or, less awkwardly, a "transitive" model of style.

Consider, for example, Wölfflin's description of Velázquez's *Infanta Margareta*, a painting which he cites as an example of the painterly style:

> Velasquez has an eye thus attuned to appearance. The dress of his little princess was embroidered in zigzag patterns: what he gives, however, is not the ornamentation in itself, but the shimmering image of the whole. Seen uniformly from a distance, yet without looking indistinct; we can see perfectly clearly what is meant, but the forms cannot be grasped, they come and go, the highlights of the fabric play over them, and the whole is dominated by the rhythm of the light waves.[12]

Superficially, this description seems explicable in terms of the adverbal model and its distinction between content and form. On that account, the subject of the painting, the little princess, would also figure as its theme or "essence"; the qualities ascribed to the subject, like "indistinctness," "shimmering image," "forms [which] cannot be grasped," would then be the means or instrument by which that subject was presented, made apparent.

But it is an obvious question whether the "subject" of the painting (to use Dewey's formulation)[13] can be intelligibly detached from its properties in this way. The obvious test here would be to see what happens if we envisage the painting without the qualities that Wölfflin identifies—inferring what, as "essential" to the painting, remains. The results of this test for Velázquez's painting seem both clear and empty: that as a viewer abstracts the supposedly adverbal qualities—the highlighting of the fabric, the distinctness of pattern, the appearance of the little princess—what remains without them, as the "Infanta herself," lacks the standing even of an abstraction. There is nothing left.

The range of examples that force similar conclusions matches the extent of stylistic discourse. As we separate out the allegedly stylistic aspects of genre, for example—not singly, but (a truer test) together—the essence that was supposed to have remained also disappears: the manners or instruments turn out to have been the thing itself. So we might inflect Barthes's metaphors: we find that the apricot has no pit, not because it is an unusual apricot but because it is, after all, an onion.[14]

This transitivity of manner, the articulation of the work as process, thus establishes a framework for the second model of style. On that model, an intrinsic connection is asserted between the "what" and the "how" of the stylistic object; the two appear as modalities of a single and common process. So Hegel, for example—for modern aesthetics and criticism, the key figure in providing a basis for this thesis—argues in one summary statement in the *Aesthetics* that "art does not lay hold of . . . [a particular] form either because it is simply there or because there is no other. The concrete context itself *implies* the presence of external and actual . . . appearance."[15] Hegel's schematization of this thesis, which traces the history of art through its "symbolic," "classical," and "romantic" phases, need not be the issue here; for even if we limit our examination to particular objects out of their historical contexts, his analysis is compelling, and not only because it proposes a remedy for the defects of the adverbial model. The "fit" between form and content as an aesthetic ideal is acknowledged in almost all accounts that speak of style at all. There is an important difference, however, between a view of that correlation as accidental and ad hoc, on the one hand, and as determinant, on the other. The significance of Hegel's analysis turns precisely on his claim for a process of reciprocal causality between form and content—a codetermination that in effect nullifies the form-content distinction as a mode of artistic analysis and thus contests the basic division on which the instrumental model of style is based. If the line between form and content is denied, the distinction between style and some inner core or stuff of which it is the instrumentality or means collapses.

This does not imply that the manner of speaking about the generic appearances of style or of any particular style necessarily changes: the formulations cited earlier—of norms, deviance, coherence—will be no less pertinent as sources for the derivation of principles of style than they would be otherwise. But those definitions *by themselves* are now shown to be either trivial or misleading—utterances that only another and more fundamental framework can make intelligible. The point is, of course, that unless stylistics is defined as a branch of linguistics or of formal logic (and even then, as some linguists and logicians would object), the consistencies or rules and deviations that mark the appearances of style do not themselves establish a ground for either the existence or understanding of style. What is missing there still is a principle to account for the *stylistic* and thus expressive significance of the regularities. In the absence of such a principle, style is *equated* with redundance or analogy, and the many counterexamples of redundancy or analogy that are *not* stylistic features— the legs of a centipede, the repetitive typeface in which a poem or novel is printed—easily confute this equation.

3. The Physiognomy of Style

The second, transitive model of style is shaped, then, by the premise that the categories or predicates of style are not auxiliary or accidental features of an otherwise integral object, but rather— transitively—precisely those features which determine that integrity for the object or work of art; there is no space between those features and the object or process itself, no internal spirit or power of which style is then a mere instrument. The latter stipulation implies that the analysis either of style as a general feature of art or of a particular artistic style will be a function of the concept of the work of art. I attempt no more here than to acknowledge this connection, and not only because of the difficulty involved in showing what the defining features of art are which then reappear in its stylistic character; if the argument until this point holds, what is important about the relation between art and style is the transitive character of that relation, *however* we define art or distinguish it from other forms of expression. For the purposes of this discussion, in fact, reference to the expressive character of art notwithstanding, the frequently cited ambiguities in the concept of expression itself may suffice; recognition of that character seems, in any event, a necessary ingredient for an adequate view of art, and few accounts of art with the exception of certain ones in the formalist tradition (that then suffer from its absence) have even attempted to do without it. Furthermore, although the claim of an intrinsic connection between style and the objects of art is independent of any particular conception of art, a number of considerations suggest (although they do not strictly imply) the component of expression as a necessary ingredient in them all.

These considerations take their point from concrete aspects of stylistic discourse: from the fact, for example, that stylistic categories are conventionally applied only to artifacts or human actions (we speak of the beauty of a sunset but not of its style);[16] and that even within the class of artifacts or human predicates, stylistic analysis pertains only to those which are referential or iconic and which are thus not merely natural (like fingerprints or voice pitch). A more basic but also more difficult point to establish emerges from the question of what—comparable in linguistic function to the phoneme or morpheme—is the basic or least unit of stylistic analysis. It is clear enough that elements as slight as individual syllables or sounds, brush strokes, individual musical notes, commas, even silences or empty spaces can be stylistically pertinent; they are pertinent, however, not in themselves (by themselves they are elements "in" or "of" the artist's style) but insofar as they both contribute to and reflect an expressive function. That function may appear at any of a number of levels of artistic scope, some of them as slight as those already named, some much larger: in the earlobe or hand of a painted figure or with the individual art work as a whole, through the work as it appears within the corpus of the artist's work, or as any of these are juxtaposed to other art forms of the same period. So a term like *baroque* is applied to units as small as a single line in a drawing and as large as the "spirit" of an historical age. The use of stylistic terms at these different levels may not be equally justified, but so far as they are *alleged* to be justified, the claim presupposes an expressive function that the various levels supposedly share; and this suggests (as I shall be arguing below) that the least unit of style—whether it be a single one, a "styleme," or one of many possible units—depends not on any single figure of speech or a gesture or statement, but on a concept of the person—without which none of the other expressive designations, whatever their scope, would be stylistically intelligible. We can, to be sure, identify these units without reference to an expressive source; but this would then be the equivalent of the botanist's description of a leaf or the engineer's account of a building site: in neither of these cases are we identifying *stylistic* features. (This proposal may seem to beg the question insofar as it assumes a means for identifying persons, but the problem of *how* that identification occurs is at least conceptually separable.)

This last stipulation of a mirroring or "doubling" effect between the single elements of the object of stylistic analysis and its source recalls the property of consistency or regularity that I earlier mentioned as a theme in recent attempts to describe the *fact* of style. Before attempting to locate the principles of the transitive model of style, we need to look more directly at this property and the evidence for its rule-like consistency (whether as deviation or, more simply, as coherence). A Brahms chord, a Picasso line (for examples) are recognizable to the practiced response even in a work encountered for the first time. This suggests the recurrence either of a single feature or set of features in each stylistic appearance, or of a "family" of features that imply a common genealogy. The former alternative—the recurrence of a single motif, color, syntactical form—is the less significant of the two stylistically and artistically: it is not mere "sameness" that produces either artistic value or stylistic quality. The consistency mentioned is better understood in terms of the second alternative and thus involves the concept of stylistic transformation: the artist's reapplication of the solution to one artistic "problem" (e.g., the rendering of an arm) to another (e.g., the rendering of facial features).[17] It is not, in such cases, that the specific results of the transformation can be predicted beforehand (although there is some probability even of this)[18]—but that retrospectively, as the viewer of a new artistic "event" reconciles his expectations to the present, a consistency is evident that implies a common generative principle. In this sense, we can speak of a "deep structure" of style. (Meyer Schapiro has argued that even this transformational consistency is sometimes lacking in style, and more certainly that it is not a necessary condition for art itself.[19] But it is possible, with respect to his examples of African art, that the supposed inconsistency is only the response of an alien eye, or that the pattern of inconsistency is itself consistent. If the phenomenon of stylistic inconsistency is actual, it would indeed follow that the objects, so far as concerns their internal structures, should not be spoken of in stylistic terms at all. It seems to me finally that the concept of what an *object* is, is at stake here as well.)

The answer to the question of how style is possible on the transitive model must then take account of at least two conditions: first, the regularity or consistency which marks the immediate appearance of style; secondly, at the level of the theory of style, the transitive and, as I have suggested, expressive function which that consistency is required to serve. The issue is not very different whether raised from the standpoint of the creator of style or of the viewer who is drawn to it: with respect to both, we look for an explanation of the lure of style—the basis for its power of evocation from creator or viewer.

I suggest that a principle that establishes the "possibility" of style in this sense is available as a version of Kierkegaard's principle of "repetition"—the activity, as he remarks in one of those rare moments where language serves as the occasion of conceptual reconstruction, of "recollection not backwards but forwards." "When the Greeks said that all knowledge is recollection, they affirmed that all that is has been; when one says that life is a repetition, one affirms that existence which has been now becomes."[20] There is, in Kierkegaard's reckoning, no inevitablility about repetition. What animates it—and also, I am suggesting, the occurrence of style as well—is the reassertion of a beginning in an open space—the development of what will be a pattern only retrospectively, with the requirement evident in the separate elements of the pattern that the common form is anticipated in them. Repetition, in other words, establishes coherence, an identity—but a coherence that takes shape only in the agency of the making, which fact itself, then, appears as part of the identity. Both of these features, located by Kierkegaard as fundamental in the human project, can be seen to underwrite the related phenomenon of style: the consistency in the stylistic pattern of one among at least several alternatives, on the one hand, and the fact that those possibilities appear even with this consistency, quite real—that the consistency is evident only retrospectively. Thus, repetition is not an act that follows from a source already completed or integral; the source is determined in the act, the determination itself communicating the detail of that process. This connection, intrinsic as well to its human source, explains how it is that style is not something apart from the object of which it is the style; it suggests, furthermore, why the discrimination of style provides not a label or moment of identification (as would any pattern that is repetitive backwards—fingerprints, carbon dating), but a means of experiencing from the inside out how a particular human identity is asserted in the first place. The repetition that becomes style is thus not the *product* of a person or of that person's vision, something made *by* him accidentally or subordinately, but the articulation of the person or vision itself.

It may be too much to claim that this principle of repetition by itself can do the work required of a transcendental account of how style is possible; if the connection I have been claiming between style and person holds, the account must also address the concept of person, and the principle of repetition does this only allusively. But the principle both acknowledges and locates that requirement, providing a basis at once for the consistency that is the signature of style and for the unpredictability or openness that distinguishes style from mere redundancy, as well as from natural or accidental matter of fact. In doing this, it also reinforces the claim often advanced in the history of aesthetics for the motif of mimesis or reduplication as the initiating impulse of art itself: style, in effect, is *also* an imitation, mimetic—but with the large difference from mere replication that the freedom of repetition requires.

In asserting a relation between the process of style and the determination of the person, the principle of repetition also provides a basis for the anthropomorphic or physiognomic character of stylistic categories referred to above. When Wölffflin, for example, marks the differences between the linear and the painterly styles, he is on his way to a distinction between the "harmony" or stasis of classical art, on the one hand, and the "movement" of the baroque, on the other;[21] without those lived qualities, the categories of the linear and the painterly make sense only as a critic-historian might out of context apply mechanically *any* categories whatever (except, of course, that he would be unlikely to). Again, in Johnson's reference to the "metaphysical" poets—a category that superficially has nothing anthropomorphic about it—we understand the reference only in terms of the "violence" he ascribes to those poets as they join discordant means. So also, to move almost randomly among more current stylistic allusions, Leonard Meyer's categories of "paraphrase, borrowing, simulation, and modeling," [22] Kenneth Clark's reference to the "severity" of the Greek nude,[23] Meyer Schapiro's more deliberate catalogue that begins with colors that are "cool" or "warm," "gay" or "sad," and extends to such complex stylistic predicates as "mannerist" or "naturalistic":[24] each of these requires either the prospect or the actual experience of a human source. (It is worth noting in this connection that semiotics, a strong recent influence on stylistic analysis, traces its own history to the Greek physicians for whom diagnosis and prognosis were based on the signs displayed—in a more literal sense, expressed—by their patients.)[25]

This does not mean that stylistic predicates are *only* subjective or emotive, although it does imply a constant subjective component. As Goodman points out, stylistic predicates often designate what *seem* to be "objective" properties (for example, the rhyme scheme of a poem).[26] But these predicates too, however objective when defined or identified out of context, are also intelligible stylistically only in terms of the shapes and intentions of their users. And this remains the case notwithstanding the space required in any stylistic setting for at least two nonexpressive elements: the material properties that may be "implied" as a consequence of initial expressive stylistic choices (so, for example, the butressing of the Gothic cathedral to meet the requirements of height and light proposed in the expressive conception); and in other instances, the evidently random choices left open within the limits fixed by the initial expressive assertion (thus Lévi-

Strauss's statement about the expressive function of cultural objects: "To say that everything in a society functions is an absurdity.")[27]

The implication of such argument, then, amounts to this: that in discriminating the features of style, the viewer follows a process and employs an idiom otherwise familiar to him from the recognition of persons—and that this provides a basis for the claim that to distinguish a style is to distinguish both a person and the field of agency or vision of that person. Stylistic categories are characteristically anthropomorphic because what they categorize is itself a human form. (In this sense, to speak of a style as "dead" is not primarily a chronological reference to the *past*.) Few works of art display this genealogy so openly as do the Byzantine mosaics in which figures are represented not as seen by an observer, but as looking at him;[28] more often the glance of art is oblique, or as Mill said about poetry—it is meant to be not heard but "overheard." But this feature, it seems evident, is a device, a diplomatic gesture or initial modesty on the part of art belied by the whole. As has been argued so insistently in philosophical attacks on the Cartesian concept of mind as a "ghost in the machine"[29]—a thinking substance inside but separate from the body—so also here. Style is not an accretion on the object, a ghost in the machine of art, but rather the object, or more precisely, the subject itself. That stylistic subject, moreover, is not only identified or named. As a cue, style is one among other telltale features of an object; unlike the other perceptual cues, however, style implies with its discovery an intersubjective relation: we both see it and see by way of it. The viewer himself "looks" (both sees and appears) as the style does; its vision becomes his own.

These last comments on the transitive conception of style that relate the apparently external features of style to the expression of its creator and of a community that includes at least the viewer, may seem to exclude by fiat some of the most common instances of stylistic practice. What, for example, of the work of the connoisseur, as in the classical studies of Giovanni Morelli when he notices the differences among ears painted by generations of Renaissnce artists?[30] Or the accounts of prosody in the standard handbooks with formulas for the various measures of the poetic foot?[31] But such examples by themselve do not, in fact, count as stylistic analysis—any more than would the attribution of a painting on the basis of the chemical composition of the paints in it, or the identification of a poet's work by the relative frequency in it of the comma. We recognize even in Morelli's detailed analysis, in fact, a larger intention to show precisely how within a work or series of works the parts constitute the whole, not as a physical object but as expressive. In the absence of such an intention, at all events, the observer's search is for history or physiology—but not for style.

The implication of what I have been saying is more than the true but trivial claim that *any* piece of human expression will naturally exemplify the human form and define a point of view. In those sources where we first find and then continue to look for style (most compellingly in the arts), we encounter a vision and the person who "has" that vision or point of view not obliquely (as the claim might go, e.g., for the role of style in scientific discourse), but because it is precisely the point of view itself and its agent that are, and are meant to be, encountered there.

4. Choice and Synonymy in Style

It may seem, even with such considerations, that the transitive conception of style, for all its rejection of the form-content distinction and its claims for the expressive character of stylistic categories, makes little difference—that it neither offers a program for stylistic analysis nor makes sense of the plentiful examples of practical criticism which do not refer to the "person" in style at all. This reservation is indisputable, it seems to me, so far as it confines its own reference to the technical idiom of applied stylistics. But as I have argued above, that technical idiom of style is itself intelligible only within a systematic and historical context—and *that* context is largely, although not completely, determined by the physiognomy of style. I suggest that this can be shown through a "spectrum" contrast that marks the relative distance between stylistic and nonstylistic terms. Consider the following critical statements:

1. The painting is beautiful.
2. The painting is a good example of the baroque.
3. The baroque coloring of the painting is always in movement and is bound up with the impression of becoming.
4. I can see by looking at it that the painting is by a follower of Velázquez, not by Velázquez himself.
5. The painting was completed in 1656.

These statements form a spectrum in which the middle one most clearly exhibits the features that have been linked in the earlier discussion here to stylistic discourse. The statements on either side of that statement move progressively away from that center, as they at least attempt to suppress one or another factor in the usual codetermination of stylistic terms. In the judgment that a painting is beautiful, the observer plays a dominant and on some accounts of value an exclusive role; at the other extreme, the assertion that the painting was completed in 1656 is almost independent of *any* critical response. In the latter statement, the role of the observer is thus put to one side, in the former, the role of the object. It is precisely the coordination of those two factors that produces the stylistic reference of the third statement and, in lesser degrees, of the second and fourth. If, as I have suggested, the intelligibility of all stylistic statements is a function of personification in an object, then that relation should be recognizable both in the stylistic idiom and in its references—and this is clearly the case for statement 3, and derivatively for statements 2 and 4. (It might be argued that the other statements also presuppose stylistic judgment for intelligibility, in effect, that stylistic criticism is the ground of *all* criticism—but for the moment it is not necessary to argue that thesis.)

The logical structure of stylistic analysis is obliged to take account of two stylistic facts of life: the possibilities that the same "thing" (content) can be expressed in different ways (styles), and that different "things" can be expressed in the same way. It might appear to follow from the transitive model of style that on its terms, neither of these "facts" *is* possible, that stylistic units not only *may* differ from each other but must, that they are untranslatable and finally even incomparable. But it also *seems* to be the case that quite different assertions can be formulated—in an apparently common manner or style, and also that a single assertion or claim can be made in a variety of ways. And if the transitive model implied that these apparent truths were simply mistaken—as Croce argued[32]—this liability in the transitive model might well be held to outweigh its other advantages.

In a minimal sense, however—as Goodman points out[33]—even the adverbal model of style must accept limitations on its use of the concept of "sameness." This qualification reflects the strictures identified by various writers in the very concept of synonymy: so, for example, Quine's conclusion that "it is not clear even in principle that it makes sense to think of words and syntax as varying from language to language while the context stays fixed."[34] The technical arguments behind this claim are not directed especially to stylistic questions, but they apply there as well as elsewhere and thus add weight to the claim advanced here against the instrumental model of style that synonymy of content cannot be established simply by abstracting the instruments of communication (if only because of the difficulty in distinguishing between content and instrument).

On the other hand, even if we assume an intrinsic disparity in all translation, that fact might not be practically crucial, since it nonetheless seems to be the case both that one *can* say quite different things in a manner or "style" that seems roughly common to them all, and that one can also make a single claim in different "ways." When Job, for example, protests that "I know that my redeemer liveth," this would obviously be at odds with the statement "I doubt that my redeemer liveth"—and the gross difference in meaning here is hardly equaled, it seems, by any like differences in style. Both statements differ in stylistically relevant ways, furthermore, from Nietzsche's assertion that "God is dead." It might seem that the adverbal model makes ready sense for understanding these differences. The variables of style and content could be said to appear in different proportions— the two Job-like statements differing from each other very much in content but slightly, if at all, in style, and both differing from Nietzsche's statement in terms of style. The differences and similarities among the statements would thus be understood in terms of the adverbal distinction between content and form.

For all its superficial plausibility, however, the instrumental model makes unwarranted assumptions that only become clear with the application of the transitive model. To assume, for instance, that the difference between "I know that my redeemer liveth" and "I doubt that my redeemer liveth" is a difference *only* in content is to take for granted that the other elements of the two expressive units (other than what is affirmed and denied) are constants and that the proportions in the two statements are identical. This *may* be the case, but it is not self-evident; and to be in a position to know it requires more than only the knowledge of the respective propositional truth values. (To assert that the latter represent "content" and everything else "style" is simply to beg the question, and this is clearly evident in the oddity of anyone's *doubting* that "my redeemer liveth"; the statement makes sense, and is stylistically consistent, but it is very unlikely because of its content.) If, however, we turn the process of analysis around by conceiving of the two elements within the expressive unit as linked rather than independent variables, the possibilities of understanding the statements come alive quite differently. Certainly this change forces recognition that the statements are bound (whether stylistically or with respect to content) to their contexts—which is no more than to say that meaning or content (and so also, the relation between content and form) is not itself explicable outside of a context. To doubt that God exists and to affirm that God exists—even if they are expressed in superficially the same "manner"—might well be to express not two different assertions but also, or even only, two quite different manners. The difference between jumping for joy and beaming with joy is almost certainly not only the difference between jumping and beaming; it has something to do with the concept of joy as well.

This does not mean that expressive units as units are incomparable—but that the modalities of comparison and of interpretation are properly applied to the units as wholes, not as divided to begin with. Rather than assuming for the expressive unit a division into form and content on the basis of a narrow and basically a priori conception of literary content as simply propositional, the transitive model requires that the unit first be considered as a whole and *then* analyzed in terms of truth or falsity which would then include under the latter consideration, relevant features of historical origins, stylistic character, and so on. To speak *then* of certain features of the object as stylistically accidental or inessential makes sense because it is the framework of the object itself that would have established them in that role.

That is to say in effect that since "style" and "content" often overlap, and since we cannot be *certain* of the distinction between them, even in those instances where they seem not to overlap, the objects of stylistic judgment should be initially conceived as wholes and *then* analyzed in terms of the pertinent modalities, including (in addition to style) truth and other evaluative predicates, practical consequence or origin, and so on. This procedure has the decisive advantage of preserving the possibility that, for any particular case, style itself may be affirmed as content—a possibility that we know is often realized in fact. And *now* if we ask whether different things can be said in the same way or the same thing in different ways, the burden is clearly laid, within the context of a *specific* judgment, on the formulation of what is meant by "same" and by "thing"; surely that is where the burden belongs. The connection between style and the expressive unit (whether the latter be a single or a corporate person—i.e., a genre, school, period)[35] is thus a necessary condition of the identification and understanding as well as of the occurrence of style.

This means of formulation also implies that the "choice" of a style— in the sense that a technique or manner of expression is consciously fitted to a supposedly determinate meaning—is not simply a choice about the means to a distinguishable end, and is hardly, in fact, a choice at all. For if what is to be expressed is a function also of the vehicle of expression, the latter affects what is expressed; the "choice" of neither is free of the other, and the articulation of the two together is a choice only in the sense that expression itself is. And *that* sense is equivocal at best—for much the same reason that one might hesitate to ascribe creations of the imagination to a process of deliberation or choice. This does not mean, of course, that the expressive function or syntax of a particular style is unintentional or accidental; it means only that, as for art as a whole, the concepts of choice and intention have a special status. The more openly deliberate the "stylistic" choices, in fact—as, for example, in substituting one word or name for another— the less significant the element is stylistically. Nor does this denial of stylistic assertion as a choice among alternative versions imply that style is independent of history or that (as Wölfflin also denies) "at any time anything is possible." For again, to speak of a history of style(s) that constrains the present by excluding certain possibilities hardly requires that what survives as stylistic "decision" is the result of choice in the ordinary sense of that term.[36] It is undoubtedly the case, as Gombrich argues in *Art and Illusion*, that both perception and artistic techniques have histories that shape even the specific artistic development, but this is far from saying that the individual development is *determined* by those histories. As Borges suggests in his story about style titled "Pierre Menard," it would undoubtedly be more improbable now for a twentieth-century novelist to write *Don Quixote* than it was for Cervantes—but a great improbability existed the first time around as well.

Beyond this formal contrast with the instrumental model, the conception of style as person provides a number of programmatic directives which I mention without discussion. For one thing, if stylistic analysis necessarily involves reference to the forms of expression, we may assume until we find otherwise that it applies to all the media of expression. I alluded earlier to the common usage of the term "style" in contexts other than that of art, but that usage, as with most expansion in linguistic practice, has in general been casual and unsystematic. Only recently have serious efforts been made to establish the warrant for such extension and to understand its forms—as it applies to the structure of science (for example, in the work of Kuhn and Feyerabend), in Lucien Goldmann's genetic-structural analysis of drama, in Hayden White's critique of historiography.[37] This work is still at its beginning, and it seems clear that one cause for its belated appearance has been the instrumental model of style in which the content of expression has, as content, simply been taken for granted.

A second programmatic implication follows from this first one: that as stylistics is applied to different expressive forms, it has new sources to draw on for categories of analysis, or at least a new sense of the extent of those sources. A ground in principle is thus available for applying stylistic categories customarily identified with one genre of expression to others, as well as for deriving new categories from the single and common source which now appears as a map of human expression. I have before this, in Chapter 2, attempted one such extension by reapplying the concept of the point of view, usually associated with the analysis of fiction and the visual arts, to philosophical writing. Many other expressive features that have been associated with particular contexts may yet be reapplied: items like intention and will, avoidance or reaction, expectation, lying, examples, mistakes—all (although perhaps not all equally) potential stylistic categories, as they are already actual categories of human expression. In following the applications of these and similar terms we also stand to learn as much from style about its source as we usually do by starting with human nature assumed as given.

This relationship, furthermore, is as informative about the past and future of style as it is about the origins of expression—and perhaps with a sharper point, given the current faith in the power, if not the virtue, of technology; one has only to follow the recent career of the term "image" to recognize how the will to control style and the pretense that such control is possible have infected what in the traditional sense of the term would be called moral discourse. The fact of the matter, of course, is quite different: that style as it is linked to expression and finally to the agency of persons simply, and certainly finally, cannot be manipulated or even anticipated. As there are no handbooks of rules which ensure the quality of a piece of writing or of a painting, there is no technology of style, no set of formulas for creating it. It follows in fact from what I have been saying and from the history of criticism itself that the categories of style are invariably retrospective and open to alternative formulation: we conceive them only after the fact, and thus find ourselves in the exposition of style always and necessarily lagging behind history—even, perhaps especially, as we attempt to anticipate it. Like expression itself, style is intrinsically contingent and unpredictable. The only means of accurately predicting any new patterns of style is by creating them—and then, of course, the prediction is quite beside the point.

This is not meant to imply that the rhetoric of persuasion or propaganda, for example, can never be effective, that political or economic forces may not succeed in constituting and imposing themselves and their styles; it means only that there is no way that they can accomplish this without doing more than they think to—without, in fact, revealing what they are doing. Fascism, to take an extreme example, is not only, but is at least, a style; seen from that perspective, Mussolini's Rome is separated from Bernini's by more than a period of three hundred years: his buildings and stadiums reveal as much as anyone has ever said discursively about the vision of fascism, with its indifference to persons, its gross self-assertion. The verbal rhetoric of

German fascism, with its references to the "final solution" *(End-lösung)*, "special treatment" *(Sonderbehandlung)*, "cleansing" *(rein-machen)*, did violence *to* language as well as through it.[38] When de Maistre writes that "every individual and national degradation is immediately heralded by a strictly proportional degradation in the language itself," he is making a general claim about social history. What I have been suggesting is that the two functions that de Maistre joins—the external manner and the content of expression—are not and could not be separate occurrences. Obviously the "idolatry of style" (Cioran's telling phrase) which sustains so much of the contemporary social structure by the symbolization of power will not be thwarted merely by the implicit communication through style of an aura of consciousness; but that aura, the sense of vision, is one, and a necessary point from which *re*vision may start—even from within; it is at any rate a characteristic by which social styles (because it is true for *all* groups and the individuals who make them up as well) inevitably betray themselves. This is true even when, as in the medium of advertising, the creators take unusual pains to conceal themselves and their motives in their work. Style, it seems, is never pristine, never without historical texture; it never attaches itself to an object without also revealing a genealogy of means. For style, intentionality is destiny.

5. The Practice of Stylistics

The question may still be raised, even granting such instances of practical application, as to what the systematic advantage of the second, transitive model of style is, since I have also acknowledged that much of what has been said here on the basis of this model is also consistent with the claims of the instrumental model. But such commonality is often the case in competing theories; it would be unusual to find two accounts of a broad and important issue that did not overlap. It is not, however, the similarities that turn out to matter, but the differences. I have suggested, for one thing, that the principles embodied in the two models of style are linked to more general philosophical principles: the connection in Aristotle's thought between the subject-predicate logic, on the one hand, and the relation between style and content, on the other, is a clear example of this. There may not be a necessary connection between the specific principles underlying conceptions of style and other principles concerning the roles of nature in general or of human nature in particular. But it is almost certainly more than accidental that there is a regular pattern among these types of principles in the accounts considered here, or that an aesthetic doctrine of style reflects the outline of a metaphysical principle. (This in itself counts as evidence for the transitive model of style, as it asserts the connection in objects between their "insides" and their "outsides.")

There are, moreover, other practical consequences that follow from the two models. It seems clear, for example, that the tradition of formalist aesthetics in such otherwise different writers as Kant and the twentieth-century critic Roger Fry presupposes an instrumental conception of style; and I think it can be shown that the liabilities of that conception show up in the implausibilities and inconsistencies in the work of those and other formalists, both systematically and in their practical criticism.

The transitive model, furthermore, sets an explicit limit to stylistic discourse, by implication, a caveat: that the analysis of style will never yield the theoretical science that many of its past practitioners have wished for it. This is to say no more than that if style is intrinsically related to the forms of expression, it can be no more determinate than are those forms—thus that the analysis of style will remain, in Aristotle's terms, a practical, not a theoretical science, the conclusions of which are limited by indeterminateness in the activity of a maker and, more important, in the objects that carry the impress of *their* makers. The failure to acknowledge the causes of this constraint provides an explanation, I think, for the eventual frustration of the efforts of the "New Critics" in the United States as well as of much in the recent work of Structuralists. Communicants of the Intentionless Fallacy, we might name these writers.

Finally, to be sure, what I have been saying reflects a purpose that is conceptual rather than programmatic. I have attempted to suggest why the question "How is style possible?" ought to be asked, and also to have marked a direction in which an answer to it will be found. That the phenomenon of style requires a principle of intelligibility is hardly a radical assertion—until we notice the many accounts that ignore or mistake that requirement. Moreover, even if the principle turns out only to reformulate the conclusions that the past analyses of particular styles have reached (this is in fact what confirmation of a principle amounts to), we will, in knowing this, understand those conclusions differently than we had before. Isaac is perplexed, in the epigraph cited for this discussion, as he tries to envision the single person composed of Jacob's voice and Esau's hands—but he does not doubt that this composition is what he must undertake. How to construct a person or its vision, with the voice or touch or look to which one has access now being the only manners of appearance of that person or vision to build on, is the task set by the discrimination of style, and even before that, as style is first created. The need to undertake this construction, and the possibility known to us from our encounters with the varieties of expression that it can be realized, are the occasions to which the question "How is style possible?" is itself a response: what makes *it* possible.

Notes

1. M. A. K. Halliday, "Linguistic Function and Literary Style," in S. Chatam, ed., *Literary Style* (Oxford: Oxford University Press, 1971), p. 330.

2. B. Block, "Linguistic Structure and Linguistic Analysis," in A. A. Mill, ed., *Report on the 4th Annual Round Table Meeting on Linguistics and Language Teaching* (Washington, D.C.: Georgetown University, 1953), p. 40.

3. E.g., L. Spitzer, "Pseudoobjective Motiviering bei Charles-Louis Philippe," in *Stilstudien* (Munich: M. Hueber, 1961), 2: 166.

4. Citations of Buffon's line from his address to the French Academy invariably ignore Buffon's assumption of a strict distinction between style and content. Thus the context of the line: ". . . Knowledge, facts, and discoveries, being easily detached, are passed on to others. . . . These things are external to the man; style is the man himself."

5. S. Johnson, *Lives of the English Poets* (Oxford: Oxford University Press, 1905), 1: 19.

6. H. Wölfflin, *Principles of Art History*, trans. M. D. Hottinger (New York: Dover, n.d.), p. 14.

7. See G. S. Kirk and J. E. Raven, *The Presocratic Philosophers* (Cambridge: Cambridge University Press, 1963), and M. Untersteiner, *The Sophists*, trans. K. Freeman (New York: Philosophical Library, 1954), Ch. 9.

8. *Rhetoric*, trans. W. Rhys Roberts, 1355al ff.

9. *Rhetoric* 1403b15 (emphasis in original text).

10. Cf., e.g., *Metaphysics*, Zeta, chs. 7–9; *Physics*, bk. 1, chs. 6–7.

11. So, for example, S. Ullmann's statement in *Style in the French Novel* (Cambridge: Cambridge University Press, 1957), which typifies this position: "There can be no question of style unless the speaker or writer has the possibility of choosing between alternate forms of expression. Synonymy, in the widest sense of the term, lies at the root of the whole problem of style" (p. 6).

12. *Principles of Art History*, pp. 47–48

13. J. Dewey, *Art as Experience* (New York: Minton, Balch, 1934), pp. 110 ff.

14. R. Barthes, in S. Chatman, ed., *Literary Style*, p. 10.

15. G. W. F. Hegel, *The Philosophy of Fine Art*, trans. F. P. B. Osmaston (London: G. Bell, 1920), 1: 97.

16. So, for example, Nelson Goodman's reference to a "Mandalaysian Sunset" (cf. "The Status of Style," *Critical Inquiry* 1 [1975]: 799–811); to which, I suppose, one might add Atlantic-ish Oceans and Yorkshire-ish Puddings.

17. See the analysis of R. Ohmann, "Generative Grammars and the Concept of Literary Style," *Word* 20 (1964: 423–99, for examples of how such transformations occur. cf. also Leonard B. Meyer, "Toward a Theory of Style" in B. Lang, ed., *The Concept of Style* (Philadelphia: University of Pennsylvania Press, 1979).

18. But not the probability that the Austrian architect Adolf Loos attached to it with the claim that "if nothing were left of an extinct race but a single button, I would be able to infer, from the shape of that button, how these people dressed, built their houses, how they lived, what was their religion, their art, their mentality." Quoted by E. H. Gombrich, "Style," in the *International Encyclopedia of the Social Sciences*, 15: 358.

19. M. Schapiro, "Style," in A. L. Kroeber, *Anthropology Today* (Chicago: University of Chicago Press, 1955), reprinted in M. Philipson, *Aesthetics Today* (New York, 1961), p. 88.

20. S. Kierkegaard, *Repetition*, tr. by W. Lowrie (Princeton, N.J.: Princeton University Press, 1941), p. 34.

21. *Principles of Art History*, p. 229.

22. L. B. Meyer, *Music, the Arts, and Ideas* (Chicago: University of Chicago Press, 1967), p. 295.

23. K. Clark, *The Nude* (Princeton, N.J.: Princeton University Press, 1972), p. 295.

24. M. Schapiro, "Style," pp. 289–90.

25. Another straw in this same wind—and how many does one need?—is the usage of the Greek χαρακτήρ, which from its early designation of the minter of coins, or of the mark made by the minter on the coins, comes to refer to "feature" or "mien" (e.g., in Theophrastus) and, in the same expansion, to "style" (although not used as commonly as λέξις).

26. N. Goodman, "The Status of Style," *Critical Inquiry* 1 (1975): 802.

27. C. Lévi-Strauss, *Anthropologie Structurale* (Paris: Plon, 1958), p. 357. Cf. also D. Shapiro, *Neurotic Styles* (New York: Basic Books, 1965), pp. 7, 88–99.

28. See on this point J. Paris, *Painting and Linguistics* (Pittsburgh, Penna.: Carnegie-Mellon, 1975), pp. 38 ff., and the ingenious argument of B. Uspenski, "'Left' and 'Right' in Icon Painting," *Semiotica 13 (1975): 33–39*.

29. As in G. Ryle, *The Concept of Mind* (New York: Barnes and Noble, 1949), ch. 1.

30. G. Morelli *Italian Painters: Critical Studies of Their Words*, trans. C. F. Ffoulkes (London: J. Murray, 1892–93), 1:34–36.

31. E.g., K. Shapiro and R. Beum, *A Prosody Handbook* (New York: Harper, 1965).

32. See B. Croce, *Aesthetic*, trans. D. Ainslee (London: Macmillan, 1922), pp. 436–58.

33. N. Goodman, "The Status of Style," p. 800.

34. W. V. O. Quine, "Meaning and Linguistics," in *From a Logical Point of View* (Cambridge, Mass.: Harvard University Press, 1953), p. 61. Cf. also M. Beardsley, "Verbal Style and Illocutionary Action," in B. Lang, ed., *The Concept of Style*. Arguing that style is important aesthetically only where synonymy is not applicable, Beardsley suggests two means (stipulation and elegant variation) by which synonymy *can* be preserved.

35. I do not mean to suggest here either the historical or the logical equivalence among these "persons," or even of the connections among them. Stylistic differences among contemporary art forms, and even within a single art form, have often been pointed out (cf., e.g., M. Schapiro, "Style," pp. 88–89, and Gombrich, "Style," p. 359); and except on the thesis of history as a unitary process that presents itself through a *Zeitgeist*, there is nothing surprising about such diversity. The surprise in fact is in the other direction: that corporate units exhibit as often as they do the consistent stylistic features of persons.

36. For a discussion of stylistic choice, cf. Meyer, *Music, the Arts, and Ideas,* and George Kubler's more radical view of stylistic choice as (always) synchronic ("Toward a Reductive Theory of Visual Style," in B. Lang, ed., *The Concept of Style.*

37. See, e.g., T. Kuhn, *The Structure of Scientific Revolutions* (Chicago: University of Chicago Press, 1963); P. Feyerabend, *Against Method* (New York: NLB, 1978); L. Goldmann, *The Hidden God,* trans. P. Thody (New York: Routledge and Kegan Paul, 1964; H. White *Metahistory* (Baltimore, Md.: Johns Hopkins Press, 1973).

38. See on the topic of political style, and especially in connection with the political uses of repetition, "Style in the Language of Politics," in H. Lasswell, N. Leites, and associates, *Language of Politics (Cambridge, Mass.: M.I.T. Press, 1965).*

7

Points of View: The Authorial Means as Literary Necessity

> A man set himself the task of depicting the world. Over many
> years he filled a space with the images of provinces, of king-
> doms, of mountains, of fish, of houses, of instruments, of stars,
> horses, persons. Shortly before he died, he realized that this
> patient labyrinth of lines traced the image of his own face.
>
> Jorge Luis Borges

Analysis of "point of view" in literary texts has inclined either toward practical criticism and thus to accounts of point of view in individual works;[1] or, more formally, toward the structural typology of point of view.[2] These lines of analysis have together provided a significant literary means, and this fact makes it more notable that the question of *why* point of view illuminates the critical process has rarely been addressed. In effect, both the occurrence and the concept of point of view have been treated as accidents: items of interest because of what is seen or accounted for by their use, but an interest joined with indifference as to what makes this true.

The latter question is potentially of great importance for literary theory, however, especially if the response to it shows that the occurrence of point of view is not an accident at all; and I shall be claiming precisely this—that point of view, in one or several of its versions, is a literary necessity, integral to the structure of the literary artifact; that a large measure of the adhesive power of the literary work depends on the way point of view functions there and on the consequent appropriation of point of view by an audience. The concept of point of view, because of the role of the *fact*, thus becomes a necessary means for understanding literary structure as well as for addressing particular texts. It may be only a slight exaggeration to claim that *all* the devices shaping the literary work are related to the role of point of view, and thus to the human, even physiognomic presence to which point of view, in its possible variations, attests. The elements of literary structure, ranging in scope from the permutations of plot and character to the figures of language and finally to the smallest "bits" of discourse, constitute a hierarchy; they vary in their importance to the quality of "literariness" in that structure. It would be reasonable (and a rudimentary form of poetic justice) that what shapes elements in that hierarchy, giving them direction, should itself appear as *literally* perspectival, a point of view—with the implication in that phrase of intention, of interest, and finally, as literary point of view comes alive in the point of view of the reader, of the power of sight or vision which the former confers on the latter.

The direction of this thesis about a source of literary structure may seem obvious. *Of course*, it will be said, the primary features of the literary work of art, with or without the claims for point of view as a literary means, are human, couriers of human expression—and what else *could* they be? But if the claims developed here have a warrant, the fact and concept of point of view yield a more specific account of the literary elements than mere expressiveness does, and a more specifically literary account than the fact of mere artifactuality does in the common assertion of an ingredient personification in literary structures.

I

1. A Theory of Types

Later in the present discussion, I attempt to identify the elements that constitute a point of view, but for the moment, point of view will be considered as a unit: a schema of articulation which expresses itself verbally or by other action and is characteristically attributed to a person. The superficial requirements for identifying a point of view reflect the parts of the phrase itself: point of view must circumscribe an area (of action or attitudes) sufficient to constitute a "point"; the view circumscribed must be sufficiently consistent to appear as a unity and thus as distinct from other points of view (and, of course, from non–points of view). These criteria are not rule-governed. The consistency required, for example, is consistency in the disposition or action of human behavior, not logical consistency; the claim that significant decisions or attitudes are in a particular case large enough to warrant ascribing a point of view is a decision for practical judgment and thus in some measure subjective. The definition of point of view, then, does not turn on a joining of necessary and sufficient conditions; this fact is itself, I hope to show, symptomatic of the referent of point of view: the person behind and in front of it (these are in some, but not in all, ways the same person).

This general and incomplete formula, which holds for both literary and extraliterary appearances of point of view, finds exemplification for literary point of view at a number of levels in the text. (I refer here specifically to the texts of imaginative literative, but an analogous argument could be made for the texts of nonfiction.) At the most concrete level, so far as individual characters (including personlike beings, such as animals in fables) are more than only names, the reader associates points of view with those names; as the characters speak and act, as their perceptions are recorded, the patterns that shape these actions emerge and become themselves part of the field of events. The delineation of literary character thus follows an unfolding pattern of representation based on the structure of semantic and even grammatical formulas, on the selection of objects to which the interest of the character is directed, on his response to events and to other characters. As these lines meet, a point of view and the character of which it is the form take shape: the vectors themselves are unintelligible without that corollary presence. Character and point of view thus appear as coextensive. The reader, prior to the reading, knows nothing of David Copperfield; as narrator, David constructs an identity, speaking about himself in a voice which is itself one among the events which he recounts. He marks off in that process of construction a point of view which the reader sees (and finally, sees by way of) if he is to understand either the line of narrative which David follows or the other characters about whom he speaks, as well as the events in which he and they act in common. Point of view at the level of literary character thus establishes a space akin to that defined by Leibniz's monads; it is not only a manner of seeing on the part of the monads (or characters) themselves, but a definition of structure and finally of existence, both of the see-er and what is seen. Like the space constituted by the monads, the universe constructed piecemeal in the literary text is the world viewed and thus constituted by each of the characters: individually perspectival, to be sure, but unified and coherent within each of the perspectives—and unified (if not complete) as the individual perspectives are later integrated by point of view in its second, "narrative" appearance.

The narrative level of point of view qualifies the points of view of individual characters and relates them to each other. So, for example, as he reads conversations carried on in the text, the reader learns what individual characters have said—and those words define both the (immediate) view and (more general) *point* of view of the characters. But the conversations reach the reader—reported either in indirect discourse, or (less obviously but no less certainly) in direct discourse—as a recitation by *another* figure whose presence is defined at least to the extent that he is known to have been in a position to hear or learn of the conversations and to have chosen to repeat them. The latter conditions shape individual character and point of view as they appear in a text by determining the frames in which the statements of conversation are set, the order and emphasis given those statements, and the responses they make, even in the description of the events to which the statements are supposed to be a response. If it is important, in recalling that line from *King Lear*, to know also *who* said "Ripeness is all," it is not less important to have understood the relation in which that speaker (and then his words) stands to the other speakers within the play—and thus also to comprehend the narrative field (the term is thus applied even to dramatic discourse) which collectively defines the individual speakers.

Insofar as discourse—the words spoken by the characters—follows the lines of narrative point of view, it is still more evident that narrative description and the standard connectives which portray literary setting and action imply the presence of a similar source. The logical possibility of alternate descriptions of any single event entails that the selection of a particular description reflects both purpose and method—and either of these is unintelligible as conceived independently of a narrator responsible for them. They do not, and cannot be understood as if they did, just occur. The narrator may appear explicitly in the text as a character (speaking in the first person or *seen* to speak as in the third person)—so, for example, David in *David Copperfield* or Kafka's Gregor Samsa. In this event, the narrator's description (and finally, his point of view) integrates the individual actions of individual characters (including his own). More usually, the narrative point of view or voice is not explicitly personified.[3] It may appear in the implied figure of an omniscient, purportedly neutral recorder who has access not only to a series of public actions but also to the private feelings and thoughts of individual characters; he will, in this omniscience, also have the power to foretell events of the action before they occur (such powers are generic in the epic narrator). Or: the implied narrator may assume his tacit role someplace between the extremes of omniscience and the view of a single character, knowing some things more than the latter might reasonably be claimed to, but not unlimited in his scope; so, for example, the narrative indefiniteness in Jane Austen's *Emma* which has led to interpretations, at one extreme, that the author, who should have been omniscient, did not recognize Emma's faults and, at the other extreme, that Emma herself is the narrator—rather than to the more accessible proposal than either of these, of a narrative figure, very much *like* Emma, who reports on all the events and characters in the novel, including Emma herself.[4] Or: the narrative voice may play several and different roles, moving, for example, between omniscience and personification in an individual character. Such, despite his claims exclusively for the former means, is Flaubert's way in *Madame Bovary* where we find the narrator speaking sometimes also in Emma's voice, thus projecting himself both into and above her consciousness. And finally, there may be more than one narrative point of view—as, for example, when a narrator who is explicitly present (as a character) is subsumed under the narrative conception of an "implied author"— the teller of the tale *including* the words of the explicit narrator. This plurality of narrative views becomes most evident when they cross each other, provide dissimilar views—for example, as between the reports by Dostoyevsky's Underground Man on *himself* and the implied author's narration of those reports (a contrast which Wayne Booth, moralizing, labels "unreliable" narration).

A third level of point of view is more difficult to isolate than the others, since it may be materially (although not formally) indistinguishable from the second level or, less often, from point of view at the level of individual character. I refer to this third level as the "resolved" point of view—in (and into) which the reader resolves the other and subordinate points of view active in the text as well as the elements which they fail to integrate. This third level of point of view has sometimes been identified with the point of view of the actual author—the reader's task being, as a consequence, to duplicate that historical perspective and understanding; this equation is avoided here mainly for the reasons argued by critics of the Intentional Fallacy.[5] It has also been represented in the figure of an "implied author" whose presence is inferred from the text itself. Almost invariably in such accounts the implied author serves a narrative role, and I have thought it more economical conceptually to include that role as one among the varieties of narrative persona—if only to distinguish it, in this theory of types, from another third level of point of view which moves beyond the narrative field altogether, beginning where narration leaves off. One reason for distinguishing the resolved point of view is, in fact, the essential incompleteness of narrative point of view. For the narrative point of view serves not only as a form or modality which shapes a content (the individual characters and *their* points of view, their emplotment and the plot as a whole); the modality of narration—*that* point of view—also stands itself as part of the content of the work, what is given in it, and thus calls attention to its own means. It thus *represents*, as well as presents, the factors which frame the other, more obviously individual elements of content, and in doing this becomes an element itself: the narrator—first-person or third-, explicit or implied—is in fact a character in the text, its differences from other characters (for example, its control over them) being differences, in terms of the literary structure, of degree rather than of kind. The narrative point of view appears in one guise as the outline of a disposition for action and character, arranging and reporting on what is said and what happens to them; in a second role, linked to the first, the narrative point of view opens itself to interpretation, suggesting to the reader, as do the other parts of the literary structure, how it—as "literally" asserted—is to be (nonliterally) understood. In effect, it asks the last in the series of questions concerning the levels of point of view—how those levels within the text are to be seen or resolved in the reader's summary point of view. The reader has sometimes been made part of the concept of point of view as "implied," and it is clear that a conception of the reader is a necessary function of point of view at the narrative level; the resolved point of view, without denying this other emphasis, introduces the reader's point of view as (part of) a conclusion to which the other points of view lead.

The basis for claiming an intrinsic incompleteness in the narrative point of view, and thus the need for something like the resolved point of view, is most obvious when the narrative point of view is ironic—since there the reader must find in the narrative presence itself not only the surface of literary detail (plot, character) but also the "fact" of irony and the specific direction in which its characteristic reversal is pointed, the object of the irony. It is true, of course, that the narrative voice itself may "be" ironic, and in the same sense that any other predicate can be ascribed to that voice; but irony may also be more subtly present than in the overt narrative point of view (in the action and character disclosed, for example—devices often used for ironic effect: for example, by Thomas Mann in *Buddenbrooks*); and in *any* event, however irony announces itself, the object of the affirmation which is the other side of denial or skepticism registered in irony remains to be located, beyond the narrative field, by the reader. Thus the end of the ironic turn is at a remove beyond the narrative view; it emerges as the narrative view, and the elements subsumed under it, *themselves* appear as representation, as they are brought together as shaping another point of view. And although such incompleteness in the narrative field may be most evident where irony is in play, it is active whatever the textual intention represented: the assertion of the text is circumscribed by the limits of assertion *in* the text, limits which in the last instance are the physical boundaries of the beginning and end of the writing. Only the reader is not bound by those limits; and this, which perhaps starts as a liability in the process of representation—the fact that representation, however artful, never becomes, or merges with, the reality of which it is a representation—turns into an unexpected asset as the reader views the cumulative assertion of the text in the figure of representation. (This may start from the reader's reaction against the physical boundaries themselves—as he asks about the line of action before the text begins or after it ends.) The narrative point of view is primarily linear, assertive; but that assertion also has an appearance, an exhibitive quality—and it is the latter, at once involving and re-presenting narrative assertion, that constitutes the resolved point of view.

There may, for any particular case, be disagreement about the form of the resolved point of view, what that last re-vision amounts to; for obvious reasons, furthermore, the resolved view is itself subject to later revision caused by change in the history of the viewer or as the objects viewed alter in time (physically, for example, as by editorial emendation, or contextually, by external developments which bear on the history of the single object). The resolved point of view which appears at any particular moment will thus be emendable historically (and an obvious question remains, if the resolved point of view is to be more than subjective impression, of its relation to the objective form of narrative point of view); but, whatever the effect of these conditions, the resolved point of view is the last point of view which the work affords—the point of view which constitutes what the reader himself sees and consequently also what he sees *through*.

The resolved point of view thus marks out a schema for understanding or viewing the narrative view and whatever is subsumed under it. The narrative point of view, beyond the specific view it discloses, gives directions as to how that disclosure itself is to be seen, and this is not identical with the point of view which was then to be articulated. Directions toward a form of understanding are not identical with the form of understanding itself; it is the latter which is disclosed in the resolved view. "This is the saddest story I have ever heard," the narrator of Ford Madox Ford's *The Good Soldier* starts out; the reader is left to discover what the force of that "sadness" is, to decide whether it is sad at all—and, if so or if not, what the point of view is of which the literary elements justifying his verdict are features.

2. The Concept of Point of View

Two characteristic features have thus been ascribed to point of view (I shall be speaking in this section of the concept of point of view generally, and thus as both within and outside the literary domain):

first, that point of view presupposes objects or an object of significant interest, what the point of view *frames;* and second, that a putative point of view must be coherent in its own terms. These conditions need to be further broken down, but their emphasis on the function of point of view draws attention again to the resemblance previously hinted at between point of view and persons. The resemblance, both the surface and more basic features of point of view indicate, is more than accidental; it reflects a natural connection or consanguinity between the literary device and what constitutes a person. Thus, the phrase "point of view" implies the existence of someone who "has" it. We do not ascribe a point of view (literary or other) to an inanimate object; and even the use, as by Spinoza, of the concept of an understanding *"sub specie æternitatis,"* takes effect only at the other extreme—as a view anchored in *no* point and precisely in that godlike respect differing from point of view as it is associated with persons. The evidence presented here so far may be insufficient for claiming that the possibility of sustaining a point of view is a condition for the existence and, consequently, identification, of a person (and vice versa), but surely the indicators suggest such a reciprocal entailment: no point of view without a person, no person without a point of view.

It would be useful for an understanding of their parallel structures to have access to the historical origins of the two concepts of person and point of view, but that history, if only because of its length, is obscure, although certain recent moments can be identified.[6] At least in part because of this historical inaccessibility, philosophical definition of the self or of persons (like, and related to, philosophical arguments for the existence of *other* persons) have usually been ahistorical in character; and what I attempt to do here, by way of distinguishing the structural elements of point of view which are presupposed in its functions, is similarly a systematic or synchronic reconstruction. I call attention in that respect to four constitutive elements.

i. In the phrase *point of view,* "view" is a metaphor.[7] Not physical seeing is required for the existence or the recognition of point of view, but per-ception realized through a medium—a joining which may reflect the activity of other of the senses than sight and which often involves or presupposes a combination of them, but which still more essentially implies an instrument of interpretation. The instrument mediating point of view is, then, not a sensory organ but an "exchange" or categorial system which supplies the form by which a given set of objects is presented to view. Point of view is thus not the product of physical sight, not even of a specific moment of understanding, but rather of a form which a combination of understanding and interest provides.

ii. The juxtaposition of "view" and "point" implies that the view in point of view is characteristically partial or perspectival—a *point*. This partiality itself is a function of two conditions referred to by the discussion in section 1. The first of these is that, however fragmentary or slight the perspective in a particular point of view is, it must be large enough (in itself or by implication) to constitute a significant unit. There are, I suggested earlier, no necessary and sufficient conditions for this "significant" unit; but the recognition of point of view is a fact even in the absence of such conditions—recognition which takes place on a spectrum of literary composition ranging from individual phonemes or morphemes (with respect to which point of view applies only derivatively, if at all) to grammatical units,[8] to the semantical units of literary meaning, and then to the larger structures of literary action and character. How we mark the location(s) on this spectrum where point of view breaks in, where the lesser units "amount to" a point of view, may be determined by no more than a rule of thumb (the rule of thumb by which we identify persons?); but *that* the discrimination is made is certain.

The second condition presupposed by the partiality of "point" in point of view is consistency. No merely random group of elements (opinions, reports of experiences, statements of intention) adequately constitutes a point of view. The elements must, it seems, reveal a connective pattern, certainly with respect to each other and, to a lesser extent, externally as well (as distinguishing them from the elements of *other* points of view). Without such consistency, there would be no reason for representing point of view as individuated at all, since the field of vision would then be drawn arbitrarily. Again, there may be no rules for testing this consistency, but practical examples of the characteristics are plentiful. A consistent commitment to inconsistency circumscribes the narrative point of view of Dostoyevsky's Underground Man—hardly less than consistency (even repetition) does for point of view in such characters of Dickens's as Micawber or Sam Weller. There is no doubt inconsistency sometimes between *levels* of point of view and, still more obviously, at the level of character, between the points of view of individual characters; and questions may occur, at any of the levels, as to what the consistency of point of view is (so, for example, the constant mystery of Hamlet); but these actual or potential inconsistencies are pertinent literarily only because of the expectation of consistency within any single point of view.

The conditions of significance and consistency are subsumable under a principle of "intentionality" or "interest"—terms which are more indicative than "partiality" of the way in which this second condition of point of view functions. The conditions of neither significance nor consistency are likely to be satisfied accidentally. They cannot, for any particular instance of point of view, be indefinitely large; the concept of a point (and also of *a* view) implies the existence of others as well (this claim is elaborated below in iv). But neither are those qualities accidental, as we recognize what accidents usually produce. In other words, the point in point of view implies an activating factor of will or intention—at least by way of an assumption that a particular point of view has been constituted for reason (which may not be but *could* be made explicit); partiality, if it is not to be, and be viewed as, simply a fragment or heap, reflects deliberation. We know little, to be sure, of the historical Homeric mind, but the intentions of the epic narrator in the *Iliad* or the *Odyssey* are clear—and the reading of those works presupposes recognition not only of the directions which those intentions supply, but before that, of both their existence and their source in an "intender." The instrumentality of point of view is then a process of activity—not merely a framing of objects which spontaneously or arbitrarily "compose" a view. As no process is intelligible apart from recognition of an ingredient source and goal (necessarily partial, insofar as the process they determine is itself partial), so point of view depends on those same factors.

iii. Implied in the concept of point of view is a condition of "extensionability." Although points of view necessarily appear in specific contexts (which may be larger points of view, as of a culture) and are thus shaped in the idiom of those contexts, the points of view are not restricted to those specific contexts; their instrumentalities, as they circumscribe a field, also define a means of transformation as *among* fields. This is not to say that any particular appearance of point of view determines or implies a claim with respect to every other context or set of objects. But insofar as point of view is distinguishable from the object(s) viewed, one way of describing that difference is in terms of potentiality or disposition for reapplication. If a supposed point of view which acted in a particular context were not dispositional—e.g., if it changed from context to context—this would be prima facie evidence that what had been isolated was not a point of view at all.

The element of extensionability once again suggests the relation of point of view to the identification of persons: in identifying persons, too, we imply expectations beyond the moment of identification (and not only expectations of physical continuity). We speak sometimes of a point of view as "limited," and we mean by this criticism that the point of view in question has not taken account of elements relevant to its own determination—that it has bought a superficially strong internal consistency at the expense of ignoring objects outside the immediate context, that it has not questioned its own applicability to objects other than those directly before it. This sometime failing in point of view suggests by implication what its excellence is.

iv. Point of view is intersubjective. This condition proposes that beyond the requirements set for the individual "holder" or source of point of view, the articulation of a point of view requires realization by another viewer, not accidentally or after the fact, but as a condition of its attribution. This claim differs from the requirement (which it resembles) that the verification of *any* asserted state of affairs presupposes that it should be translatable into empirical and thus publicly accessible terms. The very concept of a single and thus exclusive *point* of view is unintelligible; should there be such a "one," it would not be a point of view, but a, or more precisely, *the* view *simpliciter*. In other words, discrimination of a point of view presupposes not only the individuality and coherence of that point and its holder, but a plurality of points and holders (or at least one other). Nor is the latter a claim only about linguistic intelligibility—as it might be argued that *every* formal distinction implies a contrasting "other" from which the item first named is distinguished. In order for a point of view to be identified (and, before that, for the point of view to be articulated), the external criteria that have been cited are insufficient, and not only because any particular point of view is not open to definition or verification in terms of necessary and sufficient conditions. A point of view has not only to be seen but to be seen *through*—in the same sense (and on the same grounds) that, although we might confirm externally the adequacy of an individual's capacity for sight, we could infer nothing from that *alone* of what he would see at any particular moment: for *that* we would have ourselves to look at (and see) the objects before him. (The reference to physical vision affords a further analogy: How much would a blind person learn about vision from hearing a description of what it is to see?)

To put the issue in somewhat different terms: there is, with respect to the identification of a point of view, no possibility of only "knowledge by description"; what is required is "knowledge by acquaintance." The external form makes no sense except as the form of a content—and except as the corporate entity is discerned. For what is there that might simply be *described* in the phenomenon of point of view? The likely candidates are the features of consistency and magnitude; but to locate them with respect to any particular point of view is at once to define both the shape of point of view and its object(s) as viewed—that is, not only a form which determines possible views, but also the views themselves, now seen by the second viewer as well. An analogy to this connection is evident in the relation between proving a geometric theorem and "showing" the proof to somebody else: showing the proof is not different from proving it, so far as the person to whom it is shown is concerned. Recognition of point of view is, then, to see as the view itself does—and this sets conditions not only for identifying someone else's point of view (as that of a character in a novel or that of a person outside of a novel) but of *having* a point of view to begin with. Not that self-consciousness is consciousness of *another* self, but that the "doubling" effect there anticipates the intersubjectivity which is a later condition of the recognition of point of view.

I have been speaking thus far in this section about the concept of point of view in general and irrespective of context; and it is part of my thesis that this typical representation of point of view characterizes point of view in the domain of "imaginative literature," which is my main concern here. Evidence that this is the case has been presented in section 1 and will be developed further in subsequent sections, but evidence by contrast—in texts outside the domain of imaginative literature—is also available. Significant differences mark the role of point of view in "discursive" literature, and we see something more, in that contrasting role, of how the four aspects of point of view which have been distinguished function, are set in motion, on both sides of the contrast.

The distinctiveness of point of view in the texts of imaginative literature appears as sharply as it ever does by comparison with the role of point of view typically exhibited in the texts of scientific writing. I refer, as a typical example of the latter, to an article titled "Evolution of Type C Viral Genes: Evidence for an Asian Origin of Man," by R. E. Benveniste and G. J. Todaro,[9] for which the authors provide the following summary:

> Old World monkeys and apes, including man, possess as a normal component of the cellular DNA, gene sequences (virogenes) related to the RNA of a virus isolated from baboons. A comparison of the viral gene sequences and the other cellular sequences distinguishes those Old World monkeys and apes that have evolved in Africa from those that have evolved in Asia. Among the apes, only gorilla and chimpanzees seem by these criteria to be African, whereas gibbon, orang-utan and man are identified as Asian, leading us to conclude that most of man's evolution has occurred outside Africa.

The statements in the body of the article are more extended than those of the summary; but the two sets of statements are related to each other logically, by entailment, and analysis of the role of point of view in the scientific text may then draw on them both. The elements of point of view are cited in the same order followed in the characterization above.

i. The status of the concept of "view" in the scientific text seems formally identical with that described in the "literary" text. For both, "view" is a metaphor for a manner of articulation which involves more than a literal "seeing." Furthermore, the framework articulated through the scientific text is also intentional, bound to an object—at the most literal level, in the scientific text referred to, the Asian origin of man. Two large differences, however, are clear even with this first item of comparison: first, that the issue (and resolution) which occasion the scientific analysis are ascribed existence prior to and independent of the particular point of view which frames the statements of Benveniste and Todaro. Whether or not *their* account is "true," the authors assume that *some* such account rendered from the same point of view must be: the state of affairs which they attempt to describe exists independently of the specific attempt itself, and the particular account which they provide can be mistaken precisely because of the assumption of the independent existence of the objects and relations to which their point of view is directed. In the literary text, by contrast, the existence of what is viewed depends on the articulation of the point of view itself and (conversely) could not exist without it. Secondly, and a related item: the point of view applied in the account of Benveniste and Todaro has as its ideal a mirroring of the object; the point of view is essentially passive or transparent, implying in effect that the objects "intended" by the point of view and the view itself will finally coincide. If Benveniste and Todaro succeed in doing what they attempt to, by the end of their essay both their point of view and the point of view of the reader have become identical with their specific view—representing the *real* state of affairs. The difference, in this respect, from the fictional point of view is evident: point of view in the latter is recognized to influence, even to determine, its objects—not the other way round.

ii. With the second feature of point of view, the differences between its role in the literary and scientific texts emerge still more sharply. To the extent that the point of view embodied in a scientific text reveals itself as partial, as indicating a *particular* perspective or point, the work itself will be defective. Benveniste and Todaro sometimes use the pronoun "us" (e.g., ". . . leading us to conclude that . . ."), but the use of "conclude" here strongly suggests that no personal obtrusion is intended. That particular fragment could be paraphrased without loss as "leading to the conclusion that . . ." with *its* implication of a process which is at once independent of any par-

ticular observer and which requires agreement—in fact, appropriation—by any reasonable observer. The area circumscribed in their
text is obviously, in one sense, partial—since it does not involve
every possible object. Nonetheless, the "point" of view is meant to be
identical with that which might be assumed foir any and every other
object; thus, the *apparent* restriction on the extent or number of its
object(s) is hardly a restriction on point of view at all. Even the ideal
observer may see only fragments (the relation of a single item of
genetic evidence to the origins of human evolutions) of what may
seem to him a larger whole; but the fragments will be consistent with
any such larger whole or, even before that, with any other fragments
that might be discussed.

Nor is it clear what the conditions of magnitude or consistency
would amount to in the structure of the scientific text. It has, to be
sure, been asserted with respect to scientific discourse that there
exist least units of "truth," such as propositions, or, before that, in
logical axioms. But those propositions and axioms may be slight indeed; the stipulative or conventional component by which they are
defined differs both formally and materially from the natural or iconic
base that has been ascribed above to the "magnitude" of point of view
in the literary text. That "the evidence supports a claim for the (Asian)
origin of (man)" is the general assertion made by Todaro and Benveniste—but the terms set in parentheses could easily have been
replaced by any other adjective or noun, respectively, without affecting the formal status of the claim. So far as the criterion of magnitude
applies, then, it seems to be satisfied by *any* unit of intelligible discourse, and, although this is an important use of the criterion of
magnitude, it is quite different from the application of that condition
in the discrimination of point of view for which individual assertions
may or may not be sufficient and for which, in any event, there is no
sufficient *condition*.

A similar contrast affects the property of consistency, which is designed in the scientific text to reflect the denial of partiality or individuality and thus to assert its own universality. Here again we return, in scientific discourse, to a conception of *logical* consistency;
and again, as the criteria for that possess a purely formal character,
they differ significantly from the practical criteria of consistency
which have been claimed here to mark the boundaries of a (human)
point of view.

iii. The scientific work is indifferent to the requirement of extensionability and thus functions without it. Nothing is implied in its
presentation about the impulse or the capacity in the point of view of
the narrator to move beyond his immediate object: what is asserted

about the latter is either true or not—and the possibility of its being true or not is quite independent of any previous or subsequent application of the point of view within which, on *this* occasion, it appears. Since the text (and meaning) of scientific assertion resides in its own implied or explicitly stated means of verification, the words of the text and the connectives in it need be intelligible only in that sense— *whatever* their origins or later transformations (whether accidental or purposeful or with any one of a number of purposes in view). Chance or accident in fact play a more considerable role in the rhetoric of scientific formulation than they do in the discourse of imaginative literature—and this difference is in itself no accident.

We refer to a related, albeit prior, feature of the scientific text when we say that for any scientific discovery, if one person had not made it, somebody else would have—perhaps not at that time, but sooner or later (and probably sooner rather than later). The specific narrative voice, in other words, is replaceable or duplicable without loss; this replaceability is also regarded at least tacitly as an ideal, and it is thus also *likely* that the process of duplication would occur. If the narrative point of view embodied in a particular piece of work (it must be an unusual piece of scientific writing that goes below this level to the points of view of individual characters) is confined only to that work, this is no defect: its value remains intact. Whether the specific claims which emerge from the point of view applied are true or false does not depend on the reader's recognition of the applicability of that point of view to other objects (it is, after all, the denial of *a* point of view which is being asserted).

iv. The intersubjectivity of point of view, far from serving as a premise in the writing of the scientific text, is rejected even as desirable. The transaction represented in the scientific text relates a viewer (here Todaro and Benveniste act as one) to an object; the purpose acted on is to represent that object, and no other viewer is required for realizing that purpose. So far, in fact, as any other viewer happens on the view, his view, ideally, will be identical to that of the first viewer—not because the "point" of view applied requires this, but because the *point* of view is denied: there is only one view to be seen and one point of view to see with, or by, or from. (I omit the question of whether *other* elements in the writing of the scientist-narrator—e.g., the use of language itself—presuppose intersubjectivity; they almost certainly do, but in a different sense from that required by the literary point of view.) The view available to the second viewer, furthermore, is external to the first view and independent of it: a view not of what the first viewer sees *as* he sees it, but of elements reconstructed by the second viewer quite aside from what-

ever the first viewer has done or said. The surest test (and view) of
what the first viewer (supposing that there had been one) claims to
have discerned will come from the duplication of his experiments,
data, and conclusions. At the end of that process, the second viewer
sees as a disinterested observer would—not as an individual, or even
as the viewer before him saw as an individual. Had the account
written by Todaro and Benveniste been fictitious, that fact would
alter the "point of view" embedded in that account only insofar as the
claims they made would turn out (probably) to be false—a determination as likely to be made by a second or third viewer as by the first,
and none of them necessarily related to each other.

Admittedly, there may be a question as to whether these supposed
aspects of the role of point of view in scientific discourse are (or can
be) realized in practice; a case can be made that the flattening and
neutrality thus required of point of view is in principle—given the
writer's activity at all—impossible. But however this be, the *ideal*
conception of its role in scientific discourse is clear in its differences
from the role of point of view in its general definition and as it has
been identified, at the several levels, in imaginative literature. That
ideal might be summarized, with not much exaggeration, as the
elimination, or at least the neutralization, of point of view—the text
and all its elements somehow then writing themselves, disclosing at
any of its levels not a point of view but a view, or even more than that,
the view.

II

3. The Necessity of Point of View

The account in part I of this chapter has conceived of point of view
as an occasional or possible element of literary structure, and, although the specific schematization of point of view given may be
disputed, there seems little reason for doubting this more general
premise. If no more were said about it, a claim might be made for
point of view (more specifically, its permutations) as a literary figure
or even trope, and even that would be a more substantial status than
has been accorded it by many critical and theoretical analyses which
treat it as an anomalous literary device, unrelated to any other. The
claim being argued here, however, goes beyond that first step, asserting that point of view is an *intrinsic* element of literary structure and,
finally, that its then necessary occurrence also bears on the *literary*
character of that structure. Not only do we find the mechanism of
point of view in literary structure, in other words, but we do not find

literary structure *without* point of view; its presence there, moreover, is a literary rather than a structural necessity.

I do not mean by the latter claim to offer a stipulative definition of structure or of the quality of "literariness" celebrated by the Russian Formalists. It is, rather, empirical in its ground—asserting that, for literary structure (in nonfictional as well as for fictional or imaginative literature), point of view, as a *matter of fact*, is a constant feature, related to the *literary* constitution of the structure. It would be difficult to establish this general claim merely by the enumeration of individual occurrences of point of view, and indeed the claim is not easily demonstrated by any other means either; I attempt to support the claim, in fact, by three related arguments which are themselves not conclusive, but which do, taken together, make the obvious alternative assessments of the status of point of view problematic. The first of these (which follows in the present section) involves a "deduction" from the "theory of types" of point of view outlined in section 1. The second, in section 4, attempts to show how the concept of point of view underlies several important theories of genre and literary action which only obliquely refer to point of view at all; the implication drawn from that analysis asserts the general relevance of the concept of point of view to the actual practice of literary theory. The third argument, in section 5, attempts to define certain features of literariness *in general* to which the analysis of point of view otherwise presented here indicates certain obvious connections.

The first of these arguments, again, involves a deduction or systematic inference from the theory of types of point of view outlined in section 1—the first type being a function of literary character. Insofar as individual characters realize a minimal degree of autonomy (defined in the conditions cited), correspondingly individual points of view appear in the text. It may seem that we trivialize the concept of point of view by claiming a relation which apparently only replaces the traditional category of character with that of point of view. But the usefulness of the replacement becomes evident as the individual points of view of character come together and are seen to compose the narrative (and second level) point of view—a relation required for the intelligibility of the individual points of view themselves. (The latter, in this relation, are seen as social, interrelated, and not individual at all—at least so far as concerns the text as a whole.) We do, of course, often abstract the individual points of view, speaking of them as distinct from the text, e.g., "in a *Pickwickian* sense"; but we would hardly have reached that conception by following only the *one* point of view in a text to which the term most directly refers.

To be sure, point of view as it appears at the level of character is not always or necessarily a feature of the literary text. In lyric poetry, for example, a scene or event may be described in which no "characters" are named and thus no points of view ascribed to them. But this implies the absence of point of view only from that one, and not from the other, levels that have been mentioned. The narrative point of view is in fact even more likely to be evident in the absence of individual characters, since the narrator's articulation of the material then has a clear unmediated field on which to assert itself. It is evident, furthermore, that point of view at the level of character is not always unmixed or unitary. Some of the most interesting appearances of point of view in the literary text disclose "mixed" modes—shifts in point of view, for example, as a single character moves beyond the limits of what he, as individual, might be expected to know or see, to an awareness which fuses with that of the omniscient (or at least more knowing) narrator. (Here there is an interweaving even of two *levels* of point of view.)[10] These mixed modes warrant a classificatory scheme of their own; it seems likely that such classification within the broader outline of the theory of types relates directly to the conceptual distinctions presupposed in the lines separating the literary genres. I suggest how this is the case for certain standard theories of genre in section 4.

Narrative point of view is not so immediately discernible as are the points of view by which individual characters make themselves known; it might be argued, for example, that, although the reader directly "sees" the characters and relates the movement of plot to their points of view, he often can only infer the narrative presence or point of view. And surely if this claim means that the uncovering of the narrative point of view may require a constructive process which builds on other, less inclusive items (including individual points of view) in the text, this is true in the same sense that it would be of an inference drawn from a conversation overheard when the speakers involved in the conversation were unseen and otherwise unknown. But that there is a narrative source is *no more* a matter of inference in the former case than is the understanding that the conversation in the latter, is indeed "held" by *someone*. For both, recognition of the existence *and* the nature of a source is a condition of intelligibility; whether tacitly or explicitly, it affects the response of the reader or listener to what he sees or hears. In lyric poetry, even in the absence of individual characters, we can usually identify such attributes as the physical location (temporal, spatial) of the narrator who describes a scene or event. More importantly, we invariably recognize an intentionality; the purpose and animation which the narrator applies to a subject, his attitude and expectations—in short, a point of view. This

occurs not just as it happens, but necessarily, for there is no alternative—other than the possibility of accident—to the fact of this presence; and acknowledgment of that fact is part of the at least tacit
contract between reader and text. *Someone* knows, and then says,
that "she dwelt among the untrodden ways," and the reader's comprehension of that line and of those following it is thus fixed by a
constant reference to a speaker who both is in a position to say what is
said and has chosen to do so, with whatever these conditions entail as
consequences of human purpose and the selection of a means. (The
term *persona* aptly suggests that this source is "masked": all that we
directly know of the source are the words which it speaks in the text—
but this, as texts usually turn out and despite the mask, is to know a
good deal.)

Notwithstanding the other, important differences between the spoken and the written word, a deliberative source is assumed in the
comprehension of either. The discovery that a parrot has uttered the
words that we hear, or that an accident in typesetting accounts for a
statement in a text, unavoidably affects the significance we attach to
them;[11] and this could be true only if, in the larger number of cases
where no such interference occurs, comprehension on the part of an
audience presupposes the existence and assumed intention of a narrative view. Nor is the recognition of narrative presence simply a material condition which the literary structure then transcends—
reassurance to the listener or reader that he is not being "fooled":
acknowledgment of that presence is constant and itself evolves as
comprehension of the text develops; it is integral to the process of
reading. The fact that the attention of the literary reader does not
often *linger* on the figure of the narrator reflects the power of rhetorical conventions which assimilate the narrator within his representation (and undoubtedly, on the part of the audience, a desire for
such conventions)—*not* the absence of narrative structure. In looking
steadily through a filter, we may well lose all sense of the intervention
of the filter, but we have only to look again, without it or through a
different one, to see what effects the filter has had. If all utterance is
action, then even the illusion of autonomy produced by some utterance is itself a feature of action—and thus, in turn, of an agent.[12]

And lastly: the narrative point of view itself is sometimes represented as a neutral "transmitter"—a transparency which is not assertive and which simply allows the (supposedly) individual items displayed in the text to emerge. So, for example, the narrator may be
concealed as a disinterested reporter, recounting (as in the texts of
science) a sequence of events "as they actually occurred"; or he may
claim (or imply), as in the no-longer-so-experimental tradition of ex-

perimental writing, that he is only reproducing events in random sequence, and this in such a way that the narrator himself has not obtruded. Such claims, on the account given here, are invariably open to dispute. The claims for narrative nonintervention are themselves made, unavoidably, within the *frame* of a sequence of action which leaves no doubt about its composition as a view. (So, for example, the stream of consciousness technique in Virginia Woolf and in James Joyce, or the purportedly neutral vision of the New Novel of Sarrault and Robbe-Grillet. Woolf's "room with a view" was a literary and not only a personal means.) But, secondly and more importantly (since it is here that the denials of stream of consciousness and experimental writing are brought into focus most sharply), there is only one alternative to acknowledgment of the role of point of view *both* as narrative and, later, as resolved: that the process of literary understanding is essentially passive and thus common to all readers, the text simply imprinting itself—in word *and* in meaning—in the reader's consciousness. And this, I should argue, is simply false to the process of reading; reading, on this account, in the form that we know it and do it, would be quite simply impossible.

One traditional conception of reading, admittedly, has argued that words written on a page do indeed speak for themselves: that, notwithstanding their appearance as individual, discrete tokens, they nonetheless and by themselves produce a corporate structure and meaning which are then grasped apart from any presence or intention ascribed to the text. The Higher Criticism labored for centuries to show how this "Fundamentalist Fallacy" has skewed the reading of scripture, and this citing of scripture suggests a lesson about reading in general. The fact that what is supposedly devoid of narrative point of view nonetheless yields meaning which is not episodic or disjointed underscores the naiveté of the claim of textual transparency. Whenever we "understand" a sequence of words, we assume the collaboration of a voice to which we ascribe a larger potentiality even than the literal content of the words themselves; the alternative to this basis of understanding is a mystified account in which words assume the self-defining role of nature—*first* nature, not the second derivative nature which undoubtedly appears in the dualism of words and meanings.

We may not necessarily connect the reading of an individual text to the reading of other texts written by the same author, but in fact we almost invariably do this. Even in rehearsing the theme of a single novel, for example, we readily speak of "Dickens's comic vision" or "Dickens's social conscience"—and we do not refer, with this, to a particular character within the novel or to the historical figure of Dickens outside it. Rather we name a persona inhabitating the novel; we look to that persona, moreover, not only to confirm an understanding of the specific text, but because of an interest in the persona (and his point of view) that may be and often is independent of the single text. It is hardly an accident of the creative process or of literary history that the great figures in that history have almost without exception also been prolific writers; a more plausible explanation is that peripheral vision is an asset, even a requirement, for the reader in his search for a persona concealed in the text, in his capacity for recognizing or attributing literary quality—that even the concept of an "individual" text, progressively insulated in literate, and especially in technological, societies by physical framing devices and by the ideological idiom of disinterest or detachment, cannot confine the impulse of that vision. "When I read an author," J. Hillis Miller writes, "I have the conviction that my experience is most like that of encountering another human being. . . . Though the people I know are fully present in each gesture or phrase, nevertheless this presence of the whole in the part can never be understood without knowledge of the whole. . . . In the same way, a single novel or poem can be understood only if it is read in the context of other work by that author."[13]

This process of cross-reference (in a more radical current version than anything I am committed to here, "intertextuality") in textual understanding underscores the importance and the function of the resolved point of view, determined by the reader both in its immediate presence and in its potentiality for other appearances. Without an awareness of such potentiality, even the sense of immediate actuality would remain fragmented; Chomsky's distinction between "competence" and "performance" is pertinent not only for its recognition of different modalities in the activity of a narrator (implied *or* real); the ascription to the narrator (and thus to the text) of both these modalities is a condition for the comprehension by an audience of any text of imaginative literature. As the resolved point of view is realized by the reader, it assimilates the narrative view, organizing the latter's directives as to how resolution is to occur. The resolved point of view is not that of Oedipus or any other characters whom he encounters, nor of the chorus (as *it* serves a narrative function)—but of a textual intention or point or view which, as it takes shape for the reader, makes intelligible the actions or statements which emerge from both of the other levels. It is itself nowhere stated, or even, except in a manner of speaking, portrayed; the reader knows of its presence, however, as surely as he knows of the presence of the text—indeed the two objects of knowledge are finally identical, what constitute the resolved point of view.

The "necessity" of point of view in the literary text is thus asserted from two sides—by the narrative point of view in its variations (at least one of which *must* occur), articulating the individual elements in the text in so far as they are capable of being articulated at all; and by the resolved point of view which frames the narrative point of view and which is also both seen and seen through by the reader; without the resolved point of view, the structure of even the narrative point of view would remain incoherent. (As both these points of view are necessary, neither by itself is sufficient for a grasp of the text.) Admittedly, no part of this claim for the necessity of point of view in literary discourse shows *how* point of view functions *literarily;* but before that issue even comes alive we have first to acknowledge point of view as an essential, rather than an accidental, element in the literary structure.

4. Point of View as Critical Presupposition

It may be objected that, even if the claim of an intrinsic or necessary connection between point of view and the literary text were granted, that connection is so general that it does not bear on the "literariness" of texts. Like words or phonemes, it might be argued, point of view might well be a prerequisite in the making of a text without affecting the question of what distinguishes so-called literary texts from other texts—or, for that matter, texts from nontexts. Even if this point were taken, however, important consequences follow from it for certain conceptions of the ontology of the literary text (for example, in opposition to the structuralist emphasis on the impersonality of literary form). I think it can be shown, moreover, that point of view is indeed more than a necessary condition for the articulation of literary texts as texts: not only is it there, it is also a factor in defining the literariness of those texts—what marks them off from other texts and contributes to the distinctive power we associate with them. The claim for the implication of point of view in the essential character of literature occupies the two last sections of this essay—in the present section, in its appearance as a presupposition of critical theory, the discourse *about* literature.

Once again I cannot hope, in defending this claim, to base it on a sample adequate to the large number of examples or accounts of critical theory. What I attempt to do is to show that the thesis is supported by several significant and otherwise quite different works; for if, as I argue, the concept of point of view spans the substantial differences within the theory of genres as that is formulated by Lukács and by Northrop Frye; and if it also figures as a presupposition in that classical and general source for critical theory, the *Poetics* of Aristotle, we have, I believe, prima facie evidence of the systematic relevance of point of view to critical theory—evidence which stands whether one agrees or disagrees with the specific use or formulation of point of view within those several accounts. Thus, in the first instance, I shall be arguing that for both Lukács's *The Theory of the Novel* and Frye's *Anatomy of Criticism*,[14] important parts of the theoretical structures proposed are closely tied to the concept of point of view; indeed, that the structures are not accessible without the acknowledgment of that connection.

Lukács does not refer explicitly to point of view in *The Theory of the Novel* (although he does so in his later writing),[15] and the Hegelian influence which dominates *The Theory of the Novel* might seem in fact to move in the opposite direction, toward what Lukács himself speaks of as a "history of forms": the outline of an objective evolution of literary entities rather than the personalized shape of point of view within those entities. (Thus, for example, the statement, focused on the two genres principally at issue for him, that "the epic gives form to a totality of life that is rounded from within; the novel seeks, by giving form, to uncover and construct the concealed totality of life" [p. 60] and the corollary assertion that "the epic hero is, strictly speaking, never an individual" [p. 66].) But it is clear even in the development of this formal distinction that its source is ascribed, not to art merely as a form, but to consciousness, of which any of the forms of art are an expression; and on the basis of that link between formalist method and a nonformalist agent, Lukács relates his typology of individual genres to the points of view that articulate expressive content rather than to the objective transformations on which formalism otherwise might be (and has been) centered. So, for example: "The novel is the epic of an age in which the extensive totality of life is no longer directly *given*" (p. 56, emphasis added), asserting, within the novel, as well as outside it, the agency of a point of view distinguished at least by its lack of totality. The latter theme persists as Lukács argues toward his final placement of the novel vis-à-vis the epic—that "irony is the objectivity of the novel," with its source in the "writer's irony . . . found in times without a god."

What matters here is less whether Lukács refers to the historical context external to the work than that he also calls attention to a determining source also manifest *in* the novel (as evident *or* implied), and that this point of view, as it internalizes an objectivity which the epic had earlier represented, even in its external form also governs the content of the novel generically, and thus also its comprehension. To be sure, it might be argued that Lukács is here specifying point of view as a distinguishing mark *of the novel*, not *as* a category intrinsic to the theory of genres; but surely the contrast which point of view is designed to establish in this sense of its usage could only be systematically coherent in terms of the category of point of view which applies (although evidently in quite different ways) to both the epic and the novel.

It may be objected that to impose this implication on a text which explicitly insists on formal differences is to suggest an idealist prejudice (beyond Lukács's own) which would also ascribe to him an idealist epistemological commitment far beyond anything that he admits to in the work itself: Does *every* statement about social context or action entail a claim within that context for the agency of consciousness or point of view? But such a commitment, if broader than anything Lukács himself says, seems indeed to be presupposed in much that he does say; and secondly, more pertinently, Lukács himself quite explicitly anticipates it, with his insistence on the functional connection between the representations of the novel and the world reflected there: "The structural categories of the novel constitutively coincide with the world as it is today" (p. 93). Point of view, then, may not be *only* a literary device employed by the novelist—but it *is* such a means, and a significant one, as analysis reveals it, in distinguishing the generic forms of the epic and the novel.

Ostensively, Frye's conception of genres is less closely tied than is Lukács's to "natural history," his typology designating a logical permutation rather than historical ground: "The basis of generic distinctions in literature appears to be the radical of presentation. Words may be acted in front of a spectator [drama]; they may be spoken in front of a listener [epos]; they may be sung or chanted [lyric]; or they may be written for a reader [fiction]" (pp. 246–47). This formal division is also, however, assigned by Frye a natural origin, since it turns out that the principal distinctions of literary form, as they reflect variations in the radical of presentation, also reflect distinctions in archetypal imagery and thus, at an earlier remove, in man's natural capacity. And whether or not the distinctions themselves are historically or conceptually adequate for the analysis of narrative form (how illuminating is it to hear, for example, that "when Conrad employs a narrator to help him tell his story, the genre of the written word is being assimilated to that of the spoken one"?), the part of their intent which is turned to the concept of point of view is clear. The idea of the radical of presentation which appears in Frye's essay on "Theory of Genres" first as a physical concept—that is, as reflecting the manner of physical relation between a "text" and its audience—finally assumes the form of the literary and structural element, indicative of a point of view *internal* to the work. The radical of presentation becomes in effect an indicator of point of view, building literary form on what is first a means of literal staging or framework.

Admittedly, Frye often refers to the "author" as a factor governing the basic distinctions of genre, and he means in these cases not the implied author, but the design of the actual author of the text—who, for reasons alluded to in preceding sections of this chapter and *pace* Lukács, may be quite unrelated to the occurrence or form of point of view *within* the work. But this aspect of Frye's account is more than balanced by the fact that even as he emphasizes the externality of the author, both the evidence he cites and the point he argues toward suggest the presence and agency of points of view internal to the work itself, whether those of the actual author or not. The concept of the radical of presentation, even when it is internalized, limits the power of the concept of point of view which it then becomes to determining primarily formal arrangements: e.g., "The most natural unit of the lyric is the discontinuous unit of the stanza." This limitation is undoubtedly due to the fact that Frye has, before his analysis of genre, developed a "theory of modes" which is more directly concerned than is the theory of genres with the structure of literary content. But Frye, if he is not quite explicit as to *how* the "modes" and "genres" are interwoven, is nonetheless quite explicit in asserting *that* they are (e.g., p. 270)—and with this step the importance, if not the identity, of point of view internal to the work is fixed. (The "modes" themselves, it should be noted, are based on Aristotle's distinction among the objects of imitation: men who are *seen* to be better, or worse than, or on the same level as we are.)

In these two accounts, then—even in their abbreviated forms— the theory of genres turns out to be a function of permutations in the point of view of the literary persona; and this is the case even though the indicators or parameters which sponsor generic differences are located by Lukács and Frye in contexts formally quite different from each other. It might be objected, to be sure, that even granting the readings given here, the theory of genres itself is peculiarly suited to analysis in terms of the concept of point of view—that *other* critical concepts would prove less amenable, and thus that no general conclusion can meaningfully be drawn from the two examples cited. But it is

also true that the theory of genres has not traditionally been charac-
terized in terms of the concept of point of view, and that, notwithstanding this, the quite different theories cited turn out to require
that concept for their own intelligibility. The same conclusion is indicated, in the discussion immediately following this, with respect to
Aristotle's conception of plot—and these several (isolated but important) indicators of the range of critical reflection to which the concept
of point of view is not only pertinent but necessary, are not, as I argue
later, fortuitous.

A more sustained analysis would be needed, of course, to develop a
theory of literary action and to relate it to the concept of point of view
(even in Aristotle's own terms) than I can attempt here. That Aristotle
anticipated such a connection, however, is clear from the relation
between what he speaks of as the "differentiæ" of the arts (or imitation) and the "parts" of tragedy, which is the example of imitation
addressed in the *Poetics*. The differentiæ of imitation include, for
Aristotle, (1) the materials employed for imitation (rhythm, speech,
harmony); (2) the objects of imitation (e.g., either as better or worse
than "we" are); and (most pertinent to the concept of point of view and
one of its earliest formulations) (3) the *ways* in which the objects are
imitated: ". . . [1] by narrating at times and then bringing on some
dramatic character . . . the way Homer composes, or [2] with the
same person doing the imitating throughout, with no change, or [3]
with all the imitators doing their work in and through action" (*Poetics*,
1448a 19–24).[16]

None of the differentiæ may seem to be related to the six "parts" of
tragedy that Aristotle later distinguishes, but the connection at least
between the *ways* of imitation and plot, which is for Aristotle the
most important of the poetic parts, comes clear from the analysis of
plot. Thus Aristotle writes that "tragedy is an imitation not of men as
such but of an action . . . and the end [*telos*] of the story is a certain
action, not a quality. . . . Thus the course of events, the plot, is the
goal of tragedy, and the goal is the most important thing of all"
(1450a16 ff.). Events (*pragmata*) are not synonymous for Aristotle
with action (*praxis*), but the statement quoted implies that actions *are*
events, one "course" of which he regards as constitutive of plot. It
might seem from this context that Aristotle, by emphasizing the importance of action over person (i.e., the characters imitated), contradicts the thesis that has been proposed in these pages and for
which he is now cited in support—that Aristotle means in effect to
depersonalize "action," to detach it from a source. But although Aristotle speaks of "men" as the possible objects of imitation in the plural,
he speaks of "action" in the singular: tragedy is the imitation of *an*

action (cf. also 1449b25, 1449b25, 1450b25). A *sequence* of individual events, in other words, constitutes for Aristotle a *single* action, and it is such a single action which a plot—the *whole* of a plot—then imitates.

Aristotle speaks in detail in chapters 7–11 of the varieties and elements of plot, developing the concepts of simple and complex plots, peripety and recognition, of "beautiful" size and length. It is worth noting that at no point in this discussion does he explain why he chooses the term *action* to describe what he himself sometimes refers to and what might be more neutrally represented as a course or sequence of "events." It could be argued with some plausibility that his use of the concept of a single "action" in this context is metaphoric, as his reference to plot as the "psyche" of tragedy is more openly (1450a38); but whether this be so or not, Aristotle also suggests by the usage a connection between the structure of tragedy and his account of actions and agency in contexts other than that only of *poiesis*, in particular in the *Nicomachean Ethics* where at one point he explicitly joins the concepts of action and art.

In 6.2 Aristotle writes: "The origin of action . . . is choice and that of choice is desire and reasoning with a view to an end. This is why choice cannot exist either without reason and intellect or without a moral state. . . . Intellect itself, however, moves nothing, but only the intellect which aims at an end and is practical . . ." (1130a ff.). The source of action, then, is deliberative, requiring the presence of an agent who is attempting to accomplish a particular end. Action thus represents a mediation between proportionately specific sources and ends, reflecting in one the desire, in the other the understanding which together are requisites for agency.

Tragedy is not itself an action, however, but the *imitation* of an action—a difference which is summarized for Aristotle in his distinction in the *Nicomachean Ethics* between the *praxis* of moral action (as in politics or ethics) and *poiesis*. "The reasoned state of capacity to act is different from the reasoned state of the capacity to make" (1140a5). And *this* implies that the role of the agent in an action which *may be* imitated is distinguishable from the role of the agent who is the maker of the imitation—a distinction that quite exactly rehearses the grounds on which in the earlier discussion of the present essay a narrative persona or source of action was located in the literary text rather than in the writer (or maker) of that text. The agent of tragic action, in other words, acts for Aristotle *within* the plot; and this would be true, one assumes, whether the agent was explicitly identified there or, as is more certainly the case in the examples which Aristotle cites (e.g., *Oedipus Tyrannus*), his presence is known only by inference from the action which unfolds. Plot, then, as the imitation of an action is also the imitation of an agent who is not a single element or factor *within* the action but is responsible for the action as a whole. This agent who establishes the deliberative end of the poetic object may be identified—by a shift in terminology but not in concept—as the source of a point of view for the existence of which the single action constituting plot is sufficient evidence. The claim by Aristotle for the centrality of plot with respect to the other five elements of tragedy which he distinguishes is thus understandable: it is the movement of a composite action—and thus the "resolved" viewpoint, the articulation of the agent acting—which shape the character, thought, diction, even the melody and the (literal) spectacle of the tragedy.

Again, the issue here is not whether Aristotle's account of the role of plot in tragedy is adequate, or whether that account is generalizable to other literary forms. (It is possible but not self-evident that "action" might serve an equally central role, for example, in the novel or in lyric poetry.) I suggest only that, for this one influential account of dramatic action, the pertinence of the concept of point of view is integral, and that this, together with the evidence cited in the first example of genre theory, reinforces the suggestion that point of view is more than only a necessary condition of literary structure—that it is, as a matter of fact, a *literary* element in that structure. Admittedly, this evidence is still fragmentary, occasional; but it is hardly insignificant, and I indicate in the next and final section the systematic grounds which, if anything can, demonstrate its pertinence.

5. The Literariness of Point of View

The analysis of the necessity of point of view has not yet addressed the question of its "final cause" in the literary text. How, the question will go—even if point of view were everything claimed for it here—is point of view responsible for *literary* power or effect? What is its importance for literary structures as such? Such questions, it is evident, verge on the more general question of what constitutes literary or—still more generally—aesthetic quality; and for obvious reasons the latter question will be addressed here only as it relates directly to the analysis of point of view.

When we ask about the final cause of point of view, it is clear that we are presuming on the response of a reader, that we cannot fail to include this focus of point of view which has already been cited under the condition of intersubjectivity. The literary text that bears no reference to a reader (actual or implied)—if only to the writer himself as a prospective reader—is difficult even to conceive, and statements to the effect that a given author had written or would write even if he were certain that nobody would read his work are quite beside the point. The very concept of a text seems to imply the "necessity of the reader," and this is true, in any event, for texts to which the analysis of point of view developed here is pertinent. The several levels of point of view in the literary text, furthermore, have to be realized by the reader not only as it happens, but because, without that realization, the elements of the text and the text as a whole remain only unanticipated or accidental possibilities of experience—a description which describes neither texts as they are read nor the ontology of the text even as a *potential* object of reading.

In this sense, then, not only is the role of the reader anticipated, presupposed in the text; he also participates in determining the structure of the text or, more precisely, in determining that the text *has* a structure. (It would be too much to claim that the reader *creates* a structure for the work, although as invited by the latitude of interpretation which historical perspectivalism—or point of view—ensures, the reader's role is not *much* less than this.)[17] This claim for the necessity of the reader is not, it should be noted, only a comment about the process of writing and the evident truth that the author (real or implied), through that process, addresses a prospective reader (also real or implied). That claim would be true, so far as it is true at all, of everything written or said. Nor is it a version of the idealist thesis that perception or experience of an object is a condition for the reality of the object. It means more decisively that if the point(s) of view embodied in the work—and, as I have argued *necessarily* embodied in the work—are to come alive, this can only occur as a reader addresses the point(s) of view not as he perceives individual items within the text or outside of it, but when he sees as the point of view itself sees, when he sees *by way of it* (as well as, *it*). Failing this, he has no evidence that the point of view *is* a point of view or active in the work at all; and as a consequence of this failure, he could have no means of understanding the organization of plot and character for which point of view is (largely, if not exclusively) responsible.

This description of the role of the reader might be understood to imply that as the literary text is "realized," the reader "identifies" with the point(s) of view disclosed in it. But the fact that the reader comes to see by way of the text does not mean that he sees *only* by that way. The reader may appropriate (or already, to some extent, "have") any of the points of view in the text as his own; furthermore, the resolved point of view by means of which he makes sense of the other, subordinate ones is most certainly, in one obvious sense, his own. (So Poulet writes about the reader: "Whenever I read, I mentally pronounce an *I*. . . .")[18] But it is also unlikely that the reader will come to the literary structure in full possession of the point(s) of view accessible there (this is the case even after the first or successive readings: knowledge of "what happens" in the text is quite different from knowing—and still more certainly, from appropriating—the point(s) of view in the text for which the individual events are only raw material). The reader necessarily brings a point of view with him as reader—if only because he brings one with him as a human being— and *that* is not lost, even when he finds it juxtaposed to others, even contested by them. Thus, the reader's point of view persists even when he sees and sees by way of points of view within the literary structure, and even when finally he composes the resolved point of view. His appropriation of points of view from the text, in other words, is real enough—but it is not, from the reader's point of view, all of what is real. When this is not the case—that is, when *all* distance between reader and text is dissipated (a degree of identification which is less likely to occur than accounts of "aesthetic distance" usually acknowledge)—we face a literal loss of identity on either side of the relation, a merging which makes the very concept of literary text (as well as of individual reader or person) problematic.

It follows from the latter implication that the points of view encountered at any, and finally (since they converge) at all, of its possible levels qualify the actuality they represent to the reader with the modality of possibility, that they thus come to light for him as options or alternatives and thus as increments rather than replacements for his own point of view. They take this form, they appear at all, only because the reader acknowledges a constant premise of the reality of his own point of view; this is a condition for even the recognition of other points of view. But the relation here is reciprocal; and the condition mentioned is in fact perhaps the most important consequence of the intersubjective character of point of view. The recognition of other points of view is a condition even for the recognition of the reader's own: there simply *is* no discovery or having of a private point of view. Not, as in the arguments that have followed from Wittgenstein against the possibility of a private language, because of the impossibility of verifying private assertion (arguments which may or may not be valid), but because the articulation of an individual point of view, as it meets the conditions laid out for point of view, presupposes in its means—language and thought—a second, external subjectivity from which the first point of view is distinguished. That other subjectivity is presupposed in the identification of the first one as a point of view locates itself.

The encounter with point of view within the literary structure, then, quite aside from what the contents or the direction of the view are, serves as confirmation of the reader's point of view—qua point of view, but, more emphatically, as it is his. And *this* step, it seems, brings us closer to understanding the intrinsic relation of point of view to literary structure and value. For surely, it is in large measure due just to this quality of confirmation or renewal of self that the reader is drawn to the literary structure at all. As the writer so often *(literally)* writes himself into his creations, so the reader also reads himself there—partly in the familiar guise that he sees when he looks into a mirror, but more emphatically in the extraordinary changes which that guise undergoes as shaped by the writer's hand. Those changes are of such an order that at some point(s) it may not be clear to the reader whether it is his own person he is encountering or another's; but if the appropriation is sufficiently strong, that distinction will not be significant. The fact that the role of point of view in this transaction with the reader resembles what might otherwise and in a nonliterary context appear as the encounter between the reader and another *person* reflects only what we have already and repeatedly seen: the likely connection between the lure of literary structure and the concern which the reader has for persons, his own and others— for the face of the creator, for example, that Borges describes in the epigraph to this essay.

Does this speculative conclusion bring us closer, by way of the concept of point of view, to our experience of literary structures? More precisely, how does it account for the objective residue, the *Nachträglichkeit*, of that experience—the cumulation, for example, of literary history, criticism, theory, and the variety of forms that reflect that common attentiveness of them all to the literary artifact? How can we, for example, determine that a reader's interest in a literary structure in which point of view shapes the individual elements is animated, brought to life, by a challenge posed by the point of view rather than by the individual elements? Here, if we are not simply to fall back on fragmentary reports or impressions of how literature finds and leaves individual readers (and vice versa), we can only hope for clues of the presence behind the text, of the human physiognomy in terms of which point of view has been described here. The strategy directing the search for such clues seems straightforward if the claim defended is that structures on which point of view acts are of interest, at least in part, *because* of the functioning of point of view; we should then be able to verify the claim by comparing the interest in the individual elements where they are *not* accompanied or shaped by point of view—and also by comparing the interest in point of view by itself, so far as it can be distinguished from any particular or general set of individual elements. (Some evidence of comparison is already available in the account given above in section 2 of the concept of point of view as related to the scientific text in which—I have argued—the effort is apparent to *suppress* the evidence of point of view.)

Both of these possibilities can only be approximated: How, for example, can any recitation or reproduction of events be merely random if the identification of events cannot be? But we can identify two "moments" in which such recitation is *seen* as random, or at least as unshaped by point of view, and the common reaction, in those moments, is instructive. One of these is the reaction to texts whose intentions are novel or unexpected—where the point of view behind them is obscure. And here we find a moralistic as well as intellectual history of receptivity—the history of innovation in drama, and in the novel, to realism, for example, or to poetry in "plain" language and poetry in its "modern" complexity. Viewed in retrospect, the initial reaction to these developments seems not much more than puzzlement about the unusual point of view evident in them. It is not only, I believe, that the "Shock of the New" has soon worn off in these cases; it has worn off *because* of the discovery in such forms of a physiognomy that is not essentially new at all. A second item in this connection, pertinent by analogy to literary texts, is the general aesthetic distinction between natural and artifactual beauty. For any given object (a flower, even a painting), we may confuse those categories—but once we *know* that the object has been man-made or that it is natural, our way of addressing it, of reading it, is substantively determined. This could not be the case if the role of point of view in shaping the object were neutral or accidental with respect to the elements of the object itself. A third item of evidence concerns the reader's interest in narratives of events which, if there were confronted outside a narrative structure, would repel him—the problem of "horror," first put in a literary frame by Aristotle. The answer to this question (which is also Aristotle's) that the interest in such events is a function of interest in all events (the desire to know), or alternatively, that it is animated by an awareness that the events narrated are not "real," both beg the question of why there is a special and positive interest in the events as narrated. And a response which satisfies *those* conditions is the one I have been arguing for here: that the interest in the events of narration goes beyond the events to the *fact* of the narration itself and the features which *it* discloses—the point of view which figures in them all. On the one hand, the reader makes his own way into the work: its framework, like that of a door, shows him the entrances. On the other hand, the identification is not complete (since then the repulsion would win out). Thus the attachment is qualified, provisional—seen primarily as a possibility, both pointed and buffered by the contrivance of a textual medium, the articulation of a point of view in it which has an interest of its own.

What can we make of the phenomenon of "fact" of point of view as it is dissociated from any particular set of narrative events—of point of view independent of plot? The interest here is precisely an inverse function of the *lack* of interest which a set of events without a controlling point of view elicits. This is in significant ways the same interest that talk about the persona of an implied author or narrator responds to—and I have indicated before this one common critical form which that interest takes in the attraction exerted by literary biography and indeed by the interest in biography as such, literary or otherwise. It may be difficult to say *what* it is in points of view or in persons that rouses an interest independent of any particular set of features that figure in them—but about the phenomenon itself, which is, after all, much like the fact of *eros* itself, there can be little quarrel.

One last clue may be cited here that falls somewhere between events or elements represented apart from point of view, and point of view as dissociated from events or objects. And that is the case cited above in section 2, with respect to the scientific text, where point of view, although unquestionably present, is suppressed, flattened. It takes nothing away from the accomplishment of science to say that however it might wish to minimize this effect, this very effort, hidden but still evident, is integral to scientific discourse. Where scientific writing is openly instrumental, serving a practical purpose, the role of point of view—its intentions and motives—will also appear close to the surface. But even as the attempt is made to repress or to mask the author's personal sense of purpose or interest, where the emphasis is on *disinterest*, knowledge for its own sake, the reader will understand this too, ascetic and self-effacing as it may seem, still as an exemplification of the role of point of view.

These "clues," again, are symptomatic only; their significance is not self-evident, and even if it were, their implications would not be conclusive. But if we start with the observation from experience that literary structures (in preliterate hardly less than in literate societies) have been crucial in determining the forms of the most important human institutions (religious, moral, technological, aesthetic)—and that, as among these structures, it is not only the objects displayed in them but also the fact and process of articulation itself that gives them their power of evocation, then the process of point of view turns out to be more than an accidental feature of literary structure: it is in fact constitutive. We would be at a loss to devise or recognize literary structure without it—and with it, we better understand, against the background of human interests in general, the more specific but very wide interest in the institution of literature as a whole. There is a mingling of hyperbole and idolatry in the claim that what draws the reader to the literary work is the human physiognomy disclosed by it, the person he may find there—himself, perhaps, but surely others as well (if only the other whom he may yet become). But we do well to acknowledge that every representation of reality, from its "doubling" effect alone, its design to increase reality, is intrinsically hyperbolic. The discussion here of the role of point of view in literary representation has been intended to show that just such a hyperbolic multiplication of entities is a literary fact—and that persons and points of view are important among the entities that make that fact possible.

Notes

1. E.g., M. Bakhtin, *Problems of Dostoyevsky's Poetics*, trans. R. W. Rotsel (Ann Arbor, Mich.: Ardis, 1973); W. Booth, *The Rhetoric of Fiction* (Chicago: University of Chicago Press, 1961); G. Genette, *Narrative Discourse*, trans. J. E. Lewin (Ithaca, N.Y.: Cornell University Press, 1980); P. Lubbock, *The Craft of Fiction* (New York: Scribner, 1921); J. Hillis Miller, *Thomas Hardy: Distance and Desire* (Cambridge, Mass.: Harvard University Press, 1970); C. Muscatine, "Locus of Action in Medieval Narrative," *Romance Philology* 17 (1963): 115–22; R. Pascal, *The Dual Voice* (Manchester: University of Manchester Press, 1977); K. Smidt, "Point of View in Victorian Poetry," *English Studies* 38 (1957): 1–12; G. Tillotson, *Thackeray the Novelist* (Cambridge: Cambridge University Press, 1954).

2. E.g., A. Banfield, "Narrative Style and the Grammar of Direct and Indirect Speech," *Foundations of Language* 10 (1973): 1–39; W. Iser, *The Implied Reader* (Baltimore, Md.: Johns Hopkins Press, 1974); F. Kermode, "Novels: Recognition and Deception," *Critical Inquiry* 1 (1974): 103–21; J. M. Lotman, "Point of View in a Text," trans. L. M. O'Toole, *New Literary History* 6 (1975): 339–52; F. van Rossum-Huyon, "Point de vue ou perspective narrative; theories et concepts critiques," *Poetique* 4 (1970): 476–510; B. Uspensky, *The Poetics of Composition*, trans. V. Zavarian and S. Wittig (Berkeley, Calif.: University of California Press, 1973).

3. The mixing of visual and auditory metaphors has been a recurrent feature in accounts of point of view—a conflation which may be no more excusable for the fact of its recurrence. But I suggest that this mixing of metaphors is significant, reflecting an integrative function for point of view: in it, the senses are only as acute as the understanding which makes sense of *them* (see below, subsection 2).

4. Cf. Booth, *Rhetoric of Fiction*, p. 245.

5. Cf. W. K. Wimsatt and M. Beardsley, "The Intentional Fallacy," in W. K.

Wimsatt, *The Verbal Icon* (Lexington, Ky.: University of Kentucky Press, 1954); and the later discussions of that essay by I. Hungerland, "The Concept of Intention in Art Criticism," *Journal of Philosophy* 52 (1955): 733–42; R. Kuhns, "Criticism and the Problem of Intention," *Journal of Philosophy* 57 (1960): 5–25. Cf. also ch. 3 in the present volume. E. D. Hirsch is a current advocate of "intentionalism" (cf. *Validity in Interpretation* [New Haven, Conn.: Yale University Press, 1967] and *The Aims of Interpretation* [Chicago: University of Chicago Press, 1976]). And for criticism of that position in Hirsch's formulation, cf. comments by G. Dickie and M. Beardsley, *Genre* 1 (1968): 169–89. It is not crucial, in fact, whether Hirsch's arguments stand up to this criticism or not, since his position only provides an alternative description of the modality of the resolved view—it does not dispute the importance of the view itself.

6. Cf. especially E. Panofsky, "Die Perspektive als 'symbolische Form,'" *Vorträge der Bibliothek Warburg* (1924–25), pp. 258–330, and C. Guillen, "Metaphor of Perspective," in *Literature as System* (Princeton, N.J.: Princeton University Press, 1971), pp. 288–356. An incidental item in the recent history of point of view is the sharp increase in writing about the concept as from 1964 and 1965; the entries for the ten years before then in the *Social Sciences and Humanities Index* are either sparse or nonexistent.

7. S. Chatman ("Narration and Point of View in Fiction and the Cinema," *Poetica* 7 [1974]: 21–46) suggests other possible meanings for point of view, outside *and* within the literary text (the "literal" meaning, as actual seeing through someone's eyes, and the "transferred" meaning, suggesting the interest or advantage of the "viewer"); these are clearly, however, meanings peripheral to the one that has been found useful critically.

8. Cf. the connection of grammar and point of view as developed by S. Y. Kuroda, "Where Epistemology, Style and Grammar Meet: A Case Study from Japanese," in P. Kiparsky and S. Anderson, eds., *A Festschrift for Morris Halle* (New York: Holt, Rinehart, and Winston, 1973), pp. 377–91.

9. *Nature* 26 (1976): 101–8.

10. This mixed mode is more often described under the name of "free indirect discourse"; cf. P. Hernadi, "Dual Perspective: Free Indirect Discourse and Related Techniques," *Comparative Literature* 24 (1972): 32–43; and Banfield, "Narrative Style," pp. 10–13, who speaks of the "free indirect style." Cf. also the concept of "quasi-direct" discourse, as distinguished from direct and indirect discourse, as described by N. Volosinov [M. Bakhtin?], *Marxism and the Philosophy of Language*, trans. L. Matejka and I. R. Ritunik (New York: Seminar Press, 1973), pp. 141 ff.

11. See, for example, R. Gottesman and S. Bennet, eds., *Art and Error* (Bloomington, Ind.: Indiana University Press, 1970), for examples of mechanical or editorial error even in nominally standard texts (e.g., of Dickens, Mark Twain, Faulkner)—and the difference which recognition of those errors makes in the reading.

12. Bakhtin suggests *(Problems of Dostoyevsky's Poetics)* that in Dostoyevsky's "polyphony," for example, the characters speak not only for themselves but as themselves—thus, that what I call here the narrative point of view is altogether absent. (Cf. also J. Kristeva, "The Death of a Poetics," in S. Bann and J. E. Bowlt, eds., *Russian Formalism* [New York: Barnes and Noble, 1973], pp. 102–21; cf. for arguments similar to Bakhtin's in direction, but on different grounds, Banfield, "Narrative Style," and K. Walton, "Points of View in Narrative and Depictive Narration," *Nous* 10 [1976]: 50; and for a more general argument against ascribing a "persona" to the

text at all, I. Ehrenpreis, "Personae," in C. Camden, ed., *Restoration and Eighteenth-Century Literature: Essays in Honor of Alan Dugald McKillop* [Chicago: University of Chicago Press, 1963], pp. 25–37.)

13. J. Hillis Miller, "The Antithesis of Criticism," in R. Macksey, ed., *Velocities of Change* (Baltimore, Md.: Johns Hopkins University Press, 1974), p. 146. Cf. also P. Jones, *Philosophy and the Novel* (Oxford: Oxford University Press, 1975), pp. 196–197 for a more systematic analogy between the understanding of persons and of novels; and on the requirement of more than one text for identifying the author's persona, cf. G. Josipovici, *The World and the Book* (Stanford: Stanford University Press, 1971).

14. G. Lukács, *Theory of the Novel*, trans. A. Bostock (Cambridge, Mass.: M.I.T. Press, 1971); N. Frye, *Anatomy of Criticism* (Princeton, N.J.: Princeton University Press, 1957).

15. Cf., e.g., "Narrate or Describe," in *Writer and Critic*, trans. A. Kahn (New York: Grosset and Dunlap, 1970).

16. G. F. Else's translation in *Aristotle's Poetics: The Argument* (Cambridge, Mass.: Harvard University Press, 1967).

17. It will be evident that this is a diffident, even a reactionary verdict on recent emphases (such as that in Derrida) on the deconstruction of the text. If it is true that the limits of the text are not as pristine as the mythology of criticism in the nineteenth and twentieth centuries would have them, the alternative claim that no limits exist at all offers Original Sin as a cure for naiveté.

18. G. Poulet, "Criticism and the Experience of Interiority," in R. Macksey and E. Donato, eds., *The Structuralist Controversy* (Baltimore, Md.: Johns Hopkins University Press, 1972), p. 60. Poulet quickly—too quickly, it seems to me—distinguishes the "I" he pronounces from the "I" he is. Thus the actual reader also becomes for Poulet an implied reader (implied by the actual reader)—a substitution which seems both conceptually and as a matter of fact unwieldy.

PART III

Breaking into the Text

8
Nothing Comes of All: Lear-Dying

If you do not know how to die, never mind; nature will teach
you, on the spot—fully and sufficiently.

Montaigne

Bitterness is to the taste and thus not to be disputed. When I say,
then, that *King Lear* leaves a bitter taste—the taste of mortality—I
mean to suggest a premise around which the rest of this discussion
will locate itself. That premise, although unarguable, is hardly arbitrary. There has been too much talk, in the centuries of writing about
Shakespeare, of the savagery of *King Lear*, of its excessive force, for
us to mistake that response only for impression or mere sentiment.
No other of Shakespeare's tragedies—and none of the classical non-
Shakespearean tragedies—tantalizes the viewer with the prospect,
after much suffering and the recognition to which that suffering leads,
of pain sealed off, cauterized, only to have him find even in the short
time that remains (as with Cordelia's death and then Lear's), that this
is not to be, that what he is offered at a point where he hopes for
reconciliation or even only a respite is the impatience of death itself.
In the old *Leir* from which Shakespeare drew, and in Tate's revision
which improved on Shakespeare in the judgment of audiences for the
century and a half after 1681, Cordelia survives; when the king dies
(or, in Tate, lives on), he does so as kings themselves would choose to,
in honored old age. If a reader fortified with Samuel Johnson's uncommon measures of sensibility and assurance can write that "I was
many years ago so shocked by Cordelia's death, that I know not
whether I ever endured to read again the last scenes of the play till I
undertook to revise them as an editor," we are bound ourselves to
question that event and the others which lead to it. How could Shakespeare have mistaken this excess?

But we may be confident, of course, that he did not; that what for
us comes to be distinctive about *King Lear* was first and consciously

distinguished by him. And the reactions described verge, then, with a sharper edge than is usual, on a standard question asked in our skeptical readings of any complex literary structure: "Why? Why—within the structure and then from the outside, as the work is designed to act on the expectations of its audience—is what happens made to happen?" This question, we recognize, has an additional and special immediacy for the reading of *King Lear*, with respect to the beginning of the play; for however the reader may otherwise resist the artifice of critical abstraction, however he may incline to rest on the surface of the literary form, the opening moments of *King Lear* act against that disposition. In those moments, we know, the critical disagreement about the later parts or the whole of the play is at one: the first scene is a puzzle, seen as such by virtually every commentator on *King Lear* whose name is likely to mean anything to a viewer or reader—Coleridge, Bradley, Kittredge, Granville-Barker, and on and on. The question (although not the answer) is constant: Why does Lear do what he does (if there is any reason at all)—in giving away his kingdom and then cutting himself off from the people closest to him? Or, from an external view: Why did Shakespeare begin the play so, and how does that beginning serve as a beginning to the whole?

The sense of opaqueness in Act 1, Scene 1, which is reflected in these questions contrasts sharply with the larger effect referred to in my opening lines: the harsh and unequivocal strain on the audience exerted by the play as a whole. There is, then, an incongruity between the unresolved, even ambiguous opening of *King Lear* and its resolute conclusion, an incongruity which suggests that a residue is left from the attempt of the latter to dominate or tame the former; and I hope to account for the contrast between these orders of structure and consequence. I shall be arguing, in effect, that as we grasp the intentions of Scene 1 (and only by this), we realize the intentions of the play: what necessity links beginning and whole; why and how, with the realization of that necessity, the conclusion reaches a level of—one would like here to be able to use the phrase for one and a single time—unparalleled intensity; what the relation is in the process of dramatic action between genre or medium, on the one hand, and content, on the other, which assures their eventual convergence first in the character of Lear, but then also in the reader himself.

I do not mean, in emphasizing the role of the opening scene in determining these consequences, to be responsible for a general piety about the importance of artistic beginnings (later to be completed, one supposes, by assurances about middles and ends). Those claims, too, might be made, but they are hardly at issue here—where it is the incongruity between a specific, problematic beginning and a startling but unproblematic whole that directs our attention.

I

We need to be clear first on the issues which have provoked the questioning of the place or sense of Scene 1. The puzzle derives from the action, and the action at one level is simply described: the aged Lear has summoned his three daughters in order to divide his kingdom among them. He requires that the daughters claim their portions by speeches of devotion. Goneril and Regan meet his demand; Cordelia refuses, and her portion is divided between the others. She herself is "dower'd" with Lear's curse and banished—as is Kent, who is punished for speaking in her defense. The scene ends as Regan and Goneril begin to plot against Lear, who is now in their charge.

The doubts raised about the scene are represented in two sets of questions. The first of these calls attention to the character of Lear himself: Why does Lear (who is, we quickly learn, nobody's fool) act as he does—precipitously giving away his power, and then, as if troubled with the restraint of that one misstep, compounding it as he cuts himself off from the people most deserving of his attachment? Nothing in his past, as we learn of it, foretells or explains what Lear does—and little we bring from a general knowledge of human nature, outside the play, explains it—without also (as I shall attempt to show) explaining it away.

The set of "external" questions is closely related to the others: Why the compressed and causally improbable sequence of events which constitute the scene? For surely, even on the basis of the brief outline cited, it will seem more likely that this sequence—part of it or all— should have been presented by Shakespeare in retrospect, as having occurred before the play itself begins and thus as an artistic ground for more leisurely recall; or, if not that, that the sequence should have been allowed to shape a larger part of the play's action; or, even *with* these, that the events themselves—the reversals which Lear, without motive, invites and immediately suffers—should, quite simply, have been different from what they are. Could not the play as a whole have gained from a likelier beginning?

What underlies these questions and proposals, it is evident, is a common premise of incoherence or disproportion—in Lear's character, first, and then in the scene as a setting for consequent action. And the many accounts that have been given, even those which conclude that *finally* no such disproportion exists, at least agree this far about

Scene 1: that there indeed *appears* to be an improbability or discontinuity in it—apparently enough, at all events, to call for an explanation. Admittedly, this small measure of critical agreement contrasts with the larger disagreement among interpretations of the later dramatic action; but even that manner of agreement is sufficiently rare in the critical process that we do well to consider it as symptomatic.

We begin, then, with the fact of critical agreement, specifically with what turns out to be a pattern among the accounts that acknowledge the motif of disproportion. These acknowledgments fall into three groups. In the first of them we find the claim that the perceived disproportion has a basis or "objective correlative" in the work: that the disproportion in Lear's actions has a literal and real reference, defining a recognizable departure, perhaps even pathological, from the usual movement of character or behavior. The second group of accounts concludes, on the other hand, that the basis for any sense of incongruity in the work in only apparent: an appearance which can finally be integrated into, made consistent with, the other like events on the not at all disproportioned surface of the work. Neither of these accounts finally stands up, I shall be claiming here—but their mistakes are interesting, and in identifying them we lay a basis for the expansion of a third and more fruitful alternative.

The line of argument that runs through the first group of accounts mentioned is easily described—because if the disproportion, either in Lear or in the scene, is real or to be understood literally, an "explanation" of its presence need only give that element an appropriate name, assign it to a descriptive category. This is, we understand, what G. Wilson Knight intends when he describes Lear as "childish," "foolish"—and the whole of the first scene as "curious," the occasion of a "trivial domestic" quarrel in which a failure of judgment occurs which leads, as it were by accident, to later, more momentous events. This is, at an extreme which caricatures but is formally quite consistent with more measured statements of the position, what Kittredge apparently intends when he diagnoses Lear as senile; and the same point on which Allardyce Nicoll fixes his judgment of the first scene as a "failure": we do not find there, he writes, "normal and appreciable motives."

There are, to be sure, different emphases even in this single set of explanations: with one we hear that Lear is *intended* to appear as acting without normal motive; with the other, that the mechanics of Lear's character or of the scene as a whole have escaped Shakespeare. Whichever of these lines is followed, however, the critical conclusion is the same: that the Lear who appears in Scene 1, or the scene itself, embodies a gratuitousness or imbalance for which the later development of the play does not fully compensate. Consistency requires—at least—consistency; and the initial imbalance in this case remains a presence which is not made good in the interpretative conclusion.

Because of the kind of explanation which these accounts provide—in effect not explanation at all, but the naming of perception—neither the individual statements nor their common thesis is open to refutation. But it will also be evident that they are not very illuminating; that they clash with at least some of the evidence and are thus, finally, misleading. Lear foolish? Imprudent? Well, no doubt, as we might confess to ourselves about much of mankind (and perhaps ourselves). But is it because he is *only* foolish that he acts as he does? He might then as well be senile—and there is ample evidence both in Scene 1 and after it to belie that. We look for the explanation of a *particular* set of actions—and if a man is not *merely* foolish or senile (as Lear clearly is not), we have reason to expect a reason in addition to either of them: an artistic reason as well as a psychological one.

The same qualification holds, furthermore *(mutatis mutandis),* for Shakespeare himself. Even if we were to agree, for the sake of argument, that the *characters* in Scene 1 lack motive, this does not imply, as Nicoll assumes, that *Shakespeare* or (more pertinently) the *scene* lack motive. Admittedly, the part of a whole—the scene—might be a failure without making the whole a failure; but here, too, at either level, the problem remains one of arguing with a claim which is finally a report about the appearance of an intention. We are thrown back for disproof, it seems, only on the possibility that we ourselves may see again or farther than that initial report has. If the scene *were* a failure, we would expect difficulties in providing the evidence to demonstrate this; all that we can hope to do in arguing that the supposed failure is in fact a success is to show that the supposed grounds for the negative judgment (for example, Lear's lack of motive) are either not there or can be understood differently.

The second group or "nest" of interpretations of the apparent disproportion in Scene 1 concludes that the disproportion, finally, is *only* apparent; that it (the disproportion) is in fact consistent within the pattern of literal reference marked out by the dramatic events and action. Again, the accounts in this group look to different evidence as they address Lear himself or the development of the scene as an entity. Thus we hear that in Scene 1 Lear acts in character, and that the character, furthermore (with respect to its motives and actions) is consistent and intelligible—the *apparent* implausibilities notwithstanding. So, for example, Stanley Cavell suggests that the actions of Lear in Scene 1 are straightforward, fully sustained by later events.

The motivation for the structure of the scene, in particular for Lear's reaction to Cordelia's denial, is, we learn, the "avoidance of love." Lear "wants exactly what a bribe can buy: (1) false love; and (2) a public expression of love. That is: he wants something he does not have to return in kind. . . . "A. C. Bradley provides a similarly literal but less complex acknowledgment of Lear's actions which reflect, Bradley infers, a "scheme to gratify [Lear's] love of absolute power and his hunger for assurances of devotion."

Numerous other accounts move in the same direction as the last two cited. My purpose for the moment, however, is not to collect or annotate these, but to represent the form of their critical response. I do not mean to suggest, furthermore, that such accounts are simply or flatly defective—although they can be shown, I think, to leave notable lacunae: in the character they would have us recognize as Lear and in the relation to him of the apparently disjointed series of actions in the scene. For how is it, we might ask Cavell, that so many of the figures on the stage—Kent, France, Regan, Lear himself—report Lear's past love and preference for Cordelia if indeed he has "avoided" love? Are they simply mistaken? Or do they all see where he has been blind (assuming, that is, that he could have loved without himself being aware of it)? And if the events in the scene are understood to mark a sudden shift in Lear from an attitude previously held, we come back squarely, once again, to our original question about the unaccountable course that events follow: Why?

Or again: Bradley, at the same time that he argues for the plausibility of Lear's character, acknowledges that the scene in which Lear (and the play) are introduced is "strange"—"like so many of the stories on which our romantic dramas are based." But what the relation is between Lear the individual and the strangeness of context is left unquestioned—as though once having noted that strangeness, we are then simply to accept the character of Lear, whatever it may be, so long only as it is consistent with the other, more inclusive strangeness.

The claim for the value of internal consistency becomes a general principle in several influential accounts where the talk has turned from the character of Lear to the scene as a whole, and specifically, to the way in which the scene serves as preface to the remainder of the play. Surely, the contention goes, an author has a right to establish the initial premises of his own work; whatever the apparent incongruities in those premises as measured from the outside, so long as he is later consistent in realizing them internally, in the work's own terms, we ought to allow him the initial freedom. This defense of poetic insulation, it will be recognized, is for Coleridge an application of the principle which he otherwise presents as the "willing suspension of disbelief." Thus, Coleridge writes that "it [Act 1, Scene 1] is merely the canvas to the characters and passions, a mere occasion. . . ." And Granville-Barker applies the same principle more fully: the scene's "probabilities are neither here nor there. A dramatist may postulate any situation he has the means to interpret, if he will abide by the language of it after. . . . It is his starting point, the dramatist's 'let's pretend.' . . ." An apparent improbability, in other words, may be integral to the drama in the same way that premises function in a sequence of inference; even as improbable, it becomes a defect only if it is not carried forward consistently. The literary work itself defines the consistencies by which its elements are judged.

The broader question of poetic theory which underlies this contention need not be argued here. Perhaps the license of the poet extends this far as well, assuring a literal carte blanche for even the most nonliteral premises of poetic discourse. But also, if this stipulation be granted, it blankets so many and such different alternatives that we learn little from it. Premises themselves, after all, may be more or less probable—and *why*, we come round once again, even if we grant the poet this freedom, the *specific* measure and form of improbability in the opening scene of *King Lear?*

Now it may be suspected that I lay about with a broad brush in these skeptical comments only to be able to recommend more strongly the figures which I intend to paint myself—and I do not deny a basis for this suspicion. But notice also that the alternative which thus begins to emerge by attrition, as the first two possibilities falter, starts from the same premises that they accept but fail to make good. The first set of alternatives admit the apparent improbabilities of Scene 1 as real—but are then unable to account for the other, probable events which follow; the second group of alternatives find consistency in the whole—but they do this by explaining how actually probable the initial improbability is and thus by explaining it away. The third alternative, then, is given shape by these efforts: not that the improbabilities of Scene 1 should be taken literally, at face value, and given a name: senility, childishness, Shakespeare's failure. And not either that they should be transformed into a version of conventionalized probability: strangeness, the willingness to suspend disbelief about all improbability. But rather that the phenomenon of improbability itself should be recognized as a datum; that it should be understood as telling the reader, as he learns from it *what* is happening (and what may later be expected to happen), also *about* what is happening—in other words, as *re*presenting what is also and more discursively being presented. All the accounts so far cited here agree on the phenomenon of improbability or discontinuity. But after this one point of agreement, they quickly draw attention away from it—transposing the apparent improbability to a more predictable explanation that shows how *really* probable the apparent improbability is. Why not begin (as does the scene itself) with the *fact* of improbability?

II

Consider the following sentence, from which Kafka's story "The Metamorphosis" starts out: "As Gregor Samsa awoke one morning from uneasy dreams he found himself transformed in his bed into a gigantic insect." The reader will be unlikely to find anything unusual or difficult in the literal meaning either of the individual words in this sentence or of the sentence as a whole: Gregor Samsa—who we infer from the sentence had been a human being—awakes one morning to find himself an insect. To step back from this literal understanding, however, measuring this opening line, as readers are bound and meant to, by their own pasts and expectations, is also to recognize the improbability of the occurrence described. Because of Kafka's own directness, this act of recognition does not have far to move from the literal comprehension of the sentence. Yet the movement of inference, however slight, is sufficient to establish a reflective space between the meaning of the literal statement and its representation of improbability, and thus to suggest that the representation itself, the *factor* or *radical* of improbability, is intended as a generic means—a feature which although itself only exhibited and not stated, serves as a framing device for the work as a whole.

To be sure, the opening of "The Metamorphosis" is more abrupt and concise than most literary beginnings; but the use of representation as marking out a framework for artistic comprehension in itself makes no unusual formal demands on the reader. In the reading of any literary text, a development of inference is initiated and progressively refined; the reader acts to derive a whole from the single elements—a process of construction which begins, naturally enough, at the beginning of the text. Like other texts, furthermore, the process to which "The Metamorphosis" gives shape engenders factual expectations based both on what it discursively asserts (e.g., expectations about the future history of Gregor Samsa); and also on what we learn as it reflexively *points to itself* as a medium of expression, defining a means. Thus, the opening sentence that has been quoted not only *describes* an improbability but *is* itself an improbability—as measured by the conventional expectations about causality and personal identity which the reader will have brought to his reading. If we assume artistic reasons for all such effect in an artistic whole, we anticipate the presence in "The Metamorphosis" of a genre, or at least of a literary figure, for which improbability or discontinuity is a significant structural element.

For the moment I do not attempt to give a name to this artistic device, in connection either with "The Metamorphosis" or with *King Lear*, toward which the analogy is directed—in part because, in the absence of further analysis, numerous possibilities might serve; in part because it is what is common to the various possibilities that matters most immediately. Both the latter issues are complicated by the fact that discontinuity seems a characteristic feature of the separation we assume in general between art and life; *that* sense of discontinuity might easily be confused with others which are internal to specific genres or individual works.

This more general discontinuity is emblematic, in fact, of much in our understanding of the making and appreciation of art. The mechanism of intentional improbability provided Freud with a key to the interpretation of dreams—and later to his assertion of the connection between the work of the dreamer and the work of the artist; as a condition of this connection (a still longer tradition has seen), improbability, or at least dissociation, also governs the definition of the conventional literary genres and figures, from allegory at one extreme of explicitness, to metaphor and simile at the other. At every point on this spectrum, a characteristic discontinuity is both asserted and exhibited (presented and re-presented) by the genre or figure, between itself and the usual process of experience: a break which calls the reader's attention to a process which is the resultant of two related levels of discourse—the literal sequence of action and disclosure of character, on the one hand, and a set of meanings and directions revealed by that sequence as a representation which points to itself, on the other hand.

How does the description of a sequence of improbable events, such as that in "The Metamorphosis," come to serve as a representation? By defining a project for the reader—once he has admitted the literal improbability that a man should one morning wake up as an insect— of interpreting the appearance of that literal "fact"; by simultaneously calling attention to the probability of what is *not* being literally asserted, so that the fact of the improbability, and the exemplifications by which it is expressed, hint strongly at a meaning to be disclosed, and hence at the need for decodification. This directive is obviously a feature of allegory, where the literal terms of the work openly announce both a departure from conventional narrative as well as a consistency with it—by the conscientious improbability (for example) in Bunyan's *Pilgrim's Progress*, of the names Discretion, Piety, Charity, Christian; it is less obtrusive but evident nonetheless even in individual metaphors and similes—where the key lies not in the *similarity* between the elements joined in the figure but in the difference between them which reflects on that similarity. So, for example, Homer's description in the *Iliad* of the movement of the attacking Greeks who are "like clouds of buzzing, fevered flies that swarm about a cattle stall in summer when pails are splashed with milk." That the structure of simile pivots on the term *like*, tells us in effect only of one, and perhaps its lesser, component. For if the two sides of a simile were *fully* "like," we would not speak of the expression as a simile (or artful) at all, but more probably of tautology: it would hardly be worth recording that the Greeks attacking are like "soldiers going into battle." The difference (the unlikeness) between the two terms of the simile, and the contrast thus asserted which sets off the likeness, serve notice of the role of simile as artifice.

An objection previously hinted at may be raised against these formal comments, on grounds of triviality or even of inconsistency. For if what has been said so far about the role of representational discontinuity were granted for the sake of argument, it might still be objected that approximately the same claims hold for all literary fiction. By the fact that a piece of work is recognized *as* fiction, *some* characteristic indicating a deviation or exception from history must also be evident. Furthermore (and here the case for inconsistency), it has been claimed that in the encounter with the literary text, the individual events or data related there are read off against a background of general, often extraliterary, expectations which the reader brings with him. Is it not perverse to claim that such expectations are significant insofar as the work, in its improbability, fails to live up to them?

Both these objections seem to me sound—but neither is inconsistent with the thread of argument. Admittedly, there would be little surprising about the claim (if what I have been saying implies this) that the form of a literary figure like metaphor, for example, might be assigned to any literary object as a whole.[1] But what is pertinent for the present account is that however real this formal possibility, significant differences still mark the class of literary works with respect to the *specific* use they make individually of devices which contribute to the generic discontinuity between art and (for example) history. If every literary fiction is in some sense a metaphor, still, in a large number of instances, the characteristic metaphoric space—the distance between the two sides of the metaphor—is slight. The great epic fictions, for example—*War and Peace* or the *Iliad*—hardly require reference to a domain other than the ones which are explicitly represented. (This is, I take it, what Lukács means in suggesting that the drama is closer to universality, the epic to individuality.) In other literary fictions, however, the recognition of such space is crucial for comprehension. Recognition of its functioning in the work seen as representation immediately affects the process of reading; without such recognition, the latter may be unintelligible and will certainly be unintelligent. Here one might cite again *Pilgrim's Progress:* What do we understand in that text without the supposition of the well-defined—in fact, isomorphic—space of allegorical reference?

I shall be suggesting, then, that a version of metaphoric space is indicated as a medium by the disproportion of the opening scene and then turns out to be constitutive in the structure of *King Lear* as a whole. The importance of that space is underscored by the phenomenon of its progressive diminution—until, in fact, at the conclusion of *King Lear*, no distance at all remains between Lear or the reader, on the one hand, and the metaphoric reference, on the other. A more immediately practical consequence of this conception of metaphoric space is also available: that as we apply what has been noted in general about the iconic mechanisms in literary fictions, the way in which they point to themselves or "*re*present," to the apparent discontinuities or improbabilities in Scene 1 of *King Lear*, we uncover a conception of that scene which cuts between the difficulties found for the two versions described in section 1.

It will be recalled that I claim for those interpretations complementary defects: on the one hand, the rendering of contextual improbability in the opening scene of *King Lear* as literal and isolated fact and thus at the expense of other no less significant facts; on the other hand, the assimilation of that improbability to probability by a reduction which finally explained the improbability away. An opening is left here for a third alternative which bridges the apparent disjunction: proposing that the *fact* of the improbability be taken seriously, but that it be understood representationally rather than literally— pointing to its own role in setting out the generic means and expectations (or reversals of expectation) through which action and character within the play are filtered. The particular form of improbability which is thus represented, I shall be claiming, is a version of metaphoric structure; it will be important to show, then, as evidence for this claim, how individual events and developments of character are located in metaphoric space—and finally, how the force exerted by the play is a function of the diminution of the space, until, as I suggest, with its disappearance, Lear's consciousness converges on the reader's own.

A number of interpretations of *King Lear* have acknowledged the thesis of this third alternative, to the effect that the improbability in which the play originates intimates a nonliteral meaning. There is less agreement, however, about what that meaning is. So, for example, Alfred Harbage applies such terms as *ritual* and *allegory* (which he seems ready to equate): "No logical reasons appear—ritual is ritual, its logic its own. Prose is yielding to poetry, 'realism' to reality. *King Lear* is not true. It is an allegory of truth." William Frost extends the use of ritual to the boundaries of myth: "There is a 'machine-like' quality, an inevitability to the actions of ritual" which assures that "all questions of motivation are by-passed at the outset, and we start with the naked myth. . . . Given such a myth, to raise the question of motive would be to undermine the dramatic event in advance." And Jan Kott, agreeing that "when realistically treated, Lear and Glouces- ter were too ridiculous to appear [to Shakespeare's audience] as tragic heroes," argues rather for the assumption of a "philosophical" reality.

These suggestions of a direction for interpretation have a common bent, insofar as they agree that the improbability or strangeness of the opening scene points to (and is itself part of) a literary form for which improbability is integral. On the other hand, the names which they assign to that form—ritual, myth, allegory—are notoriously vague; even in their applications in context, the names hardly become more precise. This defect may, of course, be due only to the difficulty of identifying the structure described, and I do not claim that by calling that structure a metaphor I deflect the questions reasonably raised about the other terms. But to say that the improbability of Scene 1— its "magical" or "strange" quality—is indicative of metaphoric struc- ture answers at least to the requirement that we relate those literal (and improbable) events to a nonliteral ground. The claim of metaphoric structure, moreover, ensures a basis for movement in what has been described as the characteristic process of reading: that the reader's attention should be drawn simultaneously to what is being asserted or presented and to the means by which the presenta- tion is effected. The two sides of any metaphor are symmetrically referential but logically sequential; the two refer to each other—but it is invariably clear that the second term, to which comparison is made, refers back to the first, which thus serves as a fulcrum. In doing this, by interrupting the narrative flow, the second term calls attention to the process or means which is at work. It thus exemplifies what Jakobson speaks of as the characteristic poetic function: the projection of "the principle of equivalence from the axis of selection into the axis of combination." Metaphor is not alone, of course, in serving this function—but there is no question that it does so. Finally, and most important: the proposal of the use of metaphor explicitly addresses a question that the alternative possibilities cited are inclined to evade. A claim for metaphor can be only as persuasive as a supporting account of what the metaphor is a metaphor *of*. Unlike the terms *myth* or *ritual*, which imply no such reference and which consequently often have an appeal for language that has gone on holiday, the designation of *King Lear* as a metaphor opens immediately onto the question of what *King Lear* is a metaphor *of*. Failing an answer to that question, we might reasonably conclude that *King Lear* is not a metaphor at all—and perhaps that the improbabilities which the figure of metaphor was meant to explain are not improbabilities after all. The parts of an interpretative whole, it turns out, are connected (or disconnected) by logic as well as by sensibility.

III

If we ask from whose point of view the action in *King Lear* is represented, the readiest responses will undoubtedly refer either to Shakespeare or to nobody at all. None of these answers sheds much light, and this fact reflects the constraints on the question itself. The concept of point of view, we recognize, illuminating when applied to varieties of literary fiction like the novel, the short story, even the epic, has rarely been worked to advantage in respect to the drama. There, it seems, each character speaks for himself; even if the writer wanted to, it would be difficult for him to give life to an omniscient narrator (for example), manipulating or foretelling the events of the action or reporting authoritatively on what the other characters feel and why. If such a narrator *were* assigned a role, he would almost certainly turn out to be just one character to be viewed alongside others—who would then be seen as reacting to (or ignoring) his pretensions.

This would be a standard account of "point of view" as applied to drama, and, allowing for certain exceptional cases, such as the role of the chorus in Greek tragedy, it is reasonable. We recognize, to be sure, that one character in a play may come closer than others to expressing the author's views (this happens frequently in Shaw's writing, for example, and in Ibsen's). Elsewhere, furthermore, even if no single character speaks for the author, we may without much difficulty infer a statement of the *author's* point of view; this would be true, for example, in Chekhov's *Cherry Orchard*. But the point of view uncovered in such instances is at one remove from the work itself, designating what would less obliquely be termed the author's philsophical or ideological position; it is not a *structural* feature of the work itself. The point of view in drama, in other words, seems either to reduce to the points of view of a number of individual (and independent) characters—or to reach outside the work altogether, representing the author rather than the structure.

I mean to suggest, however, that this account, which serves as a general rule, does not hold for *King Lear*. Perhaps the one exception to that rule which is systematically possible occurs there—namely, that the actions of the individual characters unfold *as if* conceived or projected by only one of them, whose own role or character we then come to know by inference from the forms of the other characters. A fruitful means of following the development of plot in *King Lear* is, in fact, by construing the events which take place as if they had been first construed or seen by Lear himself—from *his* point of view. Lear's projective consciousness, moreover, is not itself constant; the changes in his point of view, as they reflect the development of events, conclude in a radical transposition of consciousness, from consciousness which addresses the prospect of death first with the detachment of a spectator to consciousness for which the imminence of that event is immediately present. This transposition, with its ingredient recognition, portends tragedy, not from its reflections *about* a series of actions, but because it *is* a series of actions—a sequence, made visible through the character of Lear, of action and of recognition. The sequence itself is not literally asserted by the statements or events in the play: those are discursive, isolated. But if we ask how the individual statements or events *become* intelligible as parts of a unity, what supports the individual and sparer lines of visible dramatic episode, what those lines *stand for*, we come (as I hope to show) to the representation of a dying Lear, or more concisely, of Lear-dying: it is on the basis of this inferred reference that I speak of the dramatic action in *King Lear* as a collective or mass metaphor— and I mean by that claim precisely this, that the play as a whole should be seen as a single, extended but nonetheless cohesive, metaphor. Even in a much slighter metaphor—the statement, for example, that "he is a lion"—the metaphor and its reference comprise a complex structure: a number of steps are required to understand why a person (and moreover that *particular* person) should be compared to a lion. And unless we do that, the statement itself is not intelligible. The number of steps required in following the development of *King Lear* is obviously much larger than for the other, but the formal process (and justification) is the same. That the drama *King Lear* may be seen as acted rather than read also makes little difference in this reckoning. It is, after all, the representational status of a literary work that opens it, ever, to the possibility and varieties of the literary figure; the fact that *King Lear* may be acted on a stage makes no more difference to its role as metaphor than does the fact that if (as I claim) it is a metaphor, it is a very large metaphor indeed.

Among the elements so far named (and reversing their order of exposition hitherto), the least problematic—because it is the one closest to the literal surface of the text—is what has been referred to as the transposition in Lear's consciousness. The beginnings of that transposition are disclosed in the opening scene, in particular with respect to the question not of why Lear *does* what he does there, but (a prior question) of what it is that he *thinks* he is doing. Two reasons are given by Lear himself as comprising the "darker purpose" behind the division of his kingdom. The first of these, as Lear describes it, is

> . . . our fast intent
> To shake all cares and business from our age,
> Conferring them on younger strengths, while we
> Unburthened crawl toward death.

It is Lear, then, who introduces death as a motif—and he does this in almost the first words that he speaks. There is no reason for us to doubt the literal importance of that motif (which is far from saying that its *only* importance is literal); and as we find it linked to the final "event" in the play which *is* in fact Lear's death, we have a prima facie basis for regarding those two markers as defining a field of action. (There is, of course, more evidence for the claim of this field of action than only those markers.)

That is not to say that the Lear of the opening scene is ready to die. Quite the contrary: we find him clinging to life, planning to dominate death if not expecting quite to escape it. This comes out explicitly in the second reason provided by Lear—his desire to see his kingdom divided while he is alive rather than to trust that it will be done after his death:

> We have this hour a constant will to publish
> Our daughters' several dowers, that future strife
> May be prevented now.

The "future strife" was in fact precipitated, not prevented, by Lear's action. But what is more immediately pertinent is the condition which his purpose would have required in order to be realized: namely, that Lear should retain, *after* the division, the authority he had when he first made it—and even beyond that, by some totemic magic, that the same measure of authority should endure after he was dead.

The two reasons of Lear's "darker purpose" thus converge on a common point—reflecting both a consciousness, however abstract, of death, and the desire to anticipate or control it. The latter impulse, or *some* such ulterior motive, seems to have determined the manner in which the division itself was made; for it is clear from Scene 1—hardly less so to the participants than to the reader—that Lear's demand of his daughters that they view for their portions by expressions of love is a charade, designed for some other end than that of competition. In the opening lines of the scene, both Kent and Gloucester are shown to be aware, before the sisters speak, that equal portions of Lear's kingdom have been allotted to Goneril and Regan. It is not quite clear from this opening conversation that Cordelia's portion is already known to be larger or more valuable than the portions of her sisters (although there is the strong suggestion that this is the case in Lear's challenge to Cordelia, which comes after her sisters have spoken but before she has:

> . . . What can you say to draw
> A third more opulent than your sisters?)

But what *is* clear here is that if the portions of Regan and Goneril have been settled before they are asked to speak, then Cordelia's portion, *whatever* its size, must have been fixed as well. Why then the charade? And more urgently, why Lear's violent reaction when what is (after all) a charade is disrupted by Cordelia's refusal to "play"?

Undoubtedly there is force in the explanation of that reaction which cites Lear's sensitivity about the king's authority; it is a fact, after all, that the charade publicly misfires. But we have also to consider the question of why the charade was initiated by Lear at all—as well as the question of why, even allowing for his sensitivity, Lear's reaction to Cordelia's words is so notably out of proportion to the words themselves, sufficiently so to be remarked on in those terms by a number of the principal characters, including Regan and Goneril, who stood only to gain by them. That overreaction is the principal element in the discontinuity noted by the otherwise various accounts that have been cited, and it cannot, I have argued, simply be explained away. It is real—as much and as brute a "fact" in the play as any other; as the alternatives arrange themselves, the disproportion must either be accounted a technical failure of Shakespeare's or assigned some nonliteral significance—and not the former until the possibilities for the latter are foreclosed.

I have already indicated the figure by which I would represent this nonliteral significance: the initiation of a metaphor which, in order to call attention both to itself and to the structure of which it is part, deliberately breaks the continuities that would be expected (and required) in a literal plane of action—the specific metaphoric content being the process of Lear-dying. Given the metaphoric framework, Lear's actions in organizing the charade and in his terrible reaction when it goes astray become intelligible. If the motif of the metaphor (what I. A. Richards calls the "tenor") is Lear-dying, then the charade of public expressions of love is understandable as an element or device in the staging of Lear's resistance—a means of giving body to his intention to dominate death. The charade would thus have been designed as part of a larger "scenario." Lear's reaction to Cordelia's words, at a literal level, is disproportionate; but it is not at all disproportionate if we understand it representationally, as a first and glimmering recognition that the fact of mortality may resist the authority even of a king; that mortality is not, as is virtually everything else in Lear's kingdom, subject to his pleasure; that eventually he must find himself located within that fact rather than outside it.

This pattern, furthermore, initiated with the acknowledgement of metaphoric structure as it shapes the opening scene, is sustained in the process of the "transposition" of Lear's consciousness: from an initial view in which Lear sees himself enacting a role, performing in another play which he himself has contrived—to its eventual and quite radical revision, initiated with Cordelia's refusal to play, where Lear's impersonal view of his dying "role" becomes a subjective and first-person consciousness for which death's full impotence, the inability in it to retrieve or to maintain anything of life, is unmistakable. Tolstoy's "Death of Ivan Ilyitch" suggests a like transposition: Ivan Ilyitch, facing the prospect of death, recalls the syllogism from his schoolboy logic in which he learned, as about creatures of another species, that "Caius is a man, men are mortal, therefore Caius is mortal." It takes three days of screaming for the dying Ivan Ilyitch to recognize that the premises of an impersonal syllogism may apply to persons, even to himself—and so, I am suggesting, with some screams of his own, the passage from consciousness of other to consciousness of self for Lear.

IV

This representational reading of a discursive or presentational theme which thus acquires the force of metaphor is supported by numerous lines of textual evidence; I deal here with only two of those lines, both of them initiated in the opening scene. The first of these concerns what might be called a "motif of vision"; the second focuses on the motif alluded to in my title—the several formulations in the play of the phrase that "nothing comes of nothing."

With respect to the former motif: it has often been remarked that as Lear in the course of the play comes to know (or see) what he did not at its beginning, that change in him is paralleled by a number of references, cumulative in their force, to vision and its organs. The subplot of *King Lear* in which Gloucester is blinded after having failed to see through Edmund's wiles, and is then led to Dover by his other son, Edgar, whom he does not recognize, is the most striking sequence of these references; as that subplot does as a unity, the other, independent references also indicate points in Lear's passage from blindness to vision. In its implication for the transposition of consciousness, the process moves from Lear physically capable of sight but actually blind as he *observes* himself—even his death—to Lear failing physically, but seeing now from the inside out. "Take my eyes," Lear says to Gloucester when, still affected by his "madness," he recognizes his blinded supporter; he has, in fact, identified Gloucester earlier (and himself as well), when he first hears Gloucester's complaints about his blindness: "What, art mad? A man may see how this world goes with no eyes."

Both the motif and the idiom of vision are set in motion in the opening scene of the play. "Dearer than eyesight" Goneril professes to hold her father, who has sought and then accepts the public pretension; "hence and avoid my sight," Lear banishes Cordelia upon her refusal to join the pretense, and then also Kent, with like words: "Out of my sight"—the two figures who, together with Gloucester, are closest to him and whom he sees again much later (in the breach of these first orders) when he has finally, and at cost, learned to see. "See better, Lear," Kent warns in these opening moments, as he risks Lear's wrath; but Lear, ignoring Cordelia's rebuke of the "still-soliciting" eyes of her sisters, gives Cordelia to France and banishes her: "nor shall ever see/that face of hers again."

The same tension between physical and moral vision recurs in later scenes—first (in Act 1 Scene 4) as Lear reacts to Goneril's indifference to his authority:

> Does any here know me? This is not Lear.
> Does Lear walk thus? Speak thus? Where are his eyes?

Again, the Fool, driving home a lesson that Lear himself now begins to acknowledge, lectures Lear on the use of a nose "i' th' middle on's face": ". . .to keep one's eyes of either side's nose, that what a man cannot smell out, he may spy into." "I did her wrong," Lear responds, seeing Cordelia in the Fool's words, when it is the thanklessness of Goneril and Regan of which he and the Fool have been speaking.

Such examples might be multiplied; they are too profuse and too pointed, especially in the brutal punishment of Gloucester which the audience is made to see, to be accidentally repetitive. In general terms, the themes that they represent are plain enough: Lear moving from blindness to sight, impelled by pain and its moral implication as those two elements animate virtually all the action of the play that touches him—that is, virtually all the action of the play. This still leaves the question of what Lear's developing sight is sight *of*, and in this connection I have mentioned a link between the transposition of consciousness and the object of that transposition in the dying Lear— namely, Lear-dying. This object of vision is clearly disclosed in the second motif I have referred to—the several occasions on which we hear what (and who) can be made of "nothing."

"Nothing, my lord," Cordelia sounds the theme in her first answer to Lear, who has asked her what she, following her sisters, will say of her love for her father.

Lear Nothing?
Cordelia Nothing.
Lear Nothing will come of nothing. Speak again.

The echo in the Gloucester subplot comes quickly, in Scene 2; Gloucester picks up Edmund's deliberately clumsy concealment of the letter he will claim to have received from Edgar:

Gloucester What paper were you reading?
Edmund Nothing, my lord.
Gloucester . . . The quality of nothing hath no such to conceal itself. Let's see. Come, if it be nothing, I shall not need spectacles.

Again, Lear responds to the Fool's didactic instruction to the bereft Lear on the value of possessions which begins with the line "Have more than thou showest . . ." (1.4):

Lear This is nothing, Fool.
Fool . . . you gave me nothing for't. Can you make no use of nothing, Nuncle?
Lear Why, no, boy. Nothing can be made out of nothing.

In these exchanges, we recognize a sharp, even lordly indifference; Lear and Gloucester, full of themselves, find no personal reference in "nothing"—nothing that could touch or move them. And this view, one might say, is reasonable, given their estates. The lines that spread out from these exchanges, however, as Lear and Gloucester are increasingly affected by the events of the drama, show an altered pattern. The focus of this change, interestingly enough, is on the character of Edgar. "Edgar I nothing am," Edgar proclaims in his disguise as Tom o'Bedlam (3.4)—and we hear next about "nothing" in the decisive moment of Lear's maddened projections of what has happened to him as, removed now from all he had "possessed," he faces the stormy night. Lear, Kent, and the Fool discover Edgar in the hovel they have entered for shelter (3.4), and Lear speaks to Edgar, who has only a blanket for cover:

> Didst thou give all to thy daughters? . . .Couldst thou save nothing? . . .
> *Kent* He hath no daughters, sir.
> *Lear* Death, traitor! Nothing could have subdued nature
> To such a lowness but his unkind daughters.
> *(to Edgar)* . . . Is man no more than this? Consider him well. Thou ow'st the worm no silk, the beast no hide, the sheep no wool, the cat no perfume. . . .Thou art the thing itself; unaccommodated man is no more but such a poor, bare, forked animal as thou art.

Lear then tears off his own clothes.

The reversal intimated in this recognition is evident; certainly it is clear that the past indifference to "nothing" has vanished—and this change, of course, affects Lear's sense of what it is that "nothing" is to be contrasted with. In the scene prior to the last one noticed (that is, in 3.3), Lear has already expanded the egocentric focus of a kingly world to find sympathy for the Fool who, alone of the king's court, has followed him. For the first time in the play, Lear conceives of the feelings, as of a self, of someone other than himself. The "nothing" that had before this begun at whatever point he himself ended now takes on life—just when mortality (and nothing) begin to catch hold of him.

> O, I have ta'en
> Too little care of this. Take physic, pomp;
> Expose thy self to feel what wretches feel,
> That thou mayst shake the superflux to them.

As king, Lear had seen himself as he would have had others see him: regal, authoritative, cloaked with power. But this figure, he recognizes as he has been driven by circumstance to live in his own skin, was not "the thing itself" to which he now pledges allegiance. "Nothing" has become a possibility—sufficiently so that the spectator's or

third-person "I" by which he had earlier defined himself has now
been transformed to that of a subject. And for *that* subject, even the
scanty accommodation of his clothing is "superflux."

I have suggested that these motifs, and indeed all the action or
events in the plot of *King Lear*, are fruitfully understood as if they
were moments in Lear's consciousness, projected on a large screen by
Lear dying—in effect, that there *is* a point of view working in the play
and that the point of view is Lear's. The transposition of consciousness—from blindness to sight, from all to nothing—is in other words
not only ascribed to Lear, not something that happens to him—but a
sequence we watch through his own eyes. This is to say more than
only that Lear is the dominant character in the play—although surely
it is relevant that by contrast the other characters in the play are flat
and restricted as initiators of action. Certainly the latter description is
true of Cordelia and her two sisters, of the Fool, Albany, Cornwall,
and Kent. Edmund and Edgar loom larger, but not enough to make a
difference (is it not a surprise, after all, to find that the subtitle of the
play is "With the Unfortunate Life of Edgar, Sonne and Heire to the
Erle of Gloster"?); and Gloucester, for whom alone a claim might be
made, is quite deliberately expended as a foil to Lear's own history
and fall. No other of Shakespeare's heroes stands so far out of the
reach of dramatic context; this too lends itself to the suggestion that
we see him, Lear, as the artificer of the context itself.

If we ask, in connection with *King Lear*, furthermore, about that
mysterious process of identification, that joining between an audience
and the *dramatis personae*, it seems clear both that there is no alternative to Lear as the object of such identification and also that Lear
invites, virtually requires, this response. It is a matter of dramatic fact
that something of Lear himself is invested in each of the actions which
occur in the entire course of the play: the causal connections are
seamless. Whatever happens in the play happens to Lear; so far as
what happens matters to the audience, it matters to them *because* it
happens to him.

It is this quality which I have intended in referring the events of
the play to a source in Lear's consciousness. That claim may seem
exaggerated; Lear is not even constantly present on stage, after all,
and events occur in his absence of which he does not, then or ever,
have knowledge (for example, the clash between Cornwall and Albany, Edgar's trip to Dover with Gloucester). The moments when he
is on stage, however, are plainly his; more than this, even when he is
not on stage, if we try to understand how it is that what takes place
occurs, the other sense of consistency persists: the whole *does* fit
together—on the assumption that its elements are being formulated

or conjured by the character whom we have come to know as Lear. Lear's world initially is overtly egocentric: he sees all of his own actions, and no less certainly those of everybody else, as they affect him. And that literal egocentricity has another, less literal, counterpart insofar as all the events that occur are either appropriated by him directly or are ingredient in some later reaction of his. In the so-called mad scenes ("so-called" because the representations of madness, like the punishments assigned in Dante's Inferno, quite lucidly represent both Lear's persona and the subsequent development of dramatic structure that reflects the persona), Lear has license openly to shape all discourse to the image of his own feeling. But this turns out to be true in his other appearances as well. In the few speeches in which he does not overtly focus the discourse on himself and his relation to the events that occur ("I," "my," "us," "our" are the almost invariable subjects of his statements), his references to other persons or events have the feel of projection, of an interest which only apparently is divested of the self. (It is the contrast with this general manner of speaking that makes the exceptional statement in his prayer cited before, "Expose thyself to feel what wretches feel," so noticeable.) This egocentricity persists even to his last lines—where Lear, mourning Cordelia, still places her in respect to himself: "Thou'lt *come* no more" (emphasis added).

The gradual modulation in this emphasis is directly related to the transposition of consciousness; it serves also as the mechanism for identification between Lear and his audience. As Lear turns from spectator of himself as regent to the much diminished subjective— and mortal—consciousness, the *spectator* of that turn unavoidably rehearses the same contraction. Can he tell (and does it matter) whose turn it is, Lear's or his? Beginning as spectator, he might, unlike Lear, also end as spectator—*unless*, as seems inevitable, the emergence of subjectivity for Lear shapes an affirmation on the part of the spectator as well. As Lear projects the events which occur in the play, so the spectator recognizes Lear himself as a projection; Lear cannot, any more than the rest of us, create himself—and that leaves only the spectator, with a new and uncertain responsibility. It is not often that he will have found himself to be part of a metaphor.

V

Now it might be objected that even if the several and cumulative levels in this account of *King Lear* were granted, there is still slight warrant for representing them as what has been interpreted here as Lear's confabulations, the result of his projection. Why make claim

for more than the figure of an egocentric king (the egocentricity perhaps part of his being king) who suffers the consequences of his own
faults, as others act on them, until those consequences conclude with
his death? Stated in this way, there is no need to think of them as
projected by the consciousness of the king himself; they might, after
all, have occurred—even to him—quite independently of that (or
any) consciousness. But I have not been suggesting that these events
do not *really* occur (as really, at any rate, as do the events of any
dramatic fiction), only that they occur always for or about Lear; and
that finally, as we recognize the difference they make *in* Lear, we best
understand that grasp (on the reader as well) as asserted, even
created, by Lear himself. We see not only what happens *to* Lear—we
see what is happening always *through* Lear. That joining of vision also
effects a joining of destiny: the reader or viewer *and* the character
now being engaged by a single process. We may perhaps explain this
end (as represented, for example, in Samuel Johnson's share of *real*
pain) by means other than the dominance of a single point of view,
namely Lear's. But that conception, at least, provides one such
means—and one which, less obliquely than do the usual alternatives,
locates a means for the reader's own entry into the plot.

A final question may be directed to the formal part of my interpretation: what need, it might be asked, even if one grants the other
interpretive commitments, to impose on *King Lear* the notion of
metaphoric structure—whether of Lear-dying or anything else? My
reasoning here, it will be recalled, set out from the nearly literal
phenomenon of improbability: the way in which the disjointed events
of the opening scene seemed, by referring to themselves, to define a
literary figure. To take that phenomenon seriously (if not literally)
seems inevitably to admit the presence of *some* literary figure, for
which discontinuity or improbability is both structurally integral and
an indicator of presence. I have not claimed, in referring to this figure
as metaphor, that no alternative figure would do; the alternatives, and
the vagaries of defining them, are too diverse even to allow an exhaus-
tive enumeration. But the fact remains that certain of those possibilities exclude themselves; allegory, for example, with the requirement (that *King Lear* obviously does not meet) of an isomorphic
parallel. The requirements for metaphor are more readily granted:
that the presence of *some* figure be indicated; that likeness and unlikeness be joined in the figure (the common "tenor" thus being implied); that the metaphoric reference have an artistic life (even if, as I
have claimed in this case, it is death which takes on that life). Finally,
to be sure, the proof of metaphoric reference is not in the eye of the
beholder but in the seeing itself—and as assurance of this one may

cite parallels, but surely no proofs. To speak of somebody as a lion suggests power and ferocity in the person because those properties are preeminent in the lion; to speak of *King Lear* as a metaphor for Lear-dying suggests that Lear-dying is what is apparent in the play as we first distinguish and then reassemble the many literal strands— the *fact* of improbability, first, which suggests the presence of the literary figure, and then the conglomerate of individual actions and statements which converge on the metaphoric point.

What thus emerges is a network of interlocking levels of critical interpretation which, originating with literal and hard facts, concludes with the abstraction of metaphor; and it may fairly be asked whether the flame is worth the candle. The reader, of course, will make his own judgment on this, but it may be well for him to have the elements of the structure reformulated in terms of their logical— rather than their apparent—connections. The first such element I have referred to is the transposition of consciousness in Lear. That change is literally described or presented in the play; little is needed even in the way of inference, to bring out the sequence. The transposition finds Lear turned from an observer of himself, even of his own impending death, into a participant—in effect a consciousness coming alive. This presents to the viewer of the play a similar project; for he, too, sets out to observe (literally) a play. So far as the process of identification, of feeling for oneself what is represented in others, is here a possibility at all, it can only settle on the process by which somebody else (Lear) turns from spectator to agent. Why, in comparison with all the deaths of other tragic drama, does Cordelia's seem especially cruel, and Lear's own death (made necessary by the other) so gratuitous and thus murderous? Not because of the fact of death in *King Lear* or because of the numbers which death claims there either—since on these grounds *King Lear* is quite unexceptional. Nor is it, given the integrity of the play, a matter of disproportion—of "overkill." The fact is that somehow—and I hope to have explained the "how"—the distance between reader and character has been so far diminished as to make the last events which take place almost (and for some readers, actually) unbearable. Between the audience outside the play and Lear within it, there is no distance at all; what in the reading of other literary works suggests a defect in or for the reader, an overt literalness or sentimentality of vision, testifies here rather to the power of the work. Lear's projects become the reader's own—and Lear himself one of them.

It is undoubtedly true of all tragedy, and indeed of all art, that in them certain measures of identification between audience and representation are effected. But that identification often (and often deliberately) is linked to an impersonal object or force. We might speak here of a "space of inference" between the viewer and the work—a space which the viewer selectively crosses as he appropriates to himself elements or characters of the drama. In Greek tragedy, that space is relatively wide; the centers of the tragedy are in the collectivity of actions and in the impersonal forces which determine them. In the transposition of consciousness which we follow in *King Lear*, the space of inference between the viewer and the character viewed comes close to the line of identity—or over that line for readers like Dr. Johnson. This is not death which we as an audience are to observe from the outside, as we do for the Greek tragedies and even for the other tragedies of Shakespeare—but death as it is experienced: dying Lear looking out on a dying world. When Donne writes that "any man's death diminishes me," he speaks, naturally enough, for the survivors: those affected by the death of others, but who even with that paring away still endure. In *King Lear* we see—*we* see, as well as Lear—that for the person dying, the other inhabitants of his world are not only diminished but dying also. Cordelia, we come to recognize, *has* to die if, as I have been claiming, it is through *Lear's* eyes, first alive, assertive, and then, later, dying, that we see her whom he "loved most." The reader thus follows Lear's consciousness as it moves inward from a view of Lear as a character in the earthly drama, a performance which he himself directs, to a view in which all that is left of the character is his consciousness—and a dying one at that.

Some writers, grasping at straws—for themselves now as much as for Lear—have suggested that *King Lear* concludes affirmatively, with a promise or implication of redemption. But it takes more than only the fact that the *audience* survives the ending of the play to warrant a conclusion that *that* is what the ending is intended to represent. (What play, after all, would be without this?) And so, as he follows the lines of the metaphor back to that view, the reader's view also is of a constant reduction, a paring away—until nothing is left. Let Edgar entice the reader, as he does Gloucester, with the prospect that "ripeness is all"; one has first to be alive to savor it. Lear, finally, is dead; everything has been taken away from him—and that leaves nothing, nothing-of-all. The reader, too, sharing Lear's portion, also knows better—if not quite so well as Lear himself. Better and bitterly.

Note

1. See, for example, W. K. Wimsatt and C. Brooks, *Literary Criticism: A Short History* (New York: A. A. Knopf, 1957), p. 750.

9

The Compleat Solipsist

It is no accident that description of art's effects often employ metaphors drawn from the idiom of physics. Not every encounter (or every audience) matches Emily Dickinson's intensity when she felt the top half of her head blown off by a good poem; but more conventional impressions may also be "compelled" or "struck" by the "force" of art. Like most apt metaphors, these do not originate or end with mere likenesses; they describe *literally* what sometimes happens. More than for almost any contemporary writer, they measure in a literal sense the work of Jorge Luis Borges. The reason for this, I think, can be made evident; it says something about the art of Borges and something about art itself.

A source for the impact of Borges's stories might first be sought among their formal qualities—for example, in their unusual economy. With the conciseness of nature in muscle compressed, his themes, even his individual sentences, wait; his reader, wandering the lazy pampas of the Argentine or a pagan kingdom millennia past, trips a release—and the here-and-now strikes. A kaleidoscope of experience and the sweep of a baroque imagination have shaped the stories. Master of Geography and History: so one might appoint Borges in school. And yet, of course, the expanse invariably converges on a point. Few writers have so equably governed the distributions of the concrete universal, of unity-in-diversity, simplicity-in-complexity.

Still, one might respond, such a manner has been affected elsewhere, by very different writers working with various idioms. Certainly the short story as a genre has bargained for economy almost more than for any other quality. So Isaac Babel, for instance, in his story with another master for a title—"Guy de Maupassant"—hints at the order of the craft as he writes of style, "of the army of words . . . in which all kinds of weapons may come into play. No iron can stab the heart with such force as a period put just at the right place." And Babel's reader finds that justice exhibited as described.

But spectacular as it is, and more fully sustained by the movements of its characters, Babel's writing does not have the stunning effect that Borges's does; and that is to say something more than that two original and scrupulous authors have not written the same stories. What is distinctive about Borges's stories—I refer especially to the early ones—appears rather in their substance and in particular in the theme of solipsism to which Borges constantly returns, inviting the reader to conceive the nonexistence of the very world from which the conception itself emerges.

This attentiveness of Borges is unusually refined. The many stories which repeat the theme do not argue the flat assertion that the selves which appear there (by indirection, the self of the reader) are alone actual in a world of detailed fictions—but only that such a solipsistic account of experience *may* hold. In restricting his claim to that of a possibility, Borges is consistent where would-be solipsists often fail—and not only with the amiable naiveté of Bertrand Russell's correspondent who complained that she was a solipsist and was disappointed that she could find so few people who agreed with her. Solipsism cannot afford to claim reality for its expositor or his world, since to do so suggests a basis beyond the self from which the actuality of the solipsist and the illusion of other existence could be measured. It is a quality of his subtlety that Borges insists only that solipsism is *possible;* the reader is asked to realize that although proof may be wanting that the world experienced is "in fact" an appearance of solipsism, this is a feature of solipsism itself: there is no way of knowing whether it is or is not. The force of a more naive solipsism comes from the uncertainty it introduces into a well-furnished and stable world; Borges's skepticism goes still further. In admitting ignorance, by stopping short, he offers uncertainty about the uncertainty—and leaves to those who would deny it only the same option.

This intimation is given, for example, in two stories in the collection *Ficciónes*—"The Circular Ruins" and "The Babylonian Lottery." In the former, a man sets himself the task of dreaming into the world a "real" being. After many failures and by subjecting himself to severe discipline, the dreamer succeeds: he dreams a man into life. As a "father," he teaches his son certain mysteries to help him on his way, blots out the memories of this education, and then sends him off. From time to time, the father hears news of his son; his fear is only that the son may discover that he is a phantom. These misgivings end abruptly. The temple where the dreamer has lived begins to burn; sensing that this is his time to die, the old man walks toward the flames—and through them. "With relief, with humiliation, with terror he understood that he also was an illusion, that someone else was dreaming him."

The narrator of "The Babylonian Lottery" traces the history of the society and institutions of a remote Babylon. That history originates in the description of a lottery, played voluntarily as a game of chance, and for small prizes. Presented to the public in these terms, the lottery arouses little interest; its organizers think to change this by interspersing a number of adverse chances—fines—among the prizes. The appeal of the lottery widens. The losers resist paying their fines, and the company administering the game offers them the alternative punishment of jail. Later, because no one chooses to pay the fine, the option is removed; losers go directly to jail. Interest in the lottery becomes more intense, and the price of the tickets is raised. The poor, resenting this disenfranchisement, rebel and overthrow the administrators; not only is the lottery to be free, but everyone will be automatically enrolled. The new company running the lottery gives the player to understand that the fates which the lottery dispenses are not, as they appear, the result of chance, but are fixed by a magical source which gives each man his due. And so on and on, until the reader discovers that metamorphoses in the lottery are responsible for each aspect of a complete society. Its judicial and penal systems, its religious beliefs, its economic divisions, even the commonplace events of every day—each is accounted for by turns in the history of the lottery.

The two stories thus converge on a common theme: that an account of the matter-of-fact world can be given which is quite plausible but not matter-of-fact at all. The evident order of that world may be the chance convergence of an indefinite randomness; its adhesive surface may cover the permeable fabric of a dream. These are live possibilities; and nothing in the world (which is, after all, as much as the reader can supply) does less than attest to them. One cannot know that one is not dreaming if one concedes the possibility that all appearances are parts of a dream; any particular semblance of order *may* be actually random if any possible order can be explained as the result of chance.

Borges's representations of this prospect are brilliant in contrivance; the same conception worked by lesser hands might amount to little more than a literary *trompe-l'oeil*. But there is also an element in the theme itself which subsidizes the metaphors of force in a reader's encounter with it. The stunning effect of the stories proposes a confrontation between solipsism, on the one hand, and an opposing movement impelled by art as art on the other. The ensuing collision between substance and form catches the reader between them; innocent or not as he stands there, he finds quickly that there is no escape.

The problem of identifying the agents in this collision (the victim we know more immediately) is linked to the question of what in art ever accounts for the force it exerts on its audience. The answers which have been given to that question are in surprisingly short supply—"surprisingly" because of the sheer mass of writing about art. Aristotle, for example, suggests that man's response is a facet of his more basic—the *most* basic—impulse to know; at the other extreme, in the formalist tradition, the response is sensuous only: it reflects a special aesthetic sensibility, perhaps, or a combination of ordinary senses. One thesis recurs in the diverging lines of these theories, whatever their disagreements: that art gives an innovative turn to experience. Either by providing a sum for the integers of the viewer's past or by opening to him a new moment in which that past is reconstructed, art leads him beyond himself. The quality of that expansion is construed differently in the several accounts; in each case, however, the process engendered by art is held to confirm in the audience a moment which had not previously signified, to replace with a consummation what had otherwise remained diffuse and remote.

It might be argued that some such condition could be ascribed to any moment of experience. But there is a distinctively personal character in art's moment: it impresses itself not as the abstract consciousness of the botanist uncovering the detail of a species, or the immediate sensation of a cool breeze on a warm day. As the artist is himself exemplified in his work, the argument goes, so the viewer finds himself exemplified—in sense or in recognition—as he faces it. Whatever in the work is said to appeal—knowledge or sensation—makes a difference to the grounds earlier laid down in the self as it responds. On any of these possibilities, art confirms as *real* (for better or worse) what the viewer has been; it thus opens for him a new and assertive present.

Other explanations of art's proximity or adhesive power have been given. But the recurrence of this one is persistent; and however else it serves, the peculiar force of Borges's writing is explicable through it. On the one hand, his writing, as art, offers the reader a confirmation of experience: it consummates for him what is otherwise diffuse in the present and merely prospective in the future. But at the same time—and here the opposing forces meet head-on—the theme of solipsism reveals the glitter of this exterior as tinsel: it argues on *its* side that what seems most real in the offer made by the stories, and in the "facts" which nourish them, is not. A gift is extended of the coherence of experience; as the stories are successful, the reader willingly accepts. But the substance of that consummation—the theme of solipsism—reveals that what has been offered, even the offer itself, amounts to no more than the substance of an illusion. The elements of experience being collected and articulated are at the same time dissociated and questioned, more radically than they had been in their prior appearance outside of art. We know from the process of Borges's stories that we do not have access even to that process. To acknowledge the possibility of the dream is to acknowledge the possibility as dream. And to conceive the order of history as chance is to chance the order of the conception itself.

The stories both present and represent: they present an organization or affirmation of the experiences which converge in them as they also represent the contradictory—a world-fiction. The synthesis is not abstract; as much as the reader, opening himself to the work, adds to himself by it, that much and more is brought into question. In the way of art, the burden remains no mere cumbrance on the work. Not only does the reader find no new affirmation of what he had been or done; he is asked to sacrifice what he had initially brought. His own starting point becomes a true point—infinitesimal in dimension.

Admittedly, the quality of this reversal is not peculiar to Borges's work. It marks much of that large body of literature which wanders back and forth over the line between illusion and reality—*Don Quixote*, for example, or *Notes from the Underground*. But many of these writings, by the richness of their detail and the variety of their narrative, bequeath to the reader something more than the skeleton uncovered in Borges's short stories. The profusion of the novel or of the novella is reassuring in its presence; such fictions seem finally to engender worlds which are real, if only in their own expanse. The economy of Borges's stories, on the other hand, leaves nothing over; one speaks of them metaphorically as breathtaking because, literally, they threaten to take it away.

10
The Politics and Art of Decency

"Good prose is like a window pane."

George Orwell

There is wisdom as well as foolishness in the moods of fashion, and both qualities have affected the critical estimates of George Orwell's work. His novels, it seems now, have found their place. The best known of them, *1984* and *Animal Farm* (something *like* a novel), are period pieces; intended didactically, they would challenge only until their lessons had been memorized—and it requires both energy and malice to forget today that social action moved by the promise of human perfectibility often succeeds in swallowing itself perfectly whole; that "communist" Russia is not (and never was) so communal after all, and that the conciseness of technological advance provides a ready vehicle for totalitarianism. Well before 1984, that novel of Orwell's threw a shadow almost as mannered as Edward Bellamy's *Looking Backward*, which conceived an improbably benign and later year 2000. The future has been moving too quickly into the present for the most radical science fiction to surprise the contemporary reader as science *or* fiction. What is startling about even an apocalyptic prediction, the contemporary reader might ask, if the one article of faith available to him asserts that everything is possible?

At least in parts, the four earlier novels—*Burmese Days, A Clergyman's Daughter, Coming Up for Air,* and *Keep the Aspidistra Flying*—deserve better than the critics have given them, but not so much better as to make an effective difference. Portraits of the artist as he becomes one, they include skeptical, occasionally lavish scenes of life in Burma, where Orwell served for five years in the colonial police, and of the class-conscious, still imperial England to which he returned after quitting that job in disgust, with few possessions or expectations other than the decision that he would be a writer. In these novels, too, a barely disguised literal assertiveness obtrudes. Orwell could not, it seems, just conceive a fictional character, and

207

display it in motion; he had also to see through it, to find for it a place among the moral ambivalences which a hyperactive sensibility revealed to him even in the mechanics of everyday commonplace. He was not, he confessed, in a letter to his friend Julian Symons, "a real novelist anyway." Disinterested, often harsh when judging his own work (at least one of the early novels, he later commented, should never have been published), he could not, would not, in writing them, leave himself and the claims of conscience out.

The argument for Orwell's stature as a writer soon turns, then, to his nonfiction—although there, again, fashion has worked to pass him by. Subtlety is the rage, and things (how *were* those Victorian philosophers Gilbert and Sullivan so canny about the dawning self-consciousness?) are "seldom what they seem." To understand the designs of a Novelist or a Politician or a General, one must have uncovered the psychological substructure; to assess the lines of social movement, political reaction, or artistic innovation, the logic of world history must have been settled beforehand. In the terms of such analysis, what is revealed by appearance as obvious or evident becomes impertinence. And to Orwell, the light of indirection was hardly to be preferred to darkness; he would cite many examples of how the one serves as well as the other to cloak ideology and self-interest. A more honest day's work would be to find—and to leave—things alone; and the instrument with which Orwell set out to accomplish this in his nonfiction was an immoderate eye for fact: for what could be *seen* in the Spanish Civil War, as opposed to what partisans of the time said was occurring there; for what it was *to be* down and out in Paris and London, in the industrial and mining town of Wigan, or in a boys' preparatory school—in their differences from what the society responsible for these institutional arrangements would have the public find in them.

The reverence for fact, however, itself suggests congruent defects of quality. *Homage to Catalonia* is a generous, the least impeachable, first-hand account of the Spanish Civil War. The faces encountered in Orwell's reports from a Lancashire mine or from his walks along the Thames Embankment settle permanently in the viewer's resolve. But the discourse of photographs is fixed in the flat lines of historical context. It no longer offers even the promise of tragic "pity and fear" to hear that Russia, anticipating a social revolution which it could not control, subverted the Spanish Republican government; or that the prosperity of the upper classes in Europe's "liberal" civilization had been paid for with deprivation for others. The claims may bear retelling—but hardly as fact or news.

Yet the impression persists, beyond such limitations, that Orwell is an important writer, an unusually resourceful craftsman of language and representation. What remains to support that impression, if we continue the recital of his work, will be found in his "smaller writings"—the four volumes of items of so many different kinds and qualities: book reviews, personal letters, letters to the editor, letters to *his* editors, and so on.[1] And in fact, a number of essays appear among these leavings which generously support the impression of a remarkable power. Those essays are as perfect as any written in this century: the principle of moral action which animates them is no less resonant than in the most compelling essays of Lawrence; their intuition of the movement of the writer's persona, as keen as that in Borges. A number of the essays are formally quite conventional. Even those, however, reflect certain of the innovations in others which mark off virtually a new genre—a revision of the neat structural closures of the conventional essay into the looser but more adhesive representations of fictional prose; they effect, in the end, an original conjunction of literary means. In accomplishing this, they also join what will be seen as disparate elements of Orwell's character as a writer—and it is important, then, both for Orwell's work and aside from it, that we should understand how these conjunctions are made.

One structural feature in particular separates the form of Orwell's essays from that of the essay which has been a characteristic presence in English literature of the last three centuries: the role of the author in the animation or action of the work. The claim of a possible variety in that role is not meant to suggest that for the work on one side of the distinction the author's presence is evident, on the other, not: even the most impersonal writing will include *that* much of the design at its source. But the figure of the author may strike various postures within the circumference of a plot, and significant differences in this respect mark Orwell's writing. Typically, in the essay's traditional form—for varied examples, in Samuel Johnson, in William Hazlitt, or Virginia Woolf—the reader quickly recognizes that the "I" who speaks from the essay is meant to be literally identified with the author. The state of affairs reconstructed in the writing, furthermore, has been previously determined by him and framed with a conclusion to which the reconstruction points: an experience leaves an impression, the work of another writer strikes a chord, past abstractions call for (or against) elaboration. The "I" of the essayist appears in the telling of such occasions as it would in a conversational report of historical or speculative event: the author, to one side—*himself* a fact—recounting a largesse of appearance located on the other side: the objects of his experience. The division between the writer and what he writes about is made plain as he segregates his data in two groups: a factual base—places, events, quotations; and the author's response—inferences, metaphors, judgments. The reader is invited to join the writer in viewing the factual base, and then to match responses with him.

In the most distinctive of Orwell's essays (I refer here for examples to "Shooting an Elephant" and "A Hanging"), the role of the author is notably different. His presence in the movement of the essays is evident; it is clear, moreover, that the details of his descriptions, even of his own part in them, are recounted as historical events. But the retelling also incorporates an unusual feature of reflexivity. The "I," the omnipresent figure of the author who traditionally moves at will within the essay, appears here not as master in that house, but as one of its occupants. The perception which discerned the events that are told lingers not as memory or theory, but in a virtual and constant present. The essayist addresses his audience less as a second observer of a scene laid open by his own sharper eye than as a participant in the scene. The author is a *persona dramatis*—part of that *persona*, of course, being a writer. Like any member of the cast, the viewpoint he opens to the reader is limited and determined within the work—one among the others. The reader thus gains access not to an independent world, not even to the author's settled habit or reflection of mind. He is admitted to a collective, still articulate process of the essay itself, a process initiated by particular objects or events which only later, through a transaction between reader and author, become a whole. The essayist, reflexively, appears as a character in the essay.

So, for example, Orwell relates an incident in "Shooting an Elephant" that might have been detachedly retold as historical narrative. During his service in Burma, an elephant that belongs to a villager runs amok, first leaving the village, then returning and killing someone in it. The elephant finally wanders out to a nearby field. His owner, who might have calmed him, has set out in the wrong direction; there is no hope that he can be recalled in time to help. Orwell sends for a rifle, intending to use it, he tells the reader, only if the elephant goes on the attack again. But in the meantime the people of the village have gathered, and when the rifle arrives, Orwell faces a spontaneous conspiracy—their expectation of sport, on the one hand (not least of all, the possibility that the elephant would get *him*), and of food, on the other. He shoots the elephant, he writes, knowing that it is unnecessary, knowing the economic loss this means for the owner—having discovered that in the role of master he is yet ruled by his subjects, that he has killed the elephant "only to avoid making a fool of myself."

In "A Hanging," the detail of narrative action is simpler yet. A native is to be hanged in the yard of a regional prison in Burma. Orwell follows the prisoner on the short walk from the condemned cells to the gallows: a dog breaks into the procession and jumps up to lick the prisoner's face; the prisoner sidesteps a puddle to avoid getting wet. The prisoner mounts the platform, chanting a last prayer; the hangman pulls the lever that releases the drop. A few macabre jokes break the tension as the small assembly disperses. Orwell finds himself laughing loudly at the jokes. "The dead man," he closes the essay, "was a hundred yards away."

As it must be for any single object of art, a report on the effectiveness of these short essays inevitably misses their art. How, especially, can a reader recount by the elements of an experience the unusual sense of dramatic integrity which he claims for the whole? But a ground for this response can be remarked in the summaries given. It is more than an accidental feature of their detail that we recognize from the expectation of the crowd, from the prisoner sidestepping a puddle, that the author himself is not freed even with the writing from the events he describes. To be sure, the abrasiveness of the events contributes to this persistence. But the reflexive posture of the author adds a factor of adhesion which the events would not by themselves. The author's "I" asserts only as much in the way of a presence as is defined in the expression of the other "I"s who appear. We hear nothing of obiter dictum or self-justification; no representation of the author acting in the present to resolve the past into abstraction; no hope of a spectator's absolution that detachment from the context, shared between the writer and reader, might bring to each. There is a great equality in the distribution of power among the characters: Orwell, the villagers, the elephant, the prison guards, the prisoner who is hanged, and finally the reader—an equality the absence of which, in these particular essays, was precisely what had set the events they describe and thus the essays themselves in motion. The writer could as well *be* the reader, at least to the extent that any reader of literary fiction discovers piecemeal elements of his identity in that representation. And surely it is just this quality of introjection, of adhesion to the reader's self by fragmentary aspects of the characters who appear before him, that enforces the lure of fiction and distinguishes its accomplishment from the comfortable disinterest evoked by the separation in the traditional essay between the objects written about and whoever is writing (or reading) about them. Orwell the author is constantly and by design also one of the author's objects; the invitation to the reader is no less modestly divided.

Not all of Orwell's essays are so equally drawn around the figure of the author as the two which have been outlined; some of them follow more closely the standard conventions by which author and reader are separated both from each other and from the events reviewed in the writing. But it is rare, even in these, that the reflexive quality by which the author assigns to himself the agency of character and to the reader a proportionately extended invitation does not come out. This is the case, for example, in "Such, Such Were the Joys," where Orwell rehearses memories of his prep school—a part of his life which he was in historical fact reluctant to revive; it is true even of the polemical piece "Benefit of Clergy," in which Orwell attacks artists in general and Salvador Dali in particular for assuming the right to stylistic carte blanche: freedom to say anything at all, so long as it is said well. The former of these essays is retrospective, the latter, more openly didactic—but in them both, the figure of the author is represented in the same terms which bind the other objects of his scrutiny: his judgments about events long past in the life of a schoolboy and about the extra-artistic obligations of the artist are judgments on Orwell himself in the virtual time of the writing. Orwell as author is still the "new" boy wetting his bed until he is beaten out of the habit; Orwell himself expresses the moral spirit of art as he separates his disgust at what Dali says from praise of Dali as a draftsman. The persona of the editorial "I" never fails to speak—but it speaks about Orwell under the same constraints which limit the other objects or characters or events of the narrative. The essayist quite explicitly denies himself the "benefit of clergy."

In this sense, it seems, the same defects that mar Orwell's novels— the conscientious intrusion of the author and the subordination of artistic license to the restrictions of fact—add an unexpected resource to the conventional form of the essay. It is as though the impulses underlying those appearances would always for Orwell distort or strain the medium of the novel; only after a search had they located a passage that would admit both Orwell's bulky grasp of the detail of experience and the moral incentive for the judgment which sustained that grasp. In the essays mentioned, these elements, which would in other forms—as in Orwell's own fiction—violate the even circle of art, redefine that circle through the status assumed by the author as one among the members of the essay's cast. This democratic appearance is too constant a feature to be accidental; elliptically, it recalls the reference of our title to the principle of decency as an item first and more openly of Orwell's politics—second and more fundamentally, of Orwell's art.

The word *decency* itself sounds quaint to the contemporary ear, and it is instructive because of this to note that Orwell returns to it in

moments when the "I" who is a character in his essays is most convincingly Orwell himself. The formal principle of decency is a constant presence in his writing. Thus, explaining his decision to fight in
Spain where he was later severely wounded, he writes: "If you had
asked me why I had joined the militia I should have answered: 'To
fight against fascism,' and if you had asked me what I was fighting *for*,
I should have answered, 'Common decency.'" Ideology itself is subordinate to the principle, he argues in *The Road to Wigan Pier:* "So
far as my experience goes, no genuine working man grasps the deeper
implications of socialism. Often, in my opinion, he is a truer Socialist
than the orthodox Marxist, because he does remember, what the
other so often forgets, that Socialism means justice and common decency." In his essay on Dickens, Orwell's criticism of Dickens as a
social thinker is mitigated by one large qualification:

> His [Dickens's] radicalism is of the vaguest kind, and yet one always
> knows that it is there. That is the difference between being a moralist and
> a politician. He has no constructive suggestions, not even a clear grasp of
> the nature of the society he is attacking, only an emotional perception that
> something is wrong. All he can finally say is, "Behave decently," which
> . . . is not so shallow as it sounds.

And in a letter soon afterwards, to Humphrey House (11 April 1940),
he identifies Dickens's commitment as his own: "The thing that
frightens me about modern intelligentsia is their inability to see that
human society must be based on common decency, whatever the
political and economic forms may be."

In one obvious sense, of course, such judgments do not move very
far. Who, after all, would dispute the claims of decency? Who, before
that, would bother to mention them? In this appeal to something
resembling a moral intuition, furthermore, we undoubtedly hear an
echo of the code of values bred to English upper-class character
which Orwell himself often contested but never escaped. ("Then are
you a gentleman?" asks the manager of the "Spike" at Lower Binfield,
in which Orwell playing the role of tramp was spending the night. "I
suppose so," Orwell replies—reluctantly conceding the inevitable.)

So far as I have been able to find, moreover, Orwell never says
what he means by the principle of decency, or gives reasons for
placing it at the basis of moral, let alone dramatic judgment. There is
other evidence, moreover, that he was quite uninterested in such
questions. ("It is the sort of thing," he writes about a section of Bertrand Russell's book *Human Knowledge*, "that makes me feel that
philosophy should be forbidden by law.") To be sure, the challenges
to decency *in effect* are named and everywhere: hypocrisy, the dou-

ble standard, the battles in Everyman between Sancho Panza and Don Quixote, suggest a Manichean presence which threatens any good of which people or societies are capable. The reports of that threat are constant, and even the fact the Orwell was acute in locating it might be viewed by the reader as inadequate compensation for the monotony of the search. This is one theme that never escapes him.

But his reiteration of the principle and its instances makes a deliberate point. For surely, among the issues affecting moral judgment, the first and largest is not *which* principle shall rule that judgment, but whether *any* principle governs it at all. The latter question Orwell saw as the most serious casualty of the subtlety of contemporary social analysis. In the attentiveness of such analysis to the causal sequence of social process, to tracing and anticipating its consequences, it had largely ignored the question of the form of the process as a whole— what the process *was* and why it had evolved as it had. Lacking the coherence that recognition of this question confers, and skewed by the dogmatic terms of ideology, the appearance of the process would necessarily be fragmented and partial. This accounts, as Orwell reviews the evidence, for the bad judgment and self-serving apologetics displayed by his contemporaries among the "intelligentsia": in their refusal to acknowledge Stalinism for the barbarism it was, in their defeatism in the early days of World War II, in their inability to find a difference between the opposing sides in that war. And if Orwell was uninterested in the derivation of the *specific* principle that might more justly determine a perspective on such cases, he never forgot, and intended that his reader should never forget, that it is with the principle of moral design that *any* analytic perspective begins and ends. Ultimately, intellectual and artistic neutrality or disinterest are fictions, and vicious ones at that. Only by admitting the role of moral principle in perception as well as in judgment does the world, for Orwell, become intelligible.

That principle, furthermore, if it has any claims at all, holds generally. Thus, for the writer, it acquires a reflexive or self-implicating quality which presents the writer himself as an important instance. The world of fact possesses for Orwell a dramatic unity which the form of his essays is designed to reenact. The facts displayed at any moment within those unities—the actuality *or* the representation— necessarily include the eye which discriminates them. Decency, Orwell might have argued, could not have it otherwise than that the written word should apply the same standards to its writer and to its reader that it lives by itself. The objects and events of history are nothing without the eye that joins or separates them; they *require* discrimination. And as that process of discrimination ought itself to appear in their representation, so also, the persons of the writer and of the reader he addresses. Drama, we know independently, extracts from all of its characters a confession of finitude—a common incompleteness which is then tested and measured by a general principle of virtue. It is a last and binding irony of his art that this measurement, which constantly forces its way beyond the artistic limits of detachment in Orwell's attempts at conventional fiction, confers, through the same excess, dramatic power on the essay—a medium which has not traditionally been a vehicle for drama at all.

The American writer to whom Orwell as essayist bears the strongest resemblance is Thoreau—a comparison that starts to their common disadvantage. Orwell was never at home with the Burmese peasants or the coal miners of Wigan or the English hoboes to whom he committed himself as a writer; the likeness that comes to mind is in a contemporary account which tells of Thoreau interrupting the austerities of Walden Pond to sneak home for some of his mother's pies. The art in both cases, it seems clear, was consciously informed, fictional, however spontaneous the germ. We find in the work of each a representation of the author that the author scarcely realized in his own person. But the integrity of the author who is a *character* in the written work is, in both writers, confirmed. The moral impulse linked almost physiologically to the eye for fact, the balking at the oversubtle consciousness, the reflexive "I" that counts itself among the objects of action in the writing, the drama located in events by their very discrimination as events: this summary humility, this uncommon decency acting on the world discerned, the representations of the two writers share. But then, the need to which Orwell answers, beyond his art, is also a bond: that there should be a knowing recluse who might penetrate the surrounding mass of artifice. Walden Pond, after all, is a metaphor of contrast. The contrast it argues, furthermore, has in subsequent history widened rather than diminished, at least by the difference between pencil making in Concord and the coal pits of Wigan.

Note

[1]*The Collected Essays, Journalism and Letters of George Orwell*, ed. Sonia Orwell and Ian Angus (New York: Harcourt, Brace, 1968).

11
The Praxis of Criticism

"How do I get to Carnegie Hall?" the stranger to New York asked. "Praxis, baby, praxis," the native replied.

I

When Hegel announced its death, he predicted that art would be survived first by religion and then by philosophy. He did not even mention criticism, and although history may yet live out the terms of this prophecy, the odds are not promising. The artists, it seems—certainly the artists of writing: the poet, dramatist, novelist—may indeed soon live only underground, invisible except for traces that require great expertise to identify; perhaps, like the Lamed-Vavniks, responsible through their selfless labors for keeping the rest of us alive and sane, but never known to us, not even discovered to themselves. But the critic, he who used to live in the Cloak of Humility, in the modest role of Handmaiden—an appurtenance, a reflection, a critic always *of* somebody or something—bestirs himself now, and finds an audience reading every move.

The turn, it seems, came with a discovery arrived at through an invalid but quite practical syllogism:

Premise 1: Art-criticism is about art. (By definition)
Premise 2: Art is about art. (Cf., eg., the Russian Formalists, the Abstract Expressionists, the Structuralists, the Post-Structuralists, the Deconstructionists, *The Anxiety of Influence*, etc.)
Conclusion: Therefore criticism is also art.
(Things about the same thing can't be far apart themselves.)

The logic is troublesome, of course, but we can hardly fault history for choosing cunning when the alternative is consistency. In any

216

event, reasons may be good even when they are not sufficient, and those are what I am after here. How has criticism come so to celebrate itself? Are its new claims possible in addition to being actual? The story is worth the telling, because even if it turns out to change nothing in the life of criticism (we can probably count on this), it may still affect the understanding with which criticism sports, plays, but cannot do without. Ours.

1. A Tale of Two

Since criticism has put little of itself into a body, we should not be surprised that it wears so many faces. The term, originally meant for "judgment," invites equivocation: Do we expect from it a verdict? An interpretation? Simply a reaction, *any* reaction? Each of these definitions, and others, has been suggested; no single motif runs through them. For example: one response to what is placed before us, one manner of judgment, is to see, and then to say, how it is made—more specifically, how it is well made. The technological impulse here has a legislative, even a moral tone, adding the attraction of taboos to the promise of order. Mainly cookbooks now deploy this manner of judgment, which served Aristotle, however, in a recipe for tragedy. There is, in any event, no ready way to elide this one purpose with that other one of appreciation, where criticism proposes to reveal to feeling the circle formed by the parallel lines of a text; or with that other, still more speculative one, which sets out, on formal grounds, the possibilities and impossibilities of literary genre. And there is no need to, either; only the housekeeper who insists that the way to keep a room clean is not to use it would tidy criticism up by telling it what tasks it shouldn't set itself.

Still, as reality has joints for the carving (so Plato arranged the menu), we ought to have our plates ready. All the more so, since in the criticism familiar to us, reality and appearance in its conclusions are so difficult to tell apart that the test we finally have to rely on, after logic and argument have had their way, is the unhappy one of indigestion: some judgments just won't go down. As we fail to locate formal differences in the immediate variety of criticism, however, we can attempt to see what more latent purposes that variety turns out to serve. And here, the matter is simpler, not historically (since in their own version of the state of nature, the functions of criticism compete with each other and encroach in disorderly fashion), but conceptually, where two alternatives are logical complements: we find the process of criticism either an end in itself or as a means to some other end.

We might, in other words, first assume that critical judgment, as intentional, has the purposes it says it has. But seen close up, those purposes turn out to be more than the saying admits, with boundaries so blurred that we can hardly tell how many, let alone where: explicative criticism, interpretive criticism, evaluative criticism, and so on. To find an order here requires that we move up a logical step, asking how to characterize the variety itself; and then a twofold division appears, at a point on which logic and history (for once) agree. Given the existence of criticism, there could be no other forms—and there *have been* these: to one side, criticism as instrument, a means merely, serving a further and so, one supposes, a higher end; to the other side, criticism as an end in itself, staking out, asserting its own claims. I speak briefly of these two together before speaking of each singly; it is not only their differences but what they have in common that will later evoke an alternative theory of criticism as praxis.

Like the history of slavery of which it is part, the idea of criticism as a means, or subordination, has formal variations within what at first glance is only a single and brute theme. For one example: the tradition here defers to the text as master—in its religious appearances, as Master; and as commentary surely is a critical genre, Biblical commentary takes life from the ideal of an absolute text where meaning is a function of every gesture of the text. (That each Hebrew letter is also a number makes this ideal more plausible—but wasn't it the idea of the absolute text, making every gesture "count," that preceded this too?) The potency of both meaning and its commentator is viewed here as inexhaustible—for the one, because of the infinite reach of its source; for the other, in the commentator's dependence on that source. The authority of the text in this version of critical subordination originally attests only to the power of its Author; but by a nifty move of Shamanism the authority of the Text survives even when its author, unsettled by the skeptical looks around him, begins to fail. His power, it turns out, is transferable (more, perhaps, an argument for than against the Author's grandiose claims; was it only an accident that the commandment against idolatry did not proscribe that one most extraordinary graven image—the written word?). Thus, as desacralization eats away at the spirit and inner life of the Church, the authority of its relics—of the past and its texts (the past itself becoming a text)—increases. So the viewer is surprised, in Titian's painting, to learn that the figure with clothes is Profane Love and the figure without them is Sacred—and so the Renaissance assumes the humanistic mission of reconstructing texts, of paring away the interpolations, notes, doodlings, absentmindedness of the scribes and clerks who had been keepers of the authorized presence and who had taken so seriously the claims of incorporeality by that presence that they would not believe that marks made on or about its words could be a violation.

The purpose of this modern scourging was purity, quite in the ritual sense. Plato's meaning (even Plato himself) is there in the text. But to reach it (and him) means to erase the marks of hands that have touched it, to authenticate the text—preferably, because less hermetically, by extratextual means. So histories are traced, the search is on for the provenance of manuscripts, biography comes to life—all the proto-versions of fingerprinting and carbon 14 that later appeared as instruments of the same process. The critic whose work turns into this process is not even obliged to read, still less to understand, the text he submits to. He has only to prepare and serve it; the consuming comes later, at other hands. It is always a mystery, with such habits, why critics know as much as they do—as much a mystery, that is, as why cooks tend to be fat.

Criticism as subordinate has not yet discovered a nonlinguistic medium, a distinctive, impersonal guise which, like any other uniform, would mark it as servant, the member of an order; but it aspires to this goal. Like the first rule of the physician, "Do no harm," the first maxim for criticism in this role is "Don't block the view." The second maxim (and there are only the two) is the refrain of Goethe dying: "More light, more light." Only so, we understand, is the object to be perceived—and that, for criticism in this office of servant, is to be. The light itself is not supposed to be part of the view—an intense, even masochistic expression of humility on the part of the agent. It is the *object* of vision, the text, that wants attention; the critic has only to make it—more precisely, to leave it—visible.

We should be in no hurry to believe that the rush of political liberals or religious antinomians has made obsolete the role of the critic as dependent on the nomos, the law of the text. The Lower and Higher Criticisms of the nineteenth century left much textual reconstruction to be done and other to be redone (there is no limit to *that*, after all); the innovations of science have provided formulas, technological devices, and a spirit which substantially increase the means of criticism as an instrument. If we ask, in fact, why critical formalism should now be in vogue when form itself is so abused in the culture, part of the answer undoubtedly lies there: form is most readily available as a means. The American "New Criticism," now itself a relic, gave good and early value to this disposition. Intention was false to the text, affect was false, paraphrase was heretical: there was only the object to be served, the text itself. The formulas of irony, paradox, tension—a critical do-it-yourself kit—were intended as much to get the critic out of the reader's way as to provide literary toeholds. That self-abnegation may not have been as noticeable in the New Critics as they supposed (their own names, after all—Tate, Ransom, Brooks— endure, and not only as titles). But their readings were devout even when they were not consistent: criticism must serve art; what the critic wills to exist is not meant to survive by itself; the original text is the thing—complex, meaningful, complete, real. Criticism, reflected from these features, is a medium, to be read *through* (in the way that glass is seen through).

The passion represented historically in this ideal of discourse as transparent may seem greater even than the allure of the original *object* of criticism; but noncritics as well are familiar with that prefer- ence for talking about somebody or -thing even when, by a slight shift in direction, the body or thing might have been addressed directly. It is the role of voyeur that the reader chooses here—perhaps, as Barthes supposes, part of the pleasure in reading *any* text, but doubled, if that is so, for the performances of criticism where we read someone else's reading of a text. The pleasures of suspicion, distance, even dominance (what pleasures, after all, would the voyeur have if he knew *he* was being watched?) begin to assert themselves here, to separate off; the reader, then the critic, begin to think of themselves. So the slave, even the slave who has been willing, finds the will taking on a life of its own, claiming the role of master. We may think of a medium as passive—but we may not, in that, be thinking the idea that the medium has of itself. And thus we find intimated the second view of criticism, in which the ideal of transparency and the role of servant give way to claims of authority, to self-assertion—a declara- tion of independence by words themselves (including, one supposes, even the words of declaration).

Here, too, there is a history—in part, the history of common sense, which is often only the recounting of brute necessity. For how, we ask (not yet referring to an actual history), *could* the critic be invisible even if he wanted to be? The critical display takes up space, its words take time. Where the *words* of an original source matter, can talk about it escape calling attention to the talk, to its own means? Can a text which might indeed be read outside any particular context be read aside from *all* contexts? The critic himself, after all, adds history to what he sees (his own history, for starters). And although his audi- ence might well deserve some indemnity for collaborating with the critic, it would hardly be reasonable to ask the critic to jump out of his skin.

Such questions have been repressed by the ideology they dispute, but they keep turning up nonetheless. They were most clearly on view in the historical parallel between the decline of authority and the greening of a self-conscious self propelled forward in the seventeenth century. Should we identify a point, for reference at least, in Descartes's dreams? That moment is already overdetermined, but no matter: not only the irony that the master of reason, of clarity and distinctness, discovers his method by way of a dream touches us, but the fact that he becomes master *in* the dream. He thus challenges the longstanding subordination of the dreamer to external source: for Joseph and his brothers; for Socrates, appealing on his last morning to a dream, in order to call his disciples beyond the incapacity which a lifetime of teaching has failed to cure. The dream is traditionally a form of commentary, a subordination—but then, in Descartes, we find the dream asserting itself, asking rather than giving deference, a reality on which the waking experience turns out to be commentary, not the other way round. "I dream, therefore I am," Descartes could have argued—since his thinking, too, might have been dreamt.

Descartes did not dream of Matthew Arnold; there is no reason why he should have. But for this second version of criticism, because language more than reason is his medium and because he rarely doubted either what he was talking about or what he said about it, Arnold appears historically as at least the preface to an ideal. Criticism in the Victorian age, where everything that language can name is also assumed to have a proper place—metaphysical etiquette—is the means by which we place ourselves in the world. Speaking about what things are is very important for their *being* what they are; and not only, then, does criticism move up to the very boundaries of art, art itself turns out to be a function of criticism. What matters in literature is thus also, whatever else it is, criticism; one could hardly require a stronger reason for deferring to criticism as an end rather than as a means, for attempting to look to it rather than through it. "Is it true," Arnold asks, "that all time given to writing critiques on the works of others would be much better employed if it were given to original composition? Is it true that Johnson had better have gone on producing more *Irenes* instead of writing his *Lives of the Poets . . .* ?" And although Arnold's denial of those possibilities is admittedly equivocal, the very question he asks clears a space that such writers as Ruskin and Pater then occupy with no equivocation at all. So Pater, for example, at once absorbing and parodying Arnold, brings the critic into full view: "The first step toward seeing one's object as it really is, is to know one's impression as it really is. . . ." The form of prose and not only that of poetry, Pater argues in his essay on style, comprises art—and how then could the prose of criticism be left out? The object itself when not viewed is unknowable; it is the view, *our* view, which always and unremittingly occupies us.

This impulse toward authority for criticism comes, moreover, from art as well as from the critic who might be suspected in making such claims of serving himself rather than art. The tradition here is if anything older than criticism itself, for in assuming criticism as a natural kind, we easily forget that if art had left it no space, criticism, historically, might never have begun. So, for example, commentaries on Homer seem obtrusions or at best redundant; Auerbach, writing about Odysseus's scar, intimates that had the Homeric style endured, interpretation need never have come into existence at all. But style did not stay constant (would there even *be* style if there were only One Style?) Turning inward, speaking more about itself and less about the world, art begins to pose and soon to leave over questions. Responding, commentary takes on body—and then, obeying the law of conservation (of energy? of inertia?), the body acts to preserve itself.

The differences between the two views of criticism,[1] then, are firm, not historically, perhaps, where lines rarely are clear, but conceptually. What is at issue between these ideas? Do they contradict each other—or is their evident disagreement mainly verbal or stipulative? Is the dialectic they combine to make—mammoth, incessant as it has been—the history of discourse or reason itself? The language we summon with such questions is metaphysics, however disguised, for in it we speculate about how certain fundamental structures—the "beings" of art—have anything to do with criticism. And the place to confront that general question seems then to be first with one of the two views we have been discussing, and then with the other.

2. Aesthetic Distance: The Myth of Immaculate Conception

The eighteenth century is the age of the encyclopedia, and of the ideas which had to be born in order to make an encyclopedia possible, one of them was the possibility of putting the objects of knowledge at a distance, constructing frames which focus, and thus celebrate, confirm, the viewer's field of vision: an order is disclosed not only in or among the objects, but *of* them as well. Museums are also encyclopedias, moreover, laid out in space rather than time, more explicitly than books putting frames to work: insulating the divisions between objects, making arrangements of and between artists or periods or topics, putting up nameplates (names themselves being an early version of the frame). The first impulse for museums admittedly seems to have been rather different, but not inconsistently so. The ruler of empire must have a place to store his acquisitions and, still more important, to show that he has acquired them. So Napoleon becomes himself a treasure of the Louvre; Catherine the Great, of the Hermitage; the Mellons (Kings of Oil and Aluminum), of the National Gallery in Washington. But what is first meant to impress by sheer mass and force also invites an order of some kind for the storing. And then distinctions appear which have to do with the character of the objects rather than with their accumulation, as though the original unsorted heap, imitating the life around it, had decided to differentiate itself, to stake out an identity.

The original impulse—indeed, all sense of origins—is soon blocked in the museum which, after we once cut through the pieties about honoring the past, turns out to recognize only the present (more like *conquering* the past). Just as the intentions of the frame quickly replace an initial character of intensification, inclusion, with the qualities of detachment, exclusion, so seriality or history in the museum turns into a single and large present tense. Objects in the museum, originally intended for specific contexts or settings, move into the setting which is a denial of settings. And what then do we know of the objects in the museum? Only that they are marked off, separated from others of their own kind and, all the more, from others of different kinds. Their value? For one, their uniqueness, their individuality. (Not only do we name *them*, we insist on the names of their makers. Forgeries are the one form of subversion feared by museums, since if they were easily and convincingly made, museums with their "originals" would be nothing but warehouses. Even a version of Angst is understandable as the condition of museums and their keepers—the consciousness that good forgeries are the ones that hang undetected.) We assume that there is no way of replicating them, not even of producing others like them in spirit but different in detail. Nor, furthermore, because they are separated in this way, can we measure them by practical standards of use or profit: what they do, what they make, even what they make of the viewer. It is a world apart—and so the frame which starts off quite modestly circling around, embellishing an object, ends egocentrically, pointing to itself. (Narcissus might indeed have been beautiful—but that fact by itself would not have told his story.)

So goes the only slightly mythic account of the origins of the Museum Theory of Art—less mythic as an account, in any event, than what the theory asserts. Kant lived immaculately, but hardly, we suppose, in his origins—and why should we credit more to his theories than to what he was unwilling to keep out of them? Yet this is the ideal to which criticism as subordinate looks: seeing as fragmentary, incomplete, dependent—opposed in each of these respects to the *object* of criticism which is complete, autonomous, removed from need and consequence, untouched by history, by intention or by consequence. "Ohne Zweck," Kant says about aesthetic judgment "without purpose"—stepping off the distance between that experience and the critical revisions or practical extensions of it, which like almost everything else man does, everything now except the sheer, self-contained aesthetic pleasure, becomes *all* "Zweck." What are the metaphysical features of the objects of aesthetic judgment? For one thing, their remoteness, their difference from others, as though they could *only* be defined negatively, by what they are not, a negative ontology. For a second thing, their willingness (in anyone else, this would be called desire) to give themselves away—insulation, frames, and all. The viewer has only to strike a posture, present himself to art in a clear show of disinterest—and art must respond. Admittedly, in answering this fastidious invitation, art turns out to have not much to show; but it cannot be faulted for holding anything back. The distance, then, is everything, the means by which the object steps outside history, outside measurement: it alone tells us what it is. That is why criticism not only can afford to be transparent, mere light, but *must* be: it is the object that is supposed to sparkle, not the critic. When the critic aspires to a character that is more than transparent, he becomes an obstruction.

An extended family of ideas is related to the theme of subordination in criticism. So, for example, *Organic Form*—that biological metaphor which first assumes the literal perfection of nature: everything in its place, to change one feature is to change them all, all surrounded, made coherent, by an impermeable membrane (an aid, surely, in immaculate conception). This sense both of necessary connection and of completeness nourishes the status of criticism as subordinate, since the critic, reflecting on the unities of art, can hardly expect to maintain them, let alone to extend the circle of their unities to his ow words. Art and criticism as subordination are thus brought together, joined by Organic Form, but ironically; they are made for each other in the way that unequals (social classes, numbers) often combine to constitute what looks like a whole.

Or again: *Faculty Psychology*, the distinctive aesthetic faculty, in particular, also known as Intuition, the Aesthetic Sense. Disengagement, after all, disinterest, is hardly the first or most evident among human impulses: we see this in the characteristics themselves, since "*eng*agement," "*int*erest" must, we suppose, logically precede them. So we then reify capacities to make room for another one, for a form of address which denies the first ones, moves beyond them, making a virtue out of the lack of necessity (of art). Thus a faculty of aesthetic judgment or sensibility is set up; and criticism in its role as instrument, even though it mediates for art, must find a different place for itself; the only real difference, when we're talking about faculties, is between one faculty and another—and this means that whatever criticism is, it's not art.

Fiction and nonfiction. The Greek myths were not, we may believe, myths for the Greeks. Only at first true and then, slowly, false. But that is a different difference from the one between fiction and nonfiction, where nonfiction may be either true or false and fiction would be—neither? Both? Something more? Something less? Is poetry fiction?—But it is too personal, too committed in its claims. Is *drama* fiction—But it is too impersonal, makes too abstract a claim. The truth of the matter is that with the distinction between fiction and nonfiction we hope to aestheticize truth altogether: fiction has nothing to do with fact, and nonfiction thinks of truth as bits of information.[2] It is fair enough, then, that fiction should come to suggest decoration, baubles, the novel as it connotes novelty, diversion, romance—the tint of scandal, the hint of a second and mysterious presence. Life, "real" life offers no such possibilities: the distances are always too short.

The intention of each of these designs is to leave intentions behind, to assume the otherworldly character that frames exemplify in themselves. Practical purpose, desire, even theorizing, abstract thinking, are if not menial, certainly mundane. Only when we move beyond them, infusing each moment with the possibility of a Sabbath outside worldly time, does man come alive, free. Those moments, art provides. Criticism, then, another mundane task, can only serve; it paves the roads that mark the distance. The language is different (ordinary); the direction is different (away from itself); the purpose is different (mainly, that there *is* one). Art is real, and criticism is only approximate; art speaks for itself, and the voice of criticism speaks only for the other. Does art on this view have parents? A lineage? Does it impinge on the history of the reader or even invite his attendance? Does it bear any other imprint of human touch? So, in adding up the answers "No," we find ourselves reinventing the Immaculate Conception.

3. Derrida Derided (or, How Original Is Original Sin?)

It requires strong will and brute force to preserve the naiveté and sweet innocence in this idea of a text which both speaks and then interprets its own words—the same power which Fundamentalists ascribe to the Bible (and even for them, that is the only text for which this is true). What, after all, could words be which had no history? Even the *concept* of a text has a beginning (and probably, in the future, also an end). Sentences, we know, exist in a time that periods and commas mark, and words themselves are flesh, body; no medium they comprise could ever be quite transparent, give itself away. And this holds as well for the other elements ingredient in words: alphabets, phonemes, the mechanical apparatus, even the shape of writing, con-texts. So long as criticism is discursive, there can be no escape from these conditions—and although it may not be clear to what extent such features obtrude on the idea of criticism as invisible, ancillary, there can be little question that barring a constant miracle, they do in fact obtrude.

For the last hundred, post-Hegelian years, a group of writers have, in a variety of languages and idioms, been making exactly this claim; they come together in as fine a point as we are likely ever to be impaled on in the works of Jacques Derrida—using his name now metonymically, even beyond what he himself recommends for authors' names, to cover a range both of his own writings and those of a group with affinities to him.[3] The diet here is rich: if Berkeley's tarwater could nourish the astringencies of British empiricism, Derrida must concentrate on creams and sauces, where the taste is for blending, for nuance, for the sustaining power of the soupçon (so Erich Heller speaks of the nineteenth- and twentieth-century "philosophers of suspicion").[4]

Exactly that traditional concept of the text which has been described, with its frames, class hierarchy, authoritarian claims, is the starting place of Derrida's thought, what he reacts against. The spaces that purportedly divide history or experience or writing as a series of texts, marked off from one another by enough distance to allow each of them to observe the others, to parse them, turn out for Derrida at each step to be only new occasions, breeding grounds, for myth, ideology. Criticism in the large becomes mythic insofar as it poses as representational, claiming a pristine object on which it—openly not pristine—reflects.

No, when Derrida thinks of texts, he thinks rather of The Text (as Heidegger insists on Being and World rather than on beings and a world: so the acquisitive impulse for Das Kapital overcomes older linguistic and social antagonisms). We think of *that*, textuality, in parts or pieces only if our thinking about it was fragmented to begin with; there is no way of establishing boundaries for discourse, because the space of reflection or consciousness required to mark them off is itself part of the artifact. We may not know exactly why a particular construction (like the myth of aesthetic distance itself) should have been made—but we know something better: why *all* constructions, including that one, are made. And the reason is precisely the opposite of detachment or disinterest, much more in the line of an unresting conatus, a common will: to power or at least to pleasure and feeling.

No text, or the reflection or consciousness in which it starts, is for Derrida more rarefied or transparent than its object: every occasion of discourse, every moment is assertive, opaque, "thick." And thus, although the sum of such moments, at some mythic later day, may be imagined to constitute a whole (Derrida is uneasy with this prospect, perhaps because he will not be there to see what he so long, with such self-denial, postponed), there is in any event no completion or detachment before then. Expression and representation make an inevitable mark, a differ*a*nce in what they express or represent—so Derrida anticipates the alteration by spelling *difference* with a difference (we shall surely hear someday about the influence of the Beatles on French thought). Thus, texts which are purportedly about other texts turn out in the end (which comes immediately) to be mainly about themselves (if, this is, they are about anything at all).

Derrida stands at an extreme in asserting this position which also has been stated here in extreme form (he is, it must be said, more radical a proponent than a practitioner; he writes about many historical figures—Plato, Husserl, Condillac—deferentially [*e*, not *a*] and lucidly). But although Derrida's account is extreme, parts of the conception of criticism (finally, of reading) which he maintains are not isolated or unique in the history of criticism. I have mentioned the quite different figures of Arnold, Ruskin, and Pater, and their claims for the hegemony of criticism; variations on that theme occur, sometimes argued, sometimes tacitly, in critics as diverse as Samuel Johnson and Lukács, Dryden and Trilling. These writers share a moral, finally a metaphysical, premise in their conceptions of criticism: namely, that since the critic, and what he relates literature to, share the life that literature has as its subject, criticism is itself literature, and the critic, an artist. The generic distinctions between the two expressive forms, even the fact that viewed as literature, criticism seems a peculiarly hybrid and ill-formed genre as compared, say, to the poem or the novel—these finally make little difference, since

what sets any genre off is the fact of its alien character rather than
what is alien about it.

I do not mean to suggest by these parallels that Derrida is the
bearer of a tradition. In addition to his distrust of the very concept of
tradition, he would have a specific objection to being identified even
with this tradition which is in some obvious ways close to him—not
because its indictment of the notion of the pristine text is misplaced
but because the indictment is not radical enough. Arnold, for example, defending the critic's role, still promises for the critic (and *his*
readers) a view of the object "as it really is"; Lukács, acknowledging
the literary significance of criticism, still views its characteristic appearance in the essay as a "preliminary" to (we assume) something
else. But for Derrida, even these modest vestiges of the logocentrism
of philosophical realism must be shed as well. It is too much to hold
that a text, in addition to speaking with its own voice, may also defer
to another; the self-assertiveness must be everything, the only thing.
Derrida, with Heidegger, fondly recalls the death of metaphysics.
Think, for example, of the traditional concept of substance, what
underwrites the definition of things in the world—and realize that
what this substance presupposes in the way of form or definition is
itself the merest of fictions: there *are* no forms to be grasped. The
hardworking mill of logocentrism—in Plato, in Aristotle—found its
grist in mistaking grammar for metaphysics, in a power of the imagination which did not recognize itself as imaginative. The very idea of
reason as dominant or even as isolable in human nature is also a
fiction: consciousness or reason are effects, traces, the detritus of will.
Thus, it is not only that man lacks the capacity to detach reason from
the will, to see or to know without motive—but that there is nothing:
no-thing, to see or to reason about: no nature, no nature*s*, not even
real fragments, which, after all, are themselves entities. As Kant's
version of the Copernican Revolution shifted the design of philosophy
from ontology to epistemology, from the question of what there is to
the question of how we can know what there is, Derrida gives the
Revolution one more turn, from epistemology to aesthesiology: from
how we can know, to the question of what is left to experience when
knowledge is cut out of it. (The next step, of course—not very far
off—must be anesthesiology.) The several faculties of mind devised to
support the naivete of aesthetic distance are replaced by one: the
capacity for pleasure which is itself a function—more literally, a
symptom—of the will.

The two great moral influences on Derrida, it comes as no surprise,
are Nietzsche and Freud. Together with them, he looks for the
Happy Science that, once and for all, will not only assert that

metaphysics is dead but will by its own example make that claim good. But is this in fact what we find in Derrida? Only if we agree that continuity is metaphysically less charged than discreteness; only if we agree that the concept of the One is coherent and without presupposition while the concept of the Many is not; only if we agree that the cure for naiveté (as for a belief in the Immaculate Conception) is the touch of Original Sin.

II

4. Upending the Mean (i.e., Praxis Makes Perfect)

The temptation is strong to take an economic view of the two ideas of criticism that have appeared here—to split the difference. And this is in fact a way that has been taken. The ideal of subordination—biblical and classical commentary, formal and formulaic criticism—has, despite itself, left traces of elaboration, new texts to be added to the old: Maimonides on the Torah, Aquinas on Aristotle; Leavis on Lawrence, Wimsatt on Samuel Johnson. The weights on the first side of these balances may not equal those on the second, but there is no question that they exist—and a similar balance appears in the other critical ideal which had hoped to elide the written past with the writing present. We recognize the past here not only as translated into the present but for itself as well. Arnold's critical ideal—to "see the object as it really is"—may be question-begging, but his nostalgia for the object is real enough; and to read Arnold on Byron, or later, Trilling on Arnold, *is* to look backward at their objects, as well as around, at the critic himself. So the liberal imagination does better, certainly *more*, than it had promised.

But this mood of compromise in practice has no counterpart in its principles, which, as between the two views of criticism, oppose each other by precept and not only by inclination. This theoretical antinomy is a division which must, I believe, be overcome by an adequate theory of criticism. As in any antinomy, resolution will not come here by finding one or the other of the opposing principles false, or by finding the whole to be a contradiction—but by discovering a ground on which the two conflicting claims are together intelligible as well as separately true. For *of course* we read criticism because of the importance of the objects about which it speaks; and *of course* we turn to criticism for the sensibility and thought of its writers themselves. A conception of criticism on which one or the other of these findings is implausible is itself, prima facie, defective. The problem, then, is to devise a structure that can house them both.

Such a structure is available in a view of criticism as "praxis" or doing,[5] in contrast to the concept of "poiesis" or making, which is, I should claim, responsible for the appearance of contradiction in the Antinomy of Criticism. The poiesis-praxis distinction is recognizably Aristotelian, although the account given it here is in its central thesis at odds with Aristotle's; namely, that art—more specifically litera- ture, including criticism—is to be understood as praxis rather than as either the product or process of poiesis. Three parts of the concept of poiesis in particular drive the antinomy—and it is their contradic- tories in the concept of praxis which, I propose, resolve it.

i. *The Ahistoricity of the object.* The object of poiesis—what is made—is set apart both from its maker and from the context of its making—and also, consequently, from its audience or critics. Histor- ical origins may be invoked as a means of explaining or understanding it, but those origins are always subordinate to the later appearances of the object which are significant instrumentally—either for producing certain practical effects or for realizing a special quality of experience. The maker himself is detached from what is made; the object has no continuing or internal consequence for him.

ii. *The lack of deliberation.* Poiesis excludes deliberation, that is, the use of general principles in the choice of means—the principles them- selves subject to revision in light of the choice itself. Poiesis appeals to two alternative procedures in avoiding the one of deliberation: the particular may be seen as an instance of general rules (so, the cook- book reading of Aristotle's *Poetics*); or, no general rules may be held to apply at all (poiesis here looks to genius or inspiration as a source). Deliberation contributes, in opposition to either of these, the con- tinuing presence for the act of criticism of the "doer": as doer, the critic is as contingent as are his choices, and he is, in fact, contingent *on* them.

iii. *The discreteness of meaning and evaluation.* The things made by poiesis are fixed at a moment. Since they are also solutions to a problem, they are judged as realizing that goal or failing to do so, and the critic's judgment here, like the success or failure itself, is attached to the moment, the problem *to be* solved. It turns out, to be sure, that both the problem and the solution are, on this view, given to the critic by the literary work itself. And as those works are individuals, separate from others, so the judgments and interpretations of them will also be.

These three features of poiesis are especially noticeable in the appearance of criticism as subordination. In contrast to the viewer with his dependence, the object, on that account, is self-contained; everything it requires—whether as a poem or a table—it provides for itself. Designed to serve an end—pleasure, usefulness—there is no reason why if that end could be otherwise realized—by an illusion or deception, by substitution, even by removal of the purpose—the object made could not be forgone. (This argument applies also to criticism itself.) To make something, in this sense, is to dissociate both maker and user (or viewer) from the object. Maker and user are each essentially complete without the object; they may be touched, but they are not altered, by changes in its status. The role of the critic is to enable, to provide for a consummation: he serves the object (like a waiter at table). The critical process, furthermore, although an activity, is in another sense passive: the object meets certain standards or not; the critic may make do *with* it, but he cannot make *it* do anything not first suggested by the object itself. And finally, the object does not endure for the viewer beyond the encounter itself except as memory (or perhaps desire, but in any case, not as present and contingent). All of these presuppositions we have seen exemplified in the conception—the Immaculate Conception—of criticism as subordinate.

On the other hand, the ideology of poiesis is broader even than the role of criticism as subordinate, and we see this quite clearly in Derrida precisely *because* of the sweep of his attack on criticism in that role. Like the account which he indicts, Derrida's account presupposes a disjunction: either knowledge—and thus criticism, as a form of knowing—must, like its objects, be clear and distinct, or it cedes any claim as knowledge (so, we might say, the dream of Descartes is still dreamt). The idea of criticism as subordinate commits itself to the first term of this disjunction: insofar as critical judgment is clear and transparent, it reveals the equally clear and distinct outlines of its objects. It is thus mimetic, representational. Derrida rejects this argument with the counterclaim that critical judgment, *all* judgment, is opaque. But in then concluding that criticism fails as knowledge, he accepts the original disjunction: a candidate for knowledge must be clear and distinct, or it has no claim to the title. Thus only the fact that there is *no* knowledge in this sense prevents criticism from qualifying; the objection has nothing to do with the criterion. What passes as knowledge in criticism turns out for Derrida to be, like other knowledge, a function of the will that prizes clarity and distinctness as it does anything else—from an interest, a *self*-interest, in the object rather than in truth.

This view is aestheticization in precisely the sense ascribed above to poiesis. In it, the consummation of action alone matters, directed to a "consumer" interested only in acting *on* the object involved. The relation involves no past or context other than that of immediacy—no integration of subject and object (because they belong to different orders), no mingling in a common project (not because they have nothing in common, but because there is no project). Where poiesis more traditionally presents itself as one activity of several open to man, one in which he is capable of making a mark that then, by dissociation, becomes a monument for him and of him, Derrida's reaction only extends this view to define man *himself* as poiesis: *he* is the object made, his *own* monument.

To this view, criticism which sees itself and its objects as aspects of praxis stands almost exactly opposed. The critic who addresses the literary text (more generally, the work of art) as a doing or action rather than a making, shapes his own work to fit: both the object and the critical judgment on it thus become "performances." Praxis implies a continuing relation between agent and action: the action is intelligible only insofar as intention and consequence appear as parts of it; the doer is himself judged in terms of what he "does." Thus, history is integral both to the work of art and to the critical process; nothing in either of them is intelligible apart from it. Because praxis involves deliberation, furthermore, its conclusions are both assertive and evaluative; and those qualities, too, rub off both on the work of art and on critical judgment. In the sense that any action is an embodiment of the agent, so the work of art too becomes a personification; it is thus distinguished not only from involuntary or chance acts but also from the larger class of actions regarded as independent of their origins. Intentions are significant in these actions, as the language if not the theory of criticism has always known; that the intentions appear first or mainly as intentions of the work of art rather than of the artist only defers the question of the relevance of origins. No *specific* history (for example, the artist's) may be presupposed for understanding a literary work, but that is far from denying the significance of history as such. Thus, the presuppositions of praxis—the unification of the self, the internal relation between subject and object, the idea of creation itself as a continuing process—openly dominate critical discourse in the same way that, before that, they dominate the process of art itself. The work of art, in other words, is itself subordinate—and so, by that fact, is the work of criticism.

The shift from poiesis to praxis has implications in "applied" criticism where the general principles cited are visible and testable. I have, for example, spoken of praxis as involving assertion and evaluation—both of them denied by poiesis with its emphasis in critical judgment on a "science" of sensibility or will. It requires no very subtle notion of assertion, in fact, to see its presence in the work of art. "The very form of a literary work," Trilling suggests, "is in itself an idea"—and surely some, if not all of the burden of proof falls on the denial of this claim, to show what either ideas or literary works *are* if they are denied this affinity. Again, a constant issue for criticism as poiesis has been the admissibility of moral criteria to the judgment of art: the latter seems diminished without them, but incoherent with them. No such incongruity occurs, however, if the structures of art are intrinsically, and not only in the eye of the beholder, related to moral action. A fictional penumbra surrounds the concepts of character and of person in general; this is only slightly denser when the moral concepts by which we address them are applied to art and to the work of criticism.

Poiesis also has difficulties in explaining historical change in critical interpretation and evaluation. Insofar as the work of art is ahistorical, its significance should be accessible at a moment, even at the first moment; it follows from the same premises, moreover, that, like judgment, critical categories are closed. But it is clear that critical consciousness, even of the individual critic, *does* evolve; critical categories contrived long after the original "fact" of the work of art may yet be apposite. This would not be surprising (indeed it is entailed) in the conception of art or criticism as praxis, since the consequences of praxis are integral to the doing: those consequences can be estimated when they are still incomplete, even at an early point; but all such judgment is defeasible. (So the maxim cited by Aristotle in the *Ethics*, "Call no man happy before he is dead," applies to art as praxis: call no art happy—or beautiful—before man is dead.) This same challenge to the ideal of organic forms also makes sense of the history of criticism as a history, where the alternative is an artificial consistency—high fiction—of inclusions and exclusions, produced from the standpoint of a mythical "ideal" observer. The latter alternative simply denies basic characteristics of the artistic medium. Like the political conceptions of Utopia, art on this account is assumed to involve completeness, irrefragability; as with the other ideal and its exemplifications, art never lives up to this one—and it is clear that art often has not even hoped to.

I do not, with these comments, mean to suggest that the ideal of criticism as praxis is new—but only that it has often been denied and still more frequently, obscured. Some of the adherents to that ideal have been named: Trilling, Arnold, Pater; and others might be added: F. R. Leavis, Kenneth Burke, Irving Howe. The strong differences among these critics would itself refute any claim for an orthodoxy, but the features of praxis that I have cited are important elements in the work of each of them. There is also one group of critics who as a *group* have significantly represented the concept of praxis. I refer here to the tradition of Marxist criticism which, as in Lukács's work on the historical novel, in Lucien Goldmann's work on Racine, in Walter Benjamin's work on the "mechanical reproduction" of art, has established a major and recognizable point of critical view. With so many critics at work, with such various practical results, often at cross-purposes to the ideologies professed, nominalism is an understandable temptation: it may seem more than enough to understand and judge them and their work individually. But there *are* generic distinctions within criticism itself—and why should we mince words here? Whatever novel or important can be said about the history or logic of linguistic forms, the interrelation of genres, the migration of literary symbols, the psychological sources or corollaries of criticism, the science of literature—all of the central promises of recent critical theory—nothing in these statements makes sense without the understanding of art and then of criticism as social action and gesture. This holds true for the critic's conception of himself no less than for his conception of what he is a critic of. Few of us, probably, escape dreams of life as Robinson Crusoe—of difference, of removal, or shrugging free from history. But no one, more certainly, can escape.

5. Non-nonviolent Criticism: Breaking into the Text

The tradition of criticism as poiesis holds to an ideal of nonviolence: in it, the critic's main concern is to avoid violating what is there—for criticism as subordinate, out of deference to the object; for criticism as autonomous, for *amour-propre*. Measured by these principles, criticism as praxis is non-nonviolent criticism: its role is *precisely* to obtrude into the work. The critic, and indeed as the critic personifies the act of reading, all readers, "force" the work—not by imposing criteria or understanding, but by hitting upon the opening which the work leaves and leaves necessarily, notwithstanding the gestures it makes toward closure. It is as if praxis were founded on a principle of incompleteness, an artistic version of Gödel's theorem: there is always a gap in the text, a requirement for an added presence in the person and grasp of the reader. The physical boundaries of the literary text are thus misleading. To view them as circumscribing the literary work is as false as it would be to say that the identity of a person is marked out by the reach of his arms and legs. In reading, we read ourselves, not in the sense that perception inevitably bears the mark of the perceiver (although this is undoubtedly, but more generally true); not even in the sense that words are always directed at someone, an implied audience (since also this, as true, is true of all words); but because the text in its composite expectation is always looking at the reader, always counting on him. He may, of course, refuse the overture—but he can hardly object that he has not been invited.

This denial of artistic closure may seem perverse—factually false for deliberately "seamless" works of art such as *Madame Bovary*, and a priori extravagant; all in all, perhaps no better than a stipulation. I concede something—but even then, not much—to the last of these claims: no theory, and not only this one, avoids a commendatory element. Insofar as this qualification is true, however, it is not *all* that is true about the theory—and that becomes evident in the examination of literary appearances, even of those works most consciously devoted to the ideals of poiesis and its distancing effects. Narration itself, we need to recognize, offers peace in its usual forms of repetition and continuity only after violence: events do not *occur* as narrated; they collect themselves under coercion, not spontaneously. Kierkegaard's parable about the tortured shrieks of the artist which, echoing from his prison, reach the ears of an audience as sweet music is surely true for the *material* of art even if we may often doubt it for the life of the artist himself. Undeniably, art often (and deliberately) conceals art—but we know this, too, only from art itself; and that *knowledge*, as well as the concealment, unavoidably figures in the attention we give art. Art, whether representational or not, has a look to it, much in the way that a face has. And what would a look—or face—be without the assumption which starts at the beginning of its history, that it would be seen? Still less, it seems, than invisible—since not evocation, not assertion, not even form would in solitude, out of all sight, be conceived as possible.

And so also for the process of criticism: the boundaries—of texts and contexts—utilized as levers by criticism are themselves projections of the critical judgment: another way of saying that what criticism criticizes cannot be dissociated or understood apart either from its history or from the person of the critic. The critic in addressing an object unavoidably speaks also of himself, thus challenging the line in critical perception between subject and object. The critic is responsible for what he says, not just because he has said it, but because what he says is unintelligible except as it acts on others. If it does not, he is not a bad critic—he is a noncritic: the distinction is worth preserving.

There is even a specific critical method dictated by these principles, although this is not the place to do more than mention it. The critic as he conceives and then tests critical possibilities is looking for a ground to the literary work—what makes its appearance, his experience, possible. The first step in this direction is in terms of coherence and consistency—reconciling the families of possible meaning both within and outside the work, excluding alternatives. What is left from this for the second step is the reconstructed look of the work in which, by that time, the critic himself appears. Having forced an entrance in the opening lines of interpretation, he easily—unavoidably—looks out of the work thereafter. Mirrors, self-portraits have had a peculiar fascination for painters, who would have their work not only reflect, but reflect the act of reflection. The writer has no such ready means of disclosure; he is often forced to tease or to taunt the reader, daring him to find the reflections, as if to suggest that there are none. It is an artifice, this challenge: the critic, seeing it, is even *meant* to see through it; with true poetic justice, he makes his way through it, by its own means, until he has the work at ground level, at *his* ground level. The critic is obliged not only to see very well, but also to see through and around, a seeing that involves a motion of the body—his body—not only of the eye, for neither, now, can (or should) criticism conceal criticism. What this amounts to, and what, I should argue, criticism must always mean is that "art is short, life is long." Why, I wonder again and again, should the critics be so reluctant to admit this? Isn't it their life, too?

> The mind never makes a great and successful effort, without a corresponding energy of the body.
>
> Thoreau

Notes

1. For statements of the work of criticism as subordination, cf. such works as C. Brooks, *The Well-Wrought Urn* (New York: Reynal and Hitchcock, 1947); J. C. Ransom, *The New Criticism* (New York, 1942); N. Frye, *Fearful Symmetry* (Princeton, N. J.: Princeton University Press, 1969); W. K. Wimsatt, *The Prose Style of Samuel Johnson* (New Haven, Conn.: Yale University Press, 1941). And for classical examples of the role of criticism as coordinate with art, cf., e.g., M. Arnold, *Essays in Criticism, First Series* (Boston: Ticknow and Fields, 1865); W. Pater, *Appreciations* (New York: Macmillan, 1905); J. E. Spingarn, *Creative Criticism* (New York: Harcourt, Brace, 1925). Cf. also G. Watson, *The Literary Critics* (Totowa, N. J.: Rowman and Littlefield, 1973) for a history of the relation between these (among other) types of criticism.

2. See for the argument of a sociological origin for the literary distinction between fiction and nonfiction, L. J. Davis, "A Social History of Fact and Fiction," in E. W. Said, ed., *Literature and Society* (Baltimore, Md.: Johns Hopkins University Press, 1980).

3. Cf., e.g., J. Derrida, *Of Grammatology*, trans. G. C. Spivak (Baltimore, Md.: Johns Hopkins University Press, 1976); *Writing and Difference*, trans. A. Bass (Chicago: University of Chicago Press, 1978), and *Glas* (Paris, 1974); R. Barthes, *The Pleasures of the Text*, trans. R. Miller (New York: Hill and Wang, 1975) and *Image-Music-Text*, trans. S. Heath (London, 1977); and the related—although not always historically or consistently—work of the "Yale School": e.g., H. Bloom, *A Map of Misreading* (New York: Oxford University Press, 1975); H. Bloom et al., *Deconstruction and Criticism* (New York: Seabury, 1979); G. Hartman, *Criticism in the Wilderness* (New Haven, Conn., Yale University Press, 1980); P. de Man, *Allegories of Reading* (New Haven, Conn., Yale University Press, 1979).

4. And so Derrida is also one of the least quotable of writers, posing a constant challenge to his reader: take all, or perhaps nothing—but at least not piecemeal. Even Hegel, more openly a disciple of the Whole, did not manage this side of his writing so efficiently.

5. Marxist writers in particular have paid considerable attention recently to the concept of praxis, but in general it has been understood, even when applied to art or criticism, to be fundamentally an ethical concept. I am claiming here that the historical and systematic distinctiveness of art and artcriticism has also to be accounted for, not only to make praxis applicable to them, but to have it applicable in other contexts as well. Cf., for general analysis of the concept, K. Axelos, *Alienation, Praxis, and Techne in the Thought of Karl Marx*, trans. R. Bruzina (Austin, Tex.: University of Texas Press, 1976); N. Lobkowicz, *Theory and Practice* (Notre Dame, Ind.: University of Notre Dame Press, 1967); P. Markovic and G. Petrovic, *Praxis* (Boston: Beacon Press, 1979); A. Sanchez Vazquez, *The Philosophy of Praxis* (New York: Humanities Press, 1977).

Bibliography

Arnold, Matthew. *Essays in Criticism*, First Series. Boston: Ticknor and Fields, 1865.

Axelos, Kostas. *Alienation, Praxis, and Techne in the Thought of Karl Marx*. Translated by R. Bruzina. Austin, Tex.: University of Texas Press, 1976.

Ayer, A. J. *Language, Truth, and Logic*. London: Gollancz, 1936.

Bakhtin, Mikhail M. *Problems of Dostoyevsky's Poetics*. Translated by R. W. Rotsel. Ann Arbor, Mich.: Ardis Publishers, 1973.

Barthes, Roland. *The Pleasures of the Text*. Translated by R. Miller. New York: Hill & Wang, 1975.

———. *Image-Music-Text*. Translated by S. Heath. New York: Hill & Wang, 1978.

Beardsley, Monroe. "Verbal Style and Illocutionary Action." In B. Lang, ed., *The Concept of Style*. Philadelphia: University of Pennsylvania Press, 1979.

Beck, L. W. "Judgments of Meaning in Art." *Journal of Philosophy* 41 (1944): 168–78.

———. "Philosophy as Literature." In B. Lang, ed., *Philosophical Style*. Chicago: Nelson-Hall, 1980.

Binkley, Timothy. *Wittgenstein's Language*. The Hague: Nijhoff, 1974.

Blanshard, Brand. *On Philosophical Style*. Manchester: Manchester University Press, 1954.

Bloom, Harold. *The Anxiety of Influence: A Theory of Poetry*. New York: Oxford University Press, 1975.

———. *A Map of Misreading*. New York: Oxford University Press, 1975.

———, et al., *Deconstruction and Criticism*. New York: Seabury Press, 1979.

Booth, Wayne C., *The Rhetoric of Fiction*. Chicago: University of Chicago Press, 1961.

Bradley, F. H. *Appearance and Reality*. New York: Macmillan, 1897.

Brooks, Cleanth. *The Well-Wrought Urn*. New York: Reynal and Hitchcock, 1947.

Brown, Richard. *A Poetic for Sociology*. New York: Cambridge University Press, 1977.

Brumbaugh, R. S., and Stallknecht, N. P. *The Compass of Philosophy*. New York: Longmans, 1954.

Chatman, Seymour, "Narration and Point of View in Fiction and the Cinema." *Poetica* 7 (1974): 21–46.

———. *Story and Discourse: Narrative Structure in Fiction and Film*. Ithaca, N. Y.: Cornell University Press, 1980.

————, ed. *Literary Style*. New York: Oxford University Press, 1971.

Church, A. "The Need for Abstract Entities in Semantic Analysis." *Proceedings of the American Academy of Arts and Sciences* 80 (1951): 100–112.

Clark, Kenneth M. *The Nude: A Study in Ideal Form*. Princeton, N. J.: Princeton University Press, 1972.

Collingwood, R. G. "Philosophy as a Branch of Literature." In *An Essay on Philosophical Method*. Oxford: Oxford University Press, 1933.

Collins, James. *Interpreting Modern Philosophy*. Princeton, N. J.: Princeton University Press, 1972.

Croce, Benedetto. *Aesthetic*. Translated by D. Ainslee. London: Macmillan, 1922.

Daniel, S. H. "A Philosophical Theory of Literary Continuity and Change." *Southern Journal of Philosophy* 18 (1980): 275–80.

Davis, Leonard J. "A Social History of Fact and Fiction." In E. S. Said, ed. *Literature and Society*. Baltimore, Md.: Johns Hopkins Press, 1980.

Derrida, Jacques. *Of Grammatology*. Translated by G. Spivak. Baltimore, Md.: Johns Hopkins Press, 1977.

————. *Writing and Difference*. Translated by A. Bass. Chicago: University of Chicago Press, 1978.

Dewey, John. *Art as Experience*. New York: Minton, Balch, 1934.

Dixon, Peter. *Rhetoric*. London: Methuen, 1971.

Donagan, Alan. "Victorian Philosophical Prose: J. S. Mill and F. H. Bradley." In S. P. Rosenbaum, ed., *English Literature and British Philosophy*. Chicago: University of Chicago Press, 1971.

Ducrot, Oswald, and Todorov, Tzvetan. *Encyclopedic Dictionary of the Sciences of Language*. Translated by C. Porter. Baltimore, Md.: Johns Hopkins Press, 1979.

Eichenbaum, Boris. "The Theory of the Formal Method." In L. Matejka and K. Pomoroska, eds., *Readings in Russian Poetics*. Cambridge, Mass.: M.I.T. Press, 1971.

Else, Gerald F. *Aristotle's Poetics: The Argument*. Cambridge, Mass.: Harvard University Press, 1967.

Feyerabend, Paul. *Against Method*. New York: Schocken, 1978.

Friedländer, Paul. *Plato*. Translated by R. Manheim. Princeton, N. J.: Princeton University Press, 1958.

Frye, Northrop. *Anatomy of Criticism*. Princeton, N. J.: Princeton University Press, 1957.

————. *Fearful Symmetry*. Princeton, N. J.: Princeton University Press, 1969.

————. "The Argument of Comedy." In D. A. Robertson, ed., *English Institute Essays*. New York: Columbia University Press, 1949.

Gadamer, H.-G. *Truth and Method*. Translated by G. Barden and J. Cumming. New York: Seabury, 1975.

Gellner, Ernest. *Words and Things*. London: Gollancz, 1959.

Genette, G. *Narrative Discourse*, Translated by J. E. Lewin. Ithaca, N. Y.: Cornell University Press, 1980.

Goldmann, Lucien. *The Hidden God*. Translated by P. Thody. New York: Routledge and Kegan Paul, 1976.

Gombrich, E. H. "Style." In *International Encyclopedia of the Social Sciences*. New York: Macmillan, 1968. Vol. 15, pp. 352–61.

———. *Art and Illusion*. Second Edition. Princeton, N. J.: Princeton University Press, 1961.

Goodman, Nelson. "On Likeness of Meaning." *Analysis* 10 (1949): 1–7.

———. *Languages of Art*. Indianapolis, Ind.: Bobbs-Merrill, 1968.

———. "The Status of Style." *Critical Inquiry* 1 (1975): 799–811.

Gottesman, R., and Bennet, S., eds. *Art and Error*. Bloomington, Ind.: Indiana University Press, 1970.

Guillen, Claudio. *Literature as System*. Princeton, N. J.: Princeton University Press, 1971.

Hartman, Geoffrey. "Crossing Over: Literary Commentary as Literature," *Comparative Literature* 28 (1976): 257–76.

———. *Criticism in the Wilderness*. New Haven, Conn.: Yale Univesity Press, 1980.

Havelock, Eric. *A Preface to Plato*. Cambridge, Mass.: Harvard University Press, 1963.

Hernadi, Paul. "Dual Perspective: Free Indirect Discourse and Related Techniques." *Comparative Literature* 24 (1972): 32–43.

———. *Beyond Genre*. Ithaca, N. Y.: Cornell University Press, 1972.

Hintikka, J. "*Cogito, Ergo Sum:* Inference or Performance?" *Philosophical Review* 71 (1962) 3–32.

Hirsch, E. D. *Validity in Interpretation*. New Haven, Conn.: Yale University Press, 1967.

———. *The Aims of Interpretation*. Chicago: University of Chicago Press, 1976.

Hospers, John. *Meaning and Truth in the Arts*. Chapel Hill, N. C.: University of North Carolina Press, 1946.

Hungerland, I. "The Concept of Intention in Art Criticism." *Journal of Philosophy* 57 (1960): 5–25.

Iser, Wolfgang. *The Implied Reader*. Baltimore, Md.: Johns Hopkins Press, 1974.

———. *The Act of Reading*. Baltimore, Md.: Johns Hopkins Press, 1978.

Jones, Peter. *Philosophy and the Novel*. Oxford: Oxford University Press, 1975.

Kermode, Frank. "Novels: Recognition and Deception." *Critical Inquiry* 1 (1974): 103–21.

Kirk, G. S., and Raven, J. E. *The Presocratic Philosophers*. Cambridge: Cambridge University Press, 1957.

Klein, Jacob. *A Commentary on Plato's Meno*. Chapel Hill, N. C.: University of North Carolina Press, 1965.

Kristeva, Julia. "The Death of a Poetics." In S. Bann and J. E. Bowlt, eds., *Russian Formalism*. New York: Barnes and Noble, 1973.

Kuhn, Thomas. *The Structure of Scientific Revolutions*. Chicago: University of Chicago Press, 1963.

Kuroda, S. Y. "Where Epistemology, Style and Grammar Meet." In P. Kiparsky and S. Anderson, eds., *A Festschrift for Morris Halle*. New York: Holt, Rinehart and Winston, 1973.

Lang, Berel. *Art and Inquiry*. Detroit, Mich.: Wayne State University Press, 1975.

Lassell, Harold; Leites, Nathan; and Associates. *Language of Politics*. Cambridge, Mass.: M.I.T. Press, 1966.

Levi, A. W. "Philosophy as Literature: The Dialogue." *Philosophy and Rhetoric* 9 (1976): 1–20.

Lobkowicz, N. *Theory and Practice*. Notre Dame, Ind.: University of Notre Dame Press, 1967.

Lord, Albert B. *The Singer of Tales*. Cambridge, Mass.: Harvard University Press, 1960.

Lotman, Juri M. "Point of View in a Text." *New Literary History* 6 (1975): 339–52.

Lubbock, Percy. *The Craft of Fiction*. New York: Scribner, 1921.

Lukács, Georg. *Theory of the Novel*. Translated by A. Bostock. Cambridge, Mass.: M.I.T. Press, 1971.

———. *Writer and Critic*. Translated by A. Kahn. New York: Grosset and Dunlap, 1970.

Mackey, Louis. "On Philosophical Form: A Tear for Adonis." *Thought* 42 (1967): 238–60.

Macksey, R., and Donato, E., eds. *The Structuralist Controversy*. Baltimore, Md.: Johns Hopkins Press, 1972.

Man, Paul de. *Allegories of Reading*. New Haven, Conn.: Yale University Press, 1979.

———. "The Rhetoric of Temporality." In C. Singleton, ed., *Interpretation*. Baltimore, Md.: Johns Hopkins Press, 1969.

Marias, J. *Philosophy as Dramatic Theory*. University Park, Penna.: Pennsylvania State University Press, 1971.

Meyer, Leonard B. *Music, the Arts, and Ideas*. Chicago: University of Chicago Press, 1969.

———. "Toward a Theory of Styles." In B. Lang, ed., *The Concept of Style*. Philadelphia: University of Pennsylvania Press, 1979.

Miller, J. Hillis. *Thomas Hardy: Distance and Desire*. Cambridge, Mass.: Harvard University Press, 1970.

———. "The Antithesis of Criticism." In R. Macksey, ed., *Velocities of Change*. Baltimore, Md.: Johns Hopkins Press, 1974.

Mink, Louis O. *Mind, History and Dialectic*. Bloomington, Ind.: Indiana University Press, 1969.

Morelli, G. *Italian Painters: Critical Studies of Their Works*. Translated by C. F. Ffoulkes. London: J. Murray, 1892–93.

Muecke, D. C. *The Compass of Irony*. London: Methuen, 1969.

Mukarovsky, Jan. *Structure, Sign, and Function*. Translated by J. Burbank and P. Steiner. New Haven, Conn.: Yale University Press, 1978.

Muscatine, Charles. "Locus of Action in Medieval Narrative." *Romance Philology* 17 (1963): 115–22.

Nelson, Lowry, Jr. "The Fictive Reader and Literary Self-Reflexiveness." In L. Nelson, Jr., P. Demetz, and T. Greene, eds., *The Discipline of Criticism*. New Haven, Conn.: Yale University Press, 1968.

Ohmann, Richard. "Generative Grammars and the Concept of Literary Style." *Word* 20 (1964): 423–99.

Ong, Walter J. *Interfaces of the Word*. Ithaca, N. Y.: Cornell University Press, 1977.

Orwell, S., and Angus, I., eds. *The Collected Essays, Journalism and Letters of George Orwell*. New York: Harcourt, Brace, 1968.

Panofsky, Erwin. "Die Perspective als 'symbolische Form.'" In *Vorträge der Bibliothek Warburg*, Neudeln/Liechtenstein 1924–25, pp. 258–330.

Paris, Jean. *Painting and Linguistics*. Pittsburgh, Penna.: Carnegie-Mellon, 1975.

Parry, Millman. *The Making of Homeric Verse*. Oxford: Oxford University Press, 1971.

Pascal, Roy. *The Dual Voice: Indirect Speech and Its Functioning in the 19th Century European Novel*. Manchester: Manchester University Press, 1977.

Pepper, Stephen. *World Hypotheses*. Berkeley, Calif.: University of California Press, 1942.

Quine, Willard V. O. *Word and Object*. Cambridge, Mass.: M.I.T. Press, 1960.

———. *From a Logical Point of View*. Cambridge, Mass.: Harvard University Press, 1961.

———. "Russell's Ontology." In E. D. Klemke, ed., *Essays on Bertrand Russell*. Urbana, Ill.: University of Illinois Press, 1970.

Ree, J.; Ayers, M.; and Westoby, A. *Philosophy and Its Past*. London: Harvester, 1978.

Rorty, Richard. "Philosophy as a Kind of Writing: An Essay on Derrida." *New Literary History* 10 (1978): 141–60.

———. *Philosophy and the Mirror of Nature*. Princeton, N. J.: Princeton University Press, 1979.

Rosen, Stanley. *Plato's Symposium*. New Haven, Conn.: Yale University Press, 1968.

Ross, Ralph. "Hobbes' Rhetoric." In R. Ross, H. Schneider, and T. Waldman, eds., *Thomas Hobbes in His time*. Minneapolis, Minn.: University of Minnesota Press, 1974.

Russell, Bertrand. *Human Knowledge: Its Scope and Limits*. New York: Simon and Schuster, 1948.

Ryle, Gilbert. *The Concept of Mind*. New York: Barnes and Noble, 1949.

Schapiro, Meyer. "Style." In A. L. Kroeber, ed., *Anthropology Today*. Chicago: University of Chicago Press, 1952.

Shapiro, David. *Neurotic Styles*. New York: Basic Books, 1965.

Shapiro, Karl, and Beum, R. *A Prosody Handbook*. New York: Harper, 1965.

Simpson, David. "Putting One's House in Order: The Career of the Self in Descartes' Method," *New Literary History* 9 (1977): 83–102.

Smidt, K. "Point of View in Victorian Poetry." *English Studies* 38 (1957): 1–12.

Spingarn, J. E. *Creative Criticism*. New York: Harcourt, Brace, 1925.

Sprague, R. K. *Plato's Use of Fallacy*. London: Routledge & Kegan Paul, 1962.

Steiner, George. "'Critic'/'Reader.'" *New Literary History* 10 (1979): 423–52.

Stevenson, C. L. *Ethics and Language*. New Haven, Conn.: Yale University Press, 1944.

Strelka, J. P. *Theories of Literary Genre*. University Park, Penna.: Pennsylvania State University Press, 1973.

Suleiman, S. R., and Crosman, I., eds. *The Reader in the Text*. Princeton, N. J.: Princeton University Press, 1980.

Thomson, James A. K. *Irony*. London: G. Allen and Unwin, 1926.

Todorov, Tzvetan. "La lecture comme construction." *Poétique* 24 (1975): 417–25.

Ullmann, Stephen. *Style in the French Novel*. Cambridge: Cambridge University Press, 1957.

Uspenski, Boris. "'Left' and 'Right' in Icon Painting." *Semiotica* 13 (1975): 33–39.

———. *The Poetics of Composition*. Translated by V. Zavarin and S. Wittig. Berkeley, Calif.: University of California Press, 1973.

Vazquez, A. Sanchez. *The Philosophy of Praxis*. Translated by M. Gonzalez. New York: Humanities Press, 1977.

Veatch, Henry. *Two Logics: The Conflict between Classical and Neo-Analytical Philosophy*. Evanston, Ill.: Northwestern University Press, 1969.

Volosinov, M. [M. Bakhtin?] *Marxism and the Philosophy of Language*. Translated by L. Matejka and I. R. Ritunik. New York: Seminar Press, 1973.

Walton, Kendall. "Points of View in Narrative and Depictive Narration." *Nous* 10 (1976).

Watson, George. *The Literary Critics*. Totowa, N. J.: Rowman and Littlefield, 1973.

White, Hayden. *Metahistory*. Baltimore, Md.: Johns Hopkins Press, 1974.

Wimsatt, William K. *The Prose Style of Samuel Johnson*. New Haven, Conn.: Yale University Press, 1941.

Wölfflin, Heinrich. *Principles of Art History*. Translated by M. D. Hottinger. New York: Dover, n.d.

Index

Lang, Berel, 43n, 45n
Leibniz, Gottfried, 27, 32–33, 73–74, 103
Lévi-Strauss, Claude, 22, 127
Lotman, Juri M., 172n
Lubbock, Percy, 172n
Lukács, Georg, 161–62, 174n

Mackey, Louis, 44n
Maimonides, Moses, 72
Marias, Julian, 44n
Marx, Karl, 79, 237n
Merleau-Ponty, Maurice, 20
Metaphor, 186–87, 199–201
Meyer, Leonard B., 126, 136n, 137n
Mink, Louis O., 45n
Moore, G. E., 26, 39, 53–54
More, Thomas, 73
Morelli, Giovanni, 127
Mukarovsky, Jan, 44n
Museum theory of art, 222–24

Nietzsche, Freidrich, 36, 63, 69

Ohmann, Richard, 136n
Ong, W. J., 44n
Organic form, 224
Orwell, George, 207–15

Panofsky, Erwin, 173n
Parry, Millman, 20
Pater, Walter, 221–22
Pepper, Stephen, 35, 44n, 80
Perelman, Charles, 44n
Plato, 20, 28, 32, 36, 57–59, 69–71, 73, 80, 84–99
Poiesis, 229–34
Point of view, 48–52, 139–50, 189–93
Poulet, Georges, 168, 174n
Praxis, 229–34
Progress, as concept, 101–3
Proposition, status of, 37–39, 118–19, 130–31

Quine, Willard Van Orman, 39, 45n, 129

Repetition, 122, 124–26
Representation, 85–86, 127–28, 184–89, 209–12
Richards, I. A., 44n
Rorty, Richard, 45n, 80
Russell, Bertrand, 26, 37
Russian formalists, 23
Ryle, Gilbert, 72

Schapiro, Meyer, 34, 126, 137n
Searle, John R., 45n
Simile, 184
Simpson, David, 44n
Solipsism, 205–6
Spinoza, B. de, 21, 82–82
Spitzer, Leo, 136n
Stallknecht, Newton P., 44n
Steiner, George, 44n
Strauss, Leo, 21
Style, adverbal, 114–22; as function of choice, 128; in identification, 24–27, 123–24, 127; in philosophical writing, 33–38, 62–65; as physiognomic, 126–28
Synonymy, 39–42, 128–31

Teaching, 107–8
Thoreau, Henry David, 215
Todaro, G. J., 150–54
Todorov, Tzvetan, 45n

Uspensky, Boris, 172n

Veatch, Henry, 45n

Watson, George, 236n
White, Hayden, 44n, 76
Wimsatt, William K., 172n, 236n
Wittgenstein, Ludwig, 21
Wölfflin, Heinrich, 115, 120, 126
Woolf, Virginia, 158

DATE DUE